"CAUGHT IN THE ACT,"
WALKING ON THE SEA,
AND
THE RELEASE OF BARABBAS REVISITED

SOUTH FLORIDA STUDIES IN THE HISTORY OF JUDAISM

Edited by
Jacob Neusner
Bruce D. Chilton, Darrell J. Fasching, William Scott Green,
Sara Mandell, James F. Strange

Number 157
"CAUGHT IN THE ACT,"
WALKING ON THE SEA,
AND
THE RELEASE OF BARABBAS REVISITED

by
Roger David Aus

19. Peter's Descending in Faith, and Naḥshon's Descending in Faith 100

20. Peter's Fear and Little Faith, and the Israelites' Fear and Little Faith..101

21. Sinking...103

22. Save Me!..104

23. Stretching Out One's Hand and Taking / Rescuing Someone Sinking in the Sea....................................105

24. The Disciples' Worshiping Jesus................................107

II.   The Messiah as Hovering Over the Water in Gen 1:2.........110

III.   The Extent of the Original Narrative..........................116

IV.   A Concrete Cause for the Origin and Date of the Original Narrative..117

V.   The Original Language and the Provenance of the Narrative 126

VI.   The Historicity and Purpose of the Narrative.................128

Appendix: The Lectionary Readings in Nisan.........................132

CHAPTER THREE

THE RELEASE OF BARABBAS REVISITED

(Mark 15:6-15; Matt 27:15-26; Luke 23:18-25; John 18:39-40)

I.   Introduction...135

II.   An Insurrection in Jerusalem in 4 BCE.......................141

    A) Herod's "Release" and "Releasing / Remitting" 142

    B) Herod's Lack of Respect for Jewish Religious Beliefs and Customs...144

    C) Herod's Fear of Insurrection and His Preventive Measures...144

    D) The Jerusalem Insurrection of 4 BCE Shortly Before Passover 145

III.   Archelaus' Handling of the Insurrection, With a Release of Prisoners...147

    1. A *bēma*...147

    2. The Crowd 148

    3. Requests / Demands...148

    4. Crying Out 148

	5.	Releasing Prisoners	148
	6.	Flattering / Conciliating	150
	7.	The Festival of Passover and Ancestral Custom	150
		a) The Festival of Passover	151
		b) Ancestral Custom	151
	8.	The King of the Jews	153
	9.	The Name Barabbas	154
IV.	The Procurator Vitellius' Release at Passover in Jerusalem		158
V.	The Original Language and Date of the Narrative		162
VI.	The Purpose of the Original Narrative, and Mark's Redaction of It		165
	A) The Purpose of the Original Narrative		165
	1) Filling a Gap		165
	2) Transferring the Roman Responsibility for Jesus' Death to the Jews		166
	3) Emphasizing Jesus' Innocence		168
	B) Mark's Redaction of It		169
Sources and Reference Works			171
Index of Modern Authors			181

Dedication

In deep gratitude to my teachers at Luther Theological Seminary, St. Paul, Minnesota, who helped me to lay a broad foundation in Biblical Studies in the 1960's,

and

my brother Stephen, who, without complaint but with deep commitment, bore the burden of loving care so many years.

Preface

The encounter of Jesus with a woman caught in the act of adultery in Jerusalem, as now described in John 7:53 – 8:11, is one of the most intriguing in the Gospels. For centuries the most varied conjectures have been made, for example, as to where in the law of Moses a command is given to stone such a person, and as to what Jesus wrote in the ground, two different times. In Chapter One I make concrete proposals, based on early Judaic traditions, in regard to both issues. The concept of "halakhah to Moses from Sinai" plays an important role here, describing a legal statement handed down for many generations outside the Bible, i.e. orally, but possessing the same validity as a written, Pentateuchal teaching.

Chapter Two deals with Jesus' walking on the Sea (of Galilee, Tiberias, Gennesaret) in Mark 6:45-52 par., including the special Petrine material found in Matt 14:28-31. I propose that most of the motifs and expressions in the narrative derive from Palestinian Judaic lore on the crossing of the Reed or Red Sea in Exodus 14-15, and on the Spirit of God as "hovering" over the water at Creation in Gen 1:2. Haggadah or non-legal Judaic traditions on the above and other Scriptures were employed to produce a narrative which is not historical, yet expresses its own religious truths. A Palestinian Jewish Christian created it in part as a foil to the maniacal Roman emperor Caligula's boast of walking as (a) god over the water in the Bay of Naples.

In Chapter Three I return to the scene of Pilate's releasing Barabbas instead of Jesus in Mark 15:6-15 par. Here I relate how the first-century Jewish historian Josephus describes in his *War* and *Jewish Antiquities* an insurrection in Jerusalem at the very end of Herod's life, in 4 BCE. Its treatment by his son and successor, Archelaus, involving a release of prisoners at the time of the Passover festival, provided most of the motifs and expressions which a Palestinian Jewish Christian employed when he first composed the Barabbas narrative in oral form. The account filled a gap present in the earliest Passion Narrative. Despite its non-historical nature, the Barabbas episode also expresses religious truths.

In the bibliography at the end of this volume I enumerate the many Judaic sources employed throughout. In the text itself only the standard abbreviations are given. An index of all the biblical and post-biblical passages cited would be rather cumbersome and stand in no relationship to the length of the volume. Nevertheless, an author index has been included to point out where I differ from much of current interpretation of the relevant pericopes. While attempting to dialogue with the most important secondary literature, I have also tried not to overburden the footnotes.

Many NT scholars today employ the genuine problem of dating rabbinic sources, which I extensively quote, as a cheap pretext for not even considering them. A complicating factor is that, in spite of many fine translations such as those of Jacob Neusner and his students, these sources are often relatively difficult to locate and read in the original Hebrew or Aramaic, not to speak of a lack of critical editions for many of them. This is one reason for my own translations, and for my quoting them extensively. I would be the first to concede that much of what is Amoraic and even some of what is ostensibly Tannaitic is late and of doubtful relevance to NT narratives. Yet a number of Judaic traditions from before 70 CE have been retained in the (patently later) rabbinic writings. Each individual tradition must be analyzed and evaluated on its own merits, which I try to do. The vexing problem of dating remains, yet so does the relevance of particular rabbinic sources.

My thanks go to Professors Étan Levine of Haifa and Peter von der Osten-Sacken of Berlin for reading Chapters One and Two, to Professor Alan Mitchell of Washington, D.C., for reading Chapter Three, and to Dr. Niko Oswald of Berlin for the same in regard to Two and Three, as well as for discussing several Aramaic expressions with me. Professor Lieselotte Kötzsche of Berlin kindly suggested that I look for three relevant illustrations from Rembrandt van Rijn (1606 – 1669), which I myself then selected. The Rev. Dr. William Downey graciously assisted me in proofreading. Finally, I would like to thank Professor Jacob Neusner for accepting this volume in the series *South Florida Studies in the History of Judaism*. It is a tribute to the ecumenical openness of an ordained Jewish rabbi that he continues to welcome relevant contributions from an ordained Christian pastor in such a series.

Chapter One above all emphasizes the role the Jew Jesus played in one particular instance in regard to an explosive issue (that of the Zealots) which shortly thereafter ended in the Jewish-Roman War of 66-70 CE. Chapters Two and Three show how Palestinian Jewish Christian narrators very creatively dealt with Judaic traditions available to them. If I have at all succeeded in elucidating how this creative process took place, my efforts will have been worthwhile.

Roger David Aus
August 1996
Berlin, Germany

"Christ and the Woman Taken in Adultery." Reproduced in O. Benesch, *The Drawings of Rembrandt* (London: The Phaidon Press, 1957) 5.297; Cat. No. 1038, figure 1253. Ca. 1658-1659.

Chapter One

"Caught in the Act" – With Whom, and By Whom? The Judaic Background of the Incident of the Adulteress in John 7:53–8:11

Introduction

This short pericope of twelve verses[1] has been called "a lost pearl of ancient tradition,"[2] a "precious little painting,"[3] "an especially worthwhile example of narrative art, singular in the literature of the gospels,"[4] a narrative of "noble beauty,"[5] and a "cause célèbre"[6] with both "tenderness and gravity."[7]

---

[1] I shall comment below in section X. on the original extent of the narrative.

[2] Cf. W. Heitmüller, *Johannesevangelium* (Die Schriften des NT, IV; Göttingen: Vandenhoeck & Ruprecht, 1908²) 789, not available to me, but cited in U. Becker, *Jesus und die Ehebrecherin*. Untersuchungen zur Text– und Überlieferungsgeschichte von Joh. 7₅₃ – 8₁₁ (BZNW 28; Berlin: Töpelmann, 1963) 3.

[3] R. Eisler, "Jesus und die ungetreue Braut" in *ZNW* 22 (1923) 305.

[4] H. Strathmann, *Das Evangelium nach Johannes* (NTD 4; Göttingen: Vandenhoeck & Ruprecht, 1959⁹) 270. He also calls it a "particularly vivid scene" (*ibid.*).

[5] H. von Campenhausen, "Zur Perikope von der Ehebrecherin (Joh 7,53 – 8,11)" in *ZNW* 68 (1977) 165. In regard to the second half, where Jesus and the woman are alone, he notes "the moving power of this quiet scene" (172). R. Schnackenburg in *Das Johannesevangelium, II. Teil* (HTKNT 4; Freiburg: Herder, 1971) 231 comments on the second half by noting the "unequaled vigor of its language," not having one word too much or too little.

[6] J. McDonald, "The So-Called 'Pericope de Adultera,'" in *NTS* 41 (1995) 415.

[7] A. McNeile, *The Gospel According to St. John* (ICC; Edinburgh: Clark, 1958) 2.716.

However, in spite of the 1963 monograph by U. Becker and more recent secondary literature,[8] many problems in the pericope remain unresolved. For example, what was the motivation of the scribes and Pharisees in bringing the adulteress to Jesus? In discussing this narrative with congregational Bible study groups, I am also invariably asked (and not just by women): "And where was the adulterer now?" In addition, what exactly did Jesus write with has finger in the earth / on the ground? Is the incident historical? Doesn't "from now on" just before "no longer sin" in 8:11 seem tautological?[9] What was the original language of the narrative? Since the pericope is clearly non-Johannine and was inserted at its present position after the completion of the Gospel,[10] what sort of Christian community handed it on?

The following study addresses these and related questions in light of early Judaic materials, many of them related to what is now still found in *m. Sanh.* 9:6, Numbers 25 and 5.

I. "Caught in the Act."

Certain scribes and Pharisees brought a woman "caught in adultery" (ἐπὶ μοιχείᾳ κατειλημμένην – John 8:3) to Jesus, who was sitting in the Temple, teaching the people (v 2). This was probably the magnificent, open-air Royal Portico or Stoa along the southern wall.[11] They placed her in the middle of the assembled people and told Jesus: "Teacher, this

---

[8] Cf. n. 2 for Becker, with literature up to then on pp. 191-203. See now also J. Becker, *Das Evangelium nach Johannes. Kapitel 1-10* (ÖTKNT 4/1; Gütersloh: Mohn; Würzburg: Echter, 1991[3]) 331-332.

[9] The RSV avoids this problem by translating: "go, and do not sin again." The NRSV more correctly renders: "Go your way, and from now on do not sin again."

[10] Cf. the extensive discussion of the lack of Johannine stylistic elements in U. Becker, *Jesus und die Ehebrecherin* 43-44, as well as 45-74. He and many others maintain that the pericope was inserted into the Fourth Gospel only in the third century CE from non-canonical tradition (39).

[11] Cf. the extensive references I cite for this, and for teachers' "sitting" there, in the "Excursus on Jesus' Sitting with the Teachers in the Temple" in regard to Luke 2:46 in my *Samuel, Saul and Jesus. Three Early Palestinian Jewish Christian Gospel Haggadoth* (SFSHJ 105; Atlanta: Scholars Press, 1994) 37-40. See also Str-B 2.625-626.

woman 'has been caught in the act,' committing adultery" (κατείληπται ἐπ' αὐτοφώρῳ μοιχευομένη – v 4).

The expression "caught in the act" is only found here in the entire NT and the LXX.[12] The term αὐτόφωρος in classical Greek appears "mostly in the phrase ἐπ' αὐτοφώρῳ λαμβάνειν, to catch 'in the act.'"[13] It is especially used of adulterers.[14] The only occurrence in this sense in Jewish literature is in Philo of Alexandria's *Spec. Leg.* 3.52. After noting that a Jewish harlot should be "stoned to death" (51),[15] he states: "The Law has rendered guilty adulteries caught 'in the act' (αὐτοφώρους) or confirmed by distinct proofs" (52). If they are not clear cases, the jealous husband causes his suspected wife to endure the rite of drinking the water of bitterness in the Jerusalem Temple, as described in Num 5:11-31 (3.52-63).

The Hebrew equivalent of the Greek phrase "to be caught in the act" in John 8:4 is נִתְפַּשׂ בִּשְׁעַת מַעֲשֶׂה.[16] The Hebrew New Testament of the United Bible Societies, for example, has here: This woman "was caught in adultery, in the very act" – נִתְפְּסָה בְּנִאוּף, בִּשְׁעַת מַעֲשֶׂה.[17]

Of the sixty-two occurrences of תפשׂ in the Hebrew Bible, only Num 5:13 deals with a person committing adultery. It states that the

---

[12] According to the Hatch-Redpath concordance, only Symmachus has αὐτόφωρος at Job 34:11.

[13] LSJ 284, with sources.

[14] Cf. the references to Xenophon, Aelianus and Achilles Tatius noted in BAGD 124. This excludes the theory of J. McDonald, "The So-Called 'Pericope de Adultera'" 426: "It is...likely...that the scribes simply seized one of the women who followed Jesus and whose compromising background was common knowledge and thrust her into the midst in an attempt to wrong-foot Jesus." She was, on the contrary, caught "in the very act" of adultery.

[15] This is not found in Deut 23:17, as F. Colson notes in the LCL edition here, but it is also attested in *Ios.* 43. It probably reflects Alexandrian Judaism's rigorous sexual mores. Punishment by stoning to death would apply all the more to adultery, which Philo has Joseph call "the greatest of crimes" (*Ios.* 44). The only other occurrence of αὐτόφωρος in Philo is in *Spec. Leg.* 4.7 regarding a thief who, breaking into a house at night, is "caught in the act"; he may be killed immediately.

[16] The phrase is also employed in modern Hebrew. Cf. R. Alcalay, *The Complete Hebrew-English Dictionary* (Tel-Aviv and Jerusalem: Massadah, 1965) 1432: "in flagrante delicto, in the very act," and *The Massada Student Dictionary, English-Hebrew* (Ramat Gan: Massada, 1978) 79.

[17] P. 258.

undetected adulteress "'was not caught' in the act" (NRSV): לֹא נִתְפָּשָׂה.[18]
"In the act" has been correctly added in the English to indicate her not
having been caught *in flagranti*, thus there were no witnesses. An early
midrash shows how dangerous the latter could be for the adulterers. R.
Yose the Galilean, a second generation Tanna,[19] notes on this passage
that "the adulterer goes in [to the woman's home] with the intent that, if
he is taken in the act, he will either kill [the enraged husband, who
discovers him,] or be killed."[20]

Judaic sources only very infrequently employ the phrase בִּשְׁעַת מַעֲשֶׂה,
"at the moment of the deed."[21] The most important passage in regard to
the Johannine pericope of the adulteress is *m. Sanh.* 9:6, as it is
interpreted in Judaic tradition in regard to the incident of Phinehas'
zealotic behavior recorded in Numbers 25.

II. *m. Sanh.* 9:6.

Verse six of section nine of the Mishnah tractate *Sanhedrin* lists five
major criminal actions to which no proper course of legal action applies,
step by step, until sentence is finally pronounced by the court or
Sanhedrin. Instead, others are entitled to take immediate action in regard
to the culprit. One example is that of a priest who served in the Temple
in a state of ritual uncleanness. Then his fellow priests do not bring him
to court. Instead, the young priests lead him outside the Temple
courtyard and split open his skull with clubs.

---

[18] Cf. BDB 1074-1075 on תָּפַשׂ. In rabbinic Hebrew both ס and שׂ are found. See
Jastrow, *A Dictionary* 1687-1688. Probably on the basis of Deut 22:28, נתפשה in
Num 5:13 was interpreted in some Tannaitic sources as "seized" (violently), i.e.
raped. See for example *Sifre* Num. Naso 7 on the verse (Horowitz 12; Neusner
1.88, who employs the RSV here; Kuhn 38, with n. 53), and *Num. Rab.* Naso 9/10
also on the verse (Mirqin 9.175; Soncino 5.257).

[19] Strack and Stemberger, *Introduction to the Talmud and Midrash* 81.

[20] Cf. *Num. Rab.* Naso 9/11 on Num 5:14, "And the spirit of jealousy come upon
him," connected to Prov 6:16 (Mirqin 9.176 – the sentence reoccurs in 9/12 on p.
177; Soncino 5.258). The translator, J. Slotki, has correctly added "in the act" to "if
he is taken." See also *Tanḥ.* Naso 1 (Eshkol 672) and *Tanḥ.* B Naso 3 (Buber 13b or
p. 26; Bietenhard 2.225). Phinehas' question regarding the Israelite Zimri,
fornicating with the heathen Cozbi, may be somehow related: "Is no one here
who will kill (him) and (as a result) be killed?" It is found in *Sifre* Num. Balak 131
on Num 25:6 (Horowitz 172; Kuhn 521).

[21] Cf. for example *t. Šabb.* 8(9):5 (Zuckermandel / Liebermann 119; Neusner 2.26);
Roš. Haš. 4(2):8 (Zuckermandel / Liebermann 213; Neusner 2.260 as 2:14); and in
the Babylonian Talmud: *Šabb.* 35a (Soncino 163); 68b (Soncino 328); *Yoma* 5b
(Soncino 20); *Zebaḥ.* 101a (Soncino 485); *Ketub.* 17b (Soncino 96) and 33a (Soncino
181, on warning false witnesses in regard to a sexual offense).

Just before this the Mishnah also notes the case of a Jewish man "who has sexual intercourse with an Aramean woman – zealots strike him down" – הַבּוֹעֵל אֲרַמִּית קַנָּאִין פּוֹגְעִין בּוֹ.[22] The latter verb, פגע,[23] does not merely mean here "fall upon" (Danby) or "beat up" (Neusner), but the same fate the priest received who performed in a state of ritual uncleanness in the Temple. Ch. Albeck explains this in a note: "those permitted to do so [zealots] kill him at the site of the deed."[24]

The term אֲרַמִּית here means "a heathen woman." Yet the same term could also mean "a Roman."[25] This is important for the identity of the man with whom the Jewish woman was caught in adultery in John 8. I shall comment on this below in section VI.

The Munich MS of the Babylonian Talmud adds to the above Hebrew phrase in *m. Sanh.* 9:6: בִּשְׁעַת מַעֲשֶׂה, "at the moment of the dead," "in the very act."[26] That is, when a Jew is caught *in flagranti* with a heathen, zealots are legally allowed to kill the Jewish person (only) if they do it on the spot and immediately.

This variant reading is preserved in the manuscript Cod. Hebr. 95 of the State Library at Munich. The latter was copied in 1343 in Paris and is the only (almost) complete MS of the Babylonian Talmud. It contains a number of variants and short comments as marginal glosses.[27] M. Krupp of Jerusalem was so kind as to consult it for me and notes that the above Hebrew phrase "was added by a later hand, presumably to clarify the real meaning."[28] A later reader did this just as the NRSV on Num 5:13 added regarding the adulteress who "was not caught": "in the act." J. Slotki also did exactly the same thing when he translated R. Yose the Galilean's statement quoted above.

---

[22] Hebrew in Albeck 4.201; English in Danby 396 and Neusner 604.

[23] Jastrow 1135.

[24] Cf. n. 22. He then points to Num 25:8 and 11. In his art. "Zealots" in *JE* (1906) 12.639, K. Kohler translates "shall be felled," i.e. killed.

[25] Cf. Jastrow 123, who cites this passage; as well as אֲרָם, Syria, often a substitute for רוֹמָא, Rome; and אַרְמָאי, Syrian, gentile, Roman (p. 122). J. Levy correctly states regarding אֲרָמִי, אֲרוֹמִי: "römisch, Römer, heidnisch; wobei man gleichzeitig an den Wortanklang von אֲרָמִי an רוֹמִי dachte." See his *Wörterbuch über die Talmudim und Midraschim* 1.168.

[26] For the reading, cf. the Goldschmidt edition, 7.342, apparatus. It is noted neither by Albeck nor by S. Krauss, *Sanhedrin-Makkot* 262-263. The Mishnah of the Jerusalem Talmud is not found as such in the text; it must be reconstructed from the gemara.

[27] Strack and Stemberger, *Introduction* 227.

[28] Private communication of 12/26/1995.

III. Numbers 25 in Judaic Tradition.

Most of the standard Mishnah editions and English translations of *Sanh.* 9:6 refer to the background of a Jew's having sexual intercourse with a heathen woman as Numbers 25, and to the zealots' killing such a person as having its precedence in the zealot Phinehas, also from that chapter. In his German translation of the Tannaitic commentary *Sifre* on Numbers, K. Kuhn even states that this midrashic presentation of the event of Numbers 25 is an apt illustration of *m. Sanh.* 9:6, "He who has sexual intercourse with a heathen woman, him the zealots can (or may) seize (and kill) at the moment of the deed [auf frischer Tat]." He thus assumes that בשעת מעשה belonged to the original Mishnaic tradition, which was pre 70 CE.[29] Indeed, one of the very infrequent occurrences of this Hebrew phrase in Judaic sources is found precisely here.

The book of Numbers describes the Israelites' forty year sojourn in the wilderness after leaving Egypt and before entering the promised Land. Chapter twenty-five states that when they dwelt at Shittim, opposite Jericho on the edge of the Jordan Valley, some 14 kilometers (8 miles) NE of the Dead Sea (Beth Peor was just south), Israelite men fornicated with Moabite women. These invited them to the sacrifices of their heathen gods, and the men ate and bowed down to the latter, among them being the Baal or fertility god of Peor.[30] This caused the LORD's anger to burn against Israel.

One striking example of how Israelite men were lured into such idolatry was the case of the Simeonite Zimri, who brought the Midianite woman Cozbi, the daughter of the prince of Midian, to the camp of the Israelites. Before the entire congregation he led her into his large vaulted tent. Seeing this, Phinehas took a spear, entered, and pierced both of them to death (through the belly, the genitals). His zealous behavior was similar to that of the LORD.

---

[29] *Sifre zu Numeri* 519.

[30] Beth Peor was also known by the later rabbis to be near the Jordan. See *Gen. Rab.* Vayyishlach 78/1 on Gen 32:27 (Theodor and Albeck 917-918; Soncino 2.715, with n. 2: "An idolatrous shrine"; Neusner 3.122). A parallel is found in *Lam. Rab.* 3:23 § 8 (Soncino 7.202). A Tannaitic tradition now found in *y. 'Avoda Zara* 1:5, 39d (Neusner 33.29-30; Wewers 19) and *Gen. Rab.* Lech Lecha 47/10 on Gen 17:27 (Theodor and Albeck 477; Soncino 1.405; Neusner 2.175) also maintains that there were three fairs. The most idolatrous was that of בוטנה, probably "Batanaea, town and district east of the Jordan" (Jastrow 145; see also בוטנן on p. 151, and the biblical Bashan in BDB 143). The site of this fair may have encouraged later rabbis to describe the incident of idolatry at Shittim and Beth Peor, east of the Jordan.

This colorful incident was retold, modified and expanded at a very early time and in many different traditions.[31] One indication of the very early date at which it was retold is found in LXX Num 25:8. It states that Phinehas took a barbed lance in his hand, entered after the Israelite man into the "furnace" (κάμινος),[32] and then pierced through both the lovers. The term "furnace," apparently making no sense here, was intended by the Greek translator to ridicule the lovers' heated passion. Zimri's "large vaulted tent" (קֻבָּה, v 8),[33] in which he and Cozbi were thought to be having very passionate intercourse, also meant in rabbinic Hebrew "tent of prostitution, brothel."[34] *Sifre* Num. Balak 131 on Num 25:1, for example, says that the Ammonite and Moabite women inside the erected brothels offered wine to an Israelite, which "burned" (בער)[35] in him. This caused him to greatly desire the woman. She was only willing to give herself to him, however, if he first worshiped the idol Baal Peor. This process was then repeated until the Israelite finally gave in.[36] *Num. Rab.* Balak 20/23 on Num 25:1-2 says that the harlot "would make him drink the wine, and the Satan would 'burn' within him, and he would be led astray after her."[37] Finally, *y. Sanh.* 10:2, 28d states regarding the proffered beverage: "When he drank it, the wine would 'burn' in him like the venom of a snake," and he would plead with the woman to surrender herself to him.[38]

---

[31] For an almost encyclopedic listing of the sources, cf. Ginzberg, *The Legends of the Jews* 3.380-389, with notes 785-804 in 6.134-138.

[32] LSJ 872, who suggest "alcove" here, which makes no sense. They note that it was proverbial of one who ate hot dishes; yet an object is definitely meant.

[33] BDB 866; it occurs only here. Cf. the root קבב.

[34] Jastrow 1323. Cf. also the Aramaic on p. 1324. *Gen. Rab.* Mikketz 91/6 on Gen 42:3 associates the term with "whores' lane" (Theodor and Albeck 1123; Soncino 2.840; Neusner 3.272 – "red-light district"). A parallel is found in *Tanḥ.* Mikketz 8 (Singermann 250-251; Eshkol 1.165). See also Num 25:1 – "to play the harlot with the daughters of Moab." *Gen. Rab.* Vayyishlach 80/10 on Gen 34:25 (Theodor and Albeck 965; Soncino 2.743, with n. 2; Neusner 3.155) interestingly asserts that Cozbi "sacrificed herself for her people," i.e. she voluntarily committed immorality with Zimri in order to help the Midianites / Moabites conquer the Israelites.

[35] The term "burning" was probably borrowed from the LORD's anger as "burning" against Israel in Num 25:3. It was for playing the harlot with the daughters of Moab and "yoking" themselves to Baal Peor.

[36] Horowitz 171; Kuhn 509-511.

[37] Mirqin 10.272; Soncino 6.821.

[38] Neusner 31.338. The sentence is later repeated.

These examples from Palestinian midrashim explain why the LXX rendered the Hebrew "large vaulted tent" of Num 25:8 as "furnace." It was the site of Zimri and Cozbi's very passionate intercourse before they were pierced through the genitals by Phinehas. The site of their debauchery was disparagingly represented as being as heated as a "furnace." The translation of the Pentateuch into Greek possibly took place already in the third century, at the latest by the middle of the second century BCE.[39] Haggadic development of Numbers 25 thus began at a very early time. It continued in the first century CE, as seen in Philo and Josephus, the latter modifying the narrative in major ways,[40] and in the Tannaitic and later midrashim. While many of the comments found in the latter are patently from a later period, others are certainly very old, as already shown by the LXX.

I shall now point out the relevance of specific aspects of Judaic interpretation of Numbers 25 (connected to the content of what later entered *m. Sanh.* 9:6) to the narrative of the adulteress in John 7:53 – 8:11.

1. *In flagranti.*

The Tannaitic midrash *Sifre* Num. Balak 131 on Num 25:8 states that Phinehas removed the tip of his (wooden) spear and put it in his money bag / hollow belt.[41] Then, leaning on the shaft (of what now appeared to be a walking stick), he proceeded to the brothel. Looking like a wanderer and employing a ruse, he gained entrance from the Simeonite guards, fellow tribesmen of Zimri. They thought he too wanted to satisfy his lust with a non-Jewish woman. "When he entered, God performed six miracles for him. The first miracle was (the following): The usual way (after intercourse) is to separate from one another, yet the angel made them cleave to each other."[42]

---

[39] Cf. O. Eissfeldt, *The Old Testament. An Introduction* (Oxford: Blackwell, 1966) 605; see also 702-703.

[40] Cf. *Mos.* 1.301-304 (in 302 Phinehas is filled with "righteous anger"); *Ebr.* 73-74; and *Mut.* 108 for Philo, and *Ant.* 4.131-155 (7-12) for Josephus, including speeches and an emphasis on the possibility of repentance. In 151 he states that Phinehas "determined...to take the law into his own hands...."

[41] Cf. Jastrow 1143 on פונדא.

[42] Horowitz 172; German in Kuhn 522-523. Cf. the parallels in *y. Sanh.* 10:2, 28d (Neusner 31.341); *b. Sanh.* 82b (Soncino 546); and *Tanḥ.* B Balak 30 (Buber 148-149, Bietenhard 2.384), where Phinehas, leaning on the wooden part of his spear as on a staff, comes to gratify his desire; here the phrase "how many miracles" occurs.

The term "cleave" here (דבק)[43] is certainly based on the synonym צמד[44] found in Num 25:3 and 5 of the Israelites' "yoking" themselves to Baal Peor. This is shown in *Tanḥ.* B Balak 27 on Num 25:3, which states that when an Israelite made a sacrifice to Peor, he ate with the non-Jewish woman, "and they cleaved (נצמדים) to each other, like yokes (of oxen)."[45]

K. Kuhn notes in regard to this first miracle in *Sifre* that the angel caused Zimri and Cozbi to continue to cleave to each other after their intercourse until Phinehas arrived "so that he could catch them in the act (according to *m. Sanh.* 9:6)."[46] This is certainly correct, since other midrashim cite this Mishnaic statement precisely at this point.[47]

One of the very infrequent occurrences of "at the moment of the deed" is then found in the continuation of *Sifre* on Num 25:8. It states that six more miracles were now performed for Phinehas. The twelfth according to the Horowitz edition was the following. It is customary for the one above (Zimri, having intercourse in the usual position, with Cozbi beneath him, both pierced through in their genitals by Phinehas' spear, yet still alive) to be lower on the spear (now held erect on Phinehas' shoulder). However, a miracle occurred, and Zimri was turned around upon Cozbi "like at the moment of the deed" (כשעת מעשה) so that all the Israelites could now see them and declare them guilty of death.[48] That is, Zimri was now again on top of Cozbi. Yet the three main MSS of *Sifre,* in addition to MS Orient. Quart 1594 of the State Library in Berlin, unknown to Horowitz, all read here: בשעת מעשה.[49] K. Kuhn correctly

---

[43] Jastrow 277. P. von der Osten-Sacken kindly calls my attention to the use of this verb in Gen 2:24, where a man "cleaves" to his wife and they become one flesh, the situation of Zimri and Cozbi.

[44] BDB 855.

[45] Buber 148; Bietenhard 2.382.

[46] *Sifre* 523, n. 149.

[47] Cf. *Tanḥ.* B Balak 30 (Buber 148, Bietenhard 2.384) on Phinehas' seeing their "deed" (מעשה); *y. Sanh.* 9:7(6), 27b (Neusner 31.307); *b. Sanh.* 82a (Soncino 546) on *m.* 9:6; and *Num. Rab.* Balak 20/25 on Num 25:7 (Mirqin 10.274; Soncino 6.824).

[48] Horowitz 173. The Latin Bible of Léon, Spain, from 1197 CE, not acquainted with this Judaic tradition, has a fine illustration of this scene with Cozbi on top of Phinehas' spear, now held upright. Cf. the art. "Phinehas" in *EJ* (1971) 13.467.

[49] On the first three, cf. Horowitz 173, apparatus: the printed edition of Venice, 1545; London, British Museum; and Rome, Vatican. See his p. XXII. On the Berlin MS, see Kuhn VII and 762 in regard to p. 173, line 5, of Horowitz.

follows them in his German translation: Zimri was turned around "im Augenblick des Geschehnisses."[50]

As I propose with additional arguments below, early Judaic haggada on Phinehas, who in his zeal pierced the Israelite Zimri through while he committed fornication with a foreign woman, is the major background for the narrative of the Jewish woman who committed adultery with another (foreign) man in John 7:53 – 8:11. She too was described by a Palestinian Jewish Christian as having been "caught 'in the very act'" (v 4). The Hebrew behind ἐπ' αὐτοφώρῳ is בְּשָׁעַת מַעֲשֶׂה, as in the Phinehas midrash.

2. *The Law of Moses.*

In John 8:5 certain scribes and Pharisees tell Jesus in regard to the adulteress they have just placed in his midst: "In the law (νόμος), Moses commanded us to stone such ones." In the final words of the pericope, Jesus tells the woman: "Sin no more" (v 8). That is, he does not dispute that she has committed the sin of adultery, in which she was caught *in flagranti* (vv 3-4).

Adultery was possible for a Jewish woman of the time only if she was already properly married, or if she was a betrothed (engaged) virgin awaiting marriage.[51] Only the latter, with her lover in a city (like Jerusalem), was to be stoned to death (Deut 22:24; cf. v 21). The punishment for an adulterous married woman was not specified in the Bible (Lev 20:10; Deut 22:22), and the traditions which later entered the Mishnah called for strangulation, the quicker, less painful and disfiguring method of killing her.[52]

In John 8:3,4,9 and 10 the Greek term γυνή is employed of the woman caught in adultery. This can mean a wife, a betrothed girl, or a woman in

---

[50] *Sifre* 524. This is labeled the eighth miracle in *Num. Rab.* Balak 20/25 (Mirqin 10.275; Soncino 6.825): "the angel turned them over at the top of the spear into proper position in order to display their disgraceful conduct to all." Miracles in connection with Phinehas became proverbial. Cf. *b. Ber.* 56b (Soncino 350): "If one sees Phinehas in a dream, a miracle will be wrought for him."

[51] Cf. the articles on "Adultery" by D. Amram in *JE* (1891) 1.216-218; J. Tigay in *EJ* (1971) 2.313-315; and "In Jewish Law" by H. Cohn in 2.315-316.

[52] Cf. the sources cited in Str-B 2.519-521. The daughter of a priest who played the harlot, in contrast, was to be burned with fire (Lev 21:9). See also Josephus, *Ant.* 4.248.

general.[53] The Hebrew equivalent is אִשָּׁה.[54] Deut 20:7 and 28:30, for example, speak of betrothing an אִשָּׁה. After she was betrothed, she was labeled a מאורשה (virgin – נערה (בתולה, as in Deut 22:23 and 25, and simply נערה in v 24. Yet she is also called a "wife" (אשה) in the latter verse. The same prevails in the LXX of these verses, which have παῖς (παρθένος) μεμνηστευμένη in 22:23 and 25, νεᾶνις in 24, and γυνή in the same verse.

A Palestinian Jewish "girl" (נַעֲרָה, νεᾶνις) was 12 to 12 1/2 years old,[55] at the end of which time she was thought to have come of age (בּוֹגֶרֶת).[56] During this time she could become "betrothed" (אֲרוּסָה or מְאָרְסָה, παῖς μεμνηστευμένη) and usually married at the age of 13 to 14. While still betrothed she *could* also be called an אשה, meaning "woman" or "wife."[57]

Yet the latter was very infrequent. In addition, the context almost always made it clear that she was definitely still betrothed. Nowhere is there a hint that the "woman" (γυνή) adulteress in John 8:3,4, 9 and 10 is a betrothed virgin of 12 to 13 years who committed adultery with a man in the city of Jerusalem.[58] If this had been the case, the Semitic original of נערה, בוגרת or ארוסה / מאורסה[59] would most probably have been translated into Greek as νεᾶνις or παῖς μεμνηστευμένη, as in the LXX at Deut 22:23-25. Only as a betrothed virgin would the biblical punishment of stoning apply to her (Deut 22:24), which the scribes and Pharisees appear to refer to in John 8:5. Rather, she was much more probably a mature wife who, for some reason dissatisfied with her marital life or simply out for adventure, decided to have an affair with a desirable adult man. The scribes and Pharisees' citation of Moses' commanding in the νόμος that such women be stoned derives from elsewhere.

---

[53] Cf. LSJ 363 and BAGD 168.

[54] Cf. BDB 61, as well as the *Hebrew New Testament* of Delitzsch 181, and that of the United Bible Societies (258).

[55] Jastrow 922.

[56] Jastrow 137 on בגר.

[57] Cf. the many sources cited by Str-B in 2.374 and 393-394. On the term "betrothed," see Jastrow 124.

[58] J. Blinzler, "Die Strafe für Ehebruch in Bibel und Halacha. Zur Auslegung von Joh. VIII.5" in *NTS* 4 (1957-1958) 32-47, argues that the adulteress is not a betrothed girl. Yet he believes stoning still prevailed for a properly married adulteress at the time of Jesus. Against this, see section VIII. below.

[59] Cf. these terms in *m. Sanh.* 7:4 and 9 (Albeck 4.191 and 193; Danby 392-393; Neusner 597 and 599; and Str-B 2.521).

Both the Hebrew New Testaments of Delitzsch and the United Bible Societies translate the νόμος of John 8:5 as "Torah," i.e. the Pentateuch.[60] Yet the Semitic original was much more probably הֲלָכָה, which is traditional, oral legal interpretation. In contrast to *haggadah*, it is thought of as "law"[61] and could then easily be translated as νόμος. The frequently occurring phrase "*halakhah* to Moses from Sinai" (הלכה למשה מסיני) sought to express the fact that the entire contents of oral teaching had the same origin as written teaching (the Bible). When legal statements could not be based upon the Bible, this phrase gave them the character of long-standing tradition.[62]

The term *halakhah* is employed in Judaic haggadah in regard to the moment before Phinehas pierces through Zimri and Cozbi with his spear. When Zimri brings the Midianite woman by the hair to Moses, he asks him whether she is forbidden or permitted. If Moses should say "forbidden," Zimri will ask him who permitted him the daughter of Jethro (the heathen Midianite priest: Exod 2:16,21; 3:1). "At that moment Moses forgot the *halakhah* [concerning intimacy with a heathen woman]..." Commenting on the verb "saw" of Num 25:7, Rab, a first generation Babylonian Amora who studied under Rabbi (Judah the Prince) in Palestine,[63] says that at this moment Phinehas "saw what was happening (מעשה, Zimri's sexual intercourse with Cozbi in the brothel), remembered the *halakhah*, and said to him (Moses): 'O great-uncle![64] Did you not teach us this on your descent from Mount Sinai: 'He who cohabits with a heathen woman – the zealots strike him down, (killing him)'?"[65]

---

[60] Cf. pp. 181 and 258, respectively.

[61] Jastrow 353, who specifically refers to *b. Sanh.* 82a twice, which I shall presently cite.

[62] Cf. W. Bacher, *Tradition und Tradenten in den Schulen Palästinas und Babyloniens* (Leipzig, 1914: reprint Berlin: de Gruyter, 1966) 21-22 and 33-34, as well as the art. "*nomos* C 4" by W. Gutbrod in *TDNT* 4.1056. See for example *b. Nid.* 45a (Soncino 312), where the students of R. Aqiva say to him: "as all the Torah is a tradition that was handed on to Moses at Sinai, so is 'the law' that a girl under the age of three years (who had intercourse) is fit for the priesthood one that was handed to Moses at Sinai." If *tōrāh* is indeed behind the *nomos* of John 8:5, it is meant as the "oral Torah" (תורה שבעל פה – Bacher, *Tradition* 22-24), which can include non-Pentateuchal *halakhah* given to Moses at Sinai.

[63] Strack and Stemberger, *Introduction* 93.

[64] Phinehas was the son of Eleazar, who was the son of Aaron, Moses' brother (Num 25:7 and 11).

[65] Cf. *b. Sanh.* 82a (Soncino 545-546, which I slightly alter); *y. Sanh.* 9:6, 27b (Neusner 31.307 as 9:7); *Num. Rab.* Balak 20/24-25 on Num 25:6-7 (Mirqin 10.273-

Here *m. Sanh.* 9:6, about zealots as having the right to strike down (and kill) a Jew who has sexual relations with a heathen woman, is cited in order to justify Phinehas' behavior. It is a "law" (*halakhah*) which Moses taught the Israelites when descending from Sinai, (where he also received the written *halakhah*, the Torah). I suggest that this terminology stands behind John 8:5. There the scribes and Pharisees maintain that "Moses commanded us in the νόμος to stone such ones" as the Jewish woman caught in the very moment of committing adultery – with a heathen man. This teaching was not a written *halakhah* already found in the Hebrew Bible, but an oral one given by God to Moses at Sinai. (On the adulterer as a Roman, see section VI., and on the punishment of stoning for such immoral behavior, equated with idolatry, see section VIII. below.)

3. *Phinehas' Zealous Behavior.*

John 8:3-6 states that certain scribes and Pharisees brought a woman caught in the very act of adultery, set her in the midst of the group of people Jesus was teaching in the Jerusalem Temple, and maintained that Moses (in the oral *halakhah*) commanded them to stone such persons. Attempting to test him in order to bring a charge against him, they then asked Jesus: "You, therefore, what do you say (in regard to her / this)?"

I suggest that the scribes and Pharisees mentioned here are Zealots who, in a *halakhah* given to Moses at Sinai now still found in *m. Sanh.* 9:6, were allowed to strike down (and kill) a Jew who fornicated with a heathen woman (and the opposite: a Jewish woman with a heathen man). Therefore they say: Moses in the oral *halakhah* commanded *us* (ἡμῖν – v 5), the Zealots, (but not others), to do so. To buttress this proposal, I shall briefly sketch Judaic interpretation of Phinehas' zealotic behavior in killing the Israelite Zimri and the heathen Cozbi, also caught in the very act of sexual intercourse. It established Phinehas as the prototype of the Zealots.[66]

274; Soncino 6.823-824); *Tanḥ.* B Balak 30 (Buber 148, Bietenhard 2.384); *Tanḥ.* Balak 20-21 (Eshkol 805-806); and *Targ. Jon.* Num 25:6-7 (Rieder 2.233, Etheridge 434).

[66] Cf. the art. "Phinehas" by M. Seligsohn in *JE* (1905) 10.18-19; the similar art. by E. Stern and M. Aberbach in *EJ* (1971) 13.465-467; the art. "Zealots" by K. Kohler in *JE* (1906) 12.639-643; the art. "Zealots" by S. Brandon in *EJ* (1971) 16.947-950; "Appendix B: The Fourth Philosophy: Sicarii and Zealots," by C. Howard in Schürer, *The history of the Jewish people in the age of Jesus Christ* 2.598-606; and M. Hengel, *The Zealots:* Investigations into the Jewish Freedom Movement in the Period from Herod I until 70 A.D. (Edinburgh: Clark, 1989), available to me as *Die Zeloten* (Leiden: Brill, 1976²). There is nothing in the index of Hengel's work in regard to John 7:53 – 8:11.

Exod 34:14 states: "You shall worship no other god, for the LORD, whose name is Jealous / Zealous (קַנָּא),[67] is a jealous / zealous God." This means the Israelite should not play the harlot after the gods of the inhabitants of the land (Canaan), nor sacrifice to their gods and, if invited, eat of the sacrifices to idols. Nor should intermarriage take place because of the danger of playing the harlot after the heathens' gods (vv 15-16). This "zeal" on the part of God applies very well to the situation of Num 25:1-2, where Israelites, later led on by Zimri, were then in grave danger of being seduced to idolatry through heathen women.

This basic thought is mirrored in *Mek.* Baḥodesh 6 on Exod 20:5. In the Second Commandment the Israelites are not to bow down to or serve any graven images / idols, "for I the LORD your God am a jealous / zealous God...." The Tannaitic midrash explains this by stating: "Zealously (בקנאה) do I exact punishment for idolatry, but in other matters I am merciful and gracious."[68]

Only two persons in later Judaic tradition on the Hebrew Bible are especially noted for their zeal for God. By killing all the prophets of Baal with the sword, Elijah showed that he had been "very zealous for the LORD, the God of hosts" (1 Kgs 18:40; 19:10 and 14).[69]

The other person was Phinehas. By piercing Zimri and Cozbi through with his spear, thereby killing them, Phinehas showed that he was "zealous for his God," making atonement for the people of Israel (Num 25:13). *Tanḥ.* B Phinehas 3 on this verse says for example: this teaches that "everyone who sheds the blood of the godless / wicked is like one who brings an offering."[70] By killing Zimri and Cozbi, Phinehas turned back God's wrath from the people of Israel, for he was "zealous" with God's "zeal" among them. Thus God did not consume the people in His "zeal" (Num 25:11).

This great emphasis on Phinehas' "zeal," carrying out God's "zeal" by killing an Israelite who in Judaic tradition fornicated with a heathen woman seeking to tempt him into idolatry, made Phinehas into the prototype of Jewish zealots.

---

[67] The root means both: BDB 888, Jastrow 1387-1388.

[68] Lauterbach 2.244. Cf. Deut 5:9 for a parallel.

[69] Jehu's zeal for the LORD in slaying the prophets of Baal, his worshipers and priests, was according to the word of the LORD which He spoke to Elijah. Cf. 2 Kgs 10:16-28.

[70] Cf. Buber 151 and Bietenhard 2.386. There is a parallel in *Tanḥ.* Phinehas 1 (Eshkol 808). In *Exod. Rab.* Terumah 33/5 on Exod 25:2, "That they take for Me an offering," like a horse in battle Phinehas risks his life "in order to sanctify God's name" (Mirqin 6.93; Soncino 3.420).

Phinehas' "interposing," according to Ps 106:28-31, was reckoned to him as righteousness forever. The fact that he was "zealous" (ἐν τῷ ζηλῶσαι αὐτόν) in the fear of the LORD made atonement for Israel (Sir 45:23). Sirach was originally written in Hebrew, in Jerusalem, in the first quarter of the second century BCE.[71] When Antiochus IV Epiphanes pillaged Jerusalem, erecting a desolating sacrilege upon the altar of burnt offering in 167 BCE (1 Macc 1:54), also forcing the Jews to serve idols (vv 43 and 47), Mattathias, the father of Judas Maccabeus, moved from Jerusalem to Modein with his family. There he in righteous anger ran and killed upon the altar a Jew who had gone forward to sacrifice (to idols) and the king's officer who was forcing the Jews to sacrifice. He also tore down the altar. 1 Macc 2:26 says "he burned with zeal (ἐζήλωσεν) for the law, as Phinehas did against Zimri the son of Salu." He then encouraged everyone "who is zealous" (ὁ ζηλῶν) for the law and supports the covenant to come out and join him (v 27) in his armed struggle against the introduction of heathen Greek religion. Upon his deathbed he encouraged others to recall that Phinehas, "because he was so deeply zealous" (ἐν τῷ ζηλῶσαι ζῆλον), received the covenant of everlasting priesthood (2:54).[72] First Maccabees was also composed in Hebrew, in Palestine, some time before the arrival of the Romans under Pompey in 63 BCE.[73]

In light of the above early Judaic sources, it can be said with certainty that Phinehas' reputation as one who in righteous zeal took the law into his own hands and killed Jewish apostates, based on Numbers 25, provided the background of the statement in *m. Sanh.* 9:6, "He who has sexual intercourse with an Aramean (heathen) woman – Zealots (קנאין) may / should strike him down, (killing him – at the very moment of the act)." Major commentators agree that the zealot Phinehas is alluded to here.[74] This is also the only occurrence of the term "zealot" in the Mishnah.

IV. The Dating of *m. Sanh.* 9:6.

The basic content of the Mishnah, usually thought to have been completed under Judah the Prince's (Rabbi's) leadership, was already set

---

[71] Cf. Nickelsburg, *Jewish Literature Between the Bible and the Mishnah* 55 and 64.

[72] It may also be noted that 4 Macc 18:12 has the mother of the seven martyred sons relate that their father had earlier told his children of the zeal of Phinehas.

[73] Nickelsburg, *Jewish Literature* 117.

[74] Cf. Krauss, *Sanhedrin-Makkot* 222-223; Albeck, *Shisha Sidre Mishnah* 4.201; Danby, *The Mishnah* 396; and Neusner, *The Mishnah* 604.

about the middle of the third century CE.[75] Yet many of the individual traditions contained in it are much older. Each must be weighed on its own merits.

M. Hengel believes the above clause in *m. Sanh.* 9:6 stems from the period 7-66 CE when, except for a short interval under Agrippa I, the right of capital punishment was taken from the Jews by the Romans. It was then a threat to those transgressors of the law who could no longer be prosecuted by a regular trial of the Sanhedrin.[76] Aside from a lack of concrete evidence for 7 CE, the beginning of the Zealotic movement (see below), a baraitha or Tannaitic tradition not found in the Mishnah maintains that the Romans took the right of capital punishment away from the Sanhedrin only forty years before the destruction of the Temple (70 CE), i.e. ca. 30 CE.[77] While this is probably a round number, the time may well be approximately correct, perhaps accounting for the emphasis in John 18:31, "It is not lawful for us to put any man to death."

The origin of *m. Sanh.* 9:6, however, is probably much older. K. Kohler speaks of it as "evidently of the Maccabean time."[78] This is because the gemara on this passage in *b. Sanh.* 82a relates the following. When R. Dimi, a fourth generation Palestinian Amora,[79] went from Palestine to Babylonia, he stated: "The court of the Hasmoneans decreed that one who cohabits with a heathen woman is liable to punishment on account of NaSHGA." This stands for *niddah*, a menstruous woman; *shifḥah*, a non-Jewish maid-servant; *goyyah*, a heathen woman; and *esheth ish*, a married woman.[80] The latter definitely meant adultery, punishable by death.

The parallel passage in *b. 'Avoda Zara* 36b discusses legal rulings by the Schools of Hillel and Shammai in regard to sexual contacts with heathens. "With all the things against which they decreed the purpose

---

[75] Cf. Strack and Stemberger, *Introduction* 155. He died in 217 CE (p. 89), so the basic redaction took place before this.

[76] *Die Zeloten* 70.

[77] Cf. *y. Sanh.* 1:1, 18a (Neusner 31.12); 7:2, 24b (Neusner 31.201); *b. Sanh.* 41a (Soncino 267); and *Šabb.* 15a (Soncino 63).

[78] Art. "Zealots" in *JE* (1906) 12.639.

[79] Strack and Stemberger, *Introduction* 104.

[80] I slightly modify the Soncino translation by H. Freedman on pp. 544-545, with his explanatory notes. After this, R. Rabin, also a fourth generation Palestinian Amora (Strack and Stemberger, *Introduction* 103), repeats the same teaching, yet with *zonah*, harlot, instead of a married wife. Post 70 CE practice may have been to leave the punishment for such an offense up to God (*Sanhedrin* 545, n. 1), yet before that time it was certainly more severe: death.

was to safeguard against idolatry."[81] They decreed against marriages with any heathen, not just Canaanites (Deut 7:3).[82] They also decreed against immoral connection with them, yet the court of Shem[83] had already done so. One could think that there was a prohibition for an Israelite woman's having intercourse with a heathen because then she would be drawn after him into idolatry, but not the reverse. Therefore the Schools of Hillel and Shammai decreed even against a Jewish man's having intercourse with a heathen woman.

Yet this prohibition, *'Avoda Zara* continues, was already a *halakhah* of Moses from Sinai, for which *m. Sanh.* 9:6 is cited. (Therefore the two Schools did not only later decree this.) It first referred to a public act like the incident (מעשה) that happened (in Num 25:6 – "in the sight of the whole congregation of the people of Israel"). The two Schools then came and prohibited even a private act (with a heathen). The Court of the Hasmoneans, however, had already decreed also against such a private act. Then the tradition related by R. Dimi above is cited.[84]

This long chain of reasoning, which continues on backwards even to the Court of David, is not intended to be historically exact. It simply wishes to express the fact that the later Schools of Hillel and Shammai did not originally decree the tradition now found in *m. Sanh.* 9:6. It had already been formulated by the Court of the Hasmoneans, i.e. in Maccabean times, in the second century BCE.[85] This is very plausible because of Jewish collaboration in Palestine with the new Greek rulers, sacrificing to idols, removing the marks of circumcision, profaning the Sabbath, and adopting the heathen Greek religion (1 Maccabees 1). The times called for very drastic measures, such as Mattathias' slaying a Jew who sacrificed (to idols). This was done in imitation of Phinehas' zealous behavior towards Zimri (2:23-26). Another drastic measure was the prohibition against sexual intercourse on the part of a Jewish man with an Aramean (heathen) woman. (This applied all the more in the patriarchal society of the time to a Jewish woman and a heathen man.)

---

[81] Soncino 176.

[82] Cf. already Ezra's demand in the fifth or fourth century BCE, that those Jews who had married gentile wives divorce them at the return from the Babylonian exile (Ezra 9-10).

[83] The son of Noah, he was thought to have an academy together with Eber. He also presided as judge at the trial of pregnant Tamar, who although promised to Shelah played the harlot (with Judah). Cf. Genesis 38, and the Judaic materials related to it in the index of Ginzberg, *Legends* 7.434.

[84] I modify and paraphrase the Soncino translation on pp. 176-177.

[85] Cf. Soncino 177, n. 7, and *Sanhedrin*, Soncino 544, n. 8.

That is, no Jew should fornicate with a Greek. The danger of being seduced into idolatry and of contaminating one's whole people was too great, as in Numbers 25.

Even if a Maccabean origin of what is still found in *m. Sanh.* 9:6 is not conceded, the latter definitely stems from a time before Jesus' ministry. As such it was known both to him and to the scribes and Pharisees who brought to him an adulteress "caught in the act." Zealots like Phinehas, they had the legal right to strike her down, i.e. to kill her.

V. The Pharisees and Zealots of Jesus' Time.

The Zealot rebellion against Rome, culminating in the Jewish-Roman War of 66-70 CE, began when Quirinius was governor of Syria, to which Judea had been annexed. When he ordered a registration of property (a census) in 6 CE, Judas the Gaulinite initiated the rebellion after having taken as his partner Zadok, a Pharisee. According to Josephus, they encouraged the Jewish nation to lay claim to its freedom (*Ant.* 18.1-4). The Jewish historian, a native of Jerusalem who himself later went over to the Romans and disparagingly called the Zealots "bandits" (λῃσταί), noted that Judas and Zadok started among the Jews an "alien fourth school of philosophy" (after the Pharisees, Sadducees and Essenes), gaining many adherents. The two leaders inspired zeal (τῷ σπουδασθέντι) among the younger people, leading to destruction (18.9-10).

Josephus also remarks that the fourth philosophy "agrees in all other respects with the opinions of the Pharisees, except that they have a passion for liberty that is almost unconquerable, since they are convinced that God alone is their leader and master" (18.23).[86]

This makes it clear why it is scribes and "Pharisees" who bring to Jesus a woman just caught in the act of adultery (John 8:3). The latter are in fact Zealots, adherents of the new religious and political movement only about twenty-five years old, who are "in principle simply a radical or particularistic wing of the Pharisees."[87] Their identification as Zealots is all the more certain if the Jewish adulteress had just had sexual intercourse with a Roman, as I shall propose below.

---

[86] Translation by L. Feldman in the LCL.

[87] R. Meyer, art. "Pharisees" in *TDNT* 9.27. The Tannaitic midrash *Sifre* Num. Balak 131 on Num 25:8 (Horowitz 172, Kuhn 522, with n. 145) has the Simeonites, guarding the brothel in which Zimri and Cozbi are fornicating, say to Phinehas when he approaches to kill the two: "Let him enter. The Pharisees (represented by Phinehas) have now declared the matter (such fornication) permitted!" There are parallels in *b. Sanh.* 82b (Soncino 546) and *y. Sanh.* 10:2, 28d (Neusner 31.340).

Behavior typical of the Pharisees is also demonstrated in John 8:9. Knowing that none of them was without sin and therefore should not cast the first stone onto the woman caught in adultery, one by one they departed, "beginning with the older ones."[88] Josephus notes that the Pharisees "show respect and deference to their elders, nor do they rashly presume to contradict their proposals" (*Ant.* 18.12).[89] Here too the younger Pharisees followed the example of their elders.

The scribes were highly respected authorities on both the written and the oral *halakhah.* Even before the fall of the Temple and Jerusalem in 70 CE and the ensuing lack of influence of the Sadducees, "the Pharisaic scribes were by far the most numerous."[90] The "scribes" of John 8:3 are most probably simply venerated Pharisaic teachers of the law, designated "scribes" to indicate that they were especially responsible for handing on both the oral and the written legal traditions, in contrast to other Pharisees. Thus they could say with astute knowledge: "In the (oral) *halakhah* Moses commanded us to stone such women" (v 5). They were referring to the oral teaching given to Moses at Sinai which is still found in *m. Sanh.* 9:6. These Pharisaic scribes were probably also Zealots, who are so labeled in the latter passage.[91]

---

[88] If "they departed" (ἐξήρχοντο) is the niphal form נפטרו in Hebrew, there may be a subtle allusion to the scribes and Pharisees' having thus "acquitted" (פטרו) the adulteress. See Jastrow 1157 on פָּטַר, niphal 2) and qal 4). M. Black in *An Aramaic Approach to the Gospels and Acts,* available to me as *Die Muttersprache Jesu. Das Aramäische der Evangelien und der Apostelgeschichte* (Stuttgart: Kohlhammer, 1982) 299, considers the phrase ἀρξάμενοι ἀπό in John 8:9 to be a Semitism. He cites the Fragment Targum on Gen 44:18, MS "P" (Klein 1.64 and 2.28): "I will begin with you" – מינך אנא מתחיל.

[89] Translation by L. Feldman in the LCL. Certainly in order to avoid such obedient following of their elders, voting on a capital case in the Sanhedrin took place "beginning from the side," i.e. with the youngest members. See *m. Sanh.* 4:2 (Albeck 4.180; Danby 387; Neusner 590), where this phrase contrasts to "beginning from the eldest," similar to John 8:9. Cf. *t. Sanh.* 7:2 (Zuckermandel / Liebermann 425-426; Neusner 4.219): In certain cases "they begin the vote from the oldest. In capital cases they begin from the side with the youngest members, so that the youngest member's opinion should not depend on the opinion of his master."

[90] Cf. J. Jeremias, *Jerusalem in the Time of Jesus* 243. He also notes that the "Pharisaic party in the Sanhedrin was composed entirely of scribes" (p. 236).

[91] Cf. Josephus, *Ant.* 13.297 for the Pharisees as "passing on to the people certain regulations handed down by former generations and not recorded in the Laws of Moses...," i.e. the oral *halakhah* given to Moses at Sinai. See also *Vita* 191 and Thackeray's note "a" on it. Thus not only the Pharisees' scribes, but also many other Pharisees, were probably acquainted with what is now still found in *m. Sanh.* 9:6.

Some of the scribes of John 8:3 may indeed have been members of the nearby Jerusalem Sanhedrin. Yet there is no indication whatsoever in the narrative that they (together with the Pharisees) had just come from the Sanhedrin, where they had accused and condemned the adulteress to death. Coming from the Sanhedrin, they are not now on the way to stone her outside the city, when they chance to come upon Jesus teaching the people. This has been proposed by many commentators, as has the opposite: they are now on the way to the Sanhedrin with her.[92]

Both views are false. The scribes and Pharisees have just now caught the adulteress in the very act. They as Zealots (the Pharisaic scribes probably, the Pharisees definitely) may only stone her to death, without taking her to the Sanhedrin, if they do so very soon. Otherwise they themselves could become guilty of murder and would have to reckon with the disapproval of the authorities.[93] Thus no "lynch justice" takes place here, as maintained by several commentators.[94] To lynch is rather "to put to death (as by hanging) by mob action without legal sanction."[95] The scribes and Zealot Pharisees are by no means a "mob,"[96] and although they do not base their behavior on the result of a proper trial in the Sanhedrin, they have legal sanction for their action: the oral *halakhah* now still found in *m. Sanh.* 9:6. It should be observed that Jesus does *not*

---

[92] Cf. already H. Meyer, *Evangelium des Johannes* (Göttingen: Vandenhoeck & Ruprecht, 1834) 109: The scribes and the Pharisees are members of the Sanhedrin who appear with Jesus as deputies of their colloquium. The woman had already been led before the Sanhedrin and accused there. Similarly J. Jeremias, "Zur Geschichtlichkeit des Verhörs Jesu vor dem Hohen Rat" in *ZNW* 43 (1950/51) 148. U. Becker, *Jesus und die Ehebrecherin* 170, says the incident takes place before the court trial. He believes the expression "scribes and Pharisees" is a later tradition borrowed from the Synoptic controversy stories (90).

[93] Cf. the discussion in *b. Sanh.* 82a, in part connected to the incident of Phinehas and Zimri (Soncino 545): it must be spontaneous. See also Philo, *Spec. Leg.* 1.55, with Phinehas referred to in 56, and 1.316: without delay. Later rabbinic opinion, after the fruitless rebellions against Rome in 66-70 and 132-135 CE, stated that Phinehas' killing Zimri and Cozbi was definitely without the Sages' approval. See for example *y. Sanh.* 9:6, 28b (Neusner 31.307).

[94] Cf. J. Derrett, "Law in the New Testament: The Story of the Woman Taken in Adultery," in *NTS* 10 (1963-64) 11. Both Krauss in *Sanhedrin-Makkot* 48, and Hengel in *Die Zeloten* 191, employ this term for *m. Sanh.* 9:6.

[95] *Webster's Ninth New Collegiate Dictionary* (Springfield, MASS: Merriam-Webster, 1987) 712.

[96] Against Derrett, "Law" 12, who speaks of "mob-execution." He also believes the crowd and the husband want the adulteress put to death (p. 11), which is not indicated by the narrative. Only the Zealots do. Luke 4:29, John 8:59 and Acts 14:5, in contrast, are examples of attempted mob execution.

contest the legal basis for the Zealots' action.[97] Instead, he appeals to their sense of shame by writing the beginnings of two relevant biblical verses in the earth (see section VII. below). This causes them to leave, one by one.

VI. The Identity of the Adulterer.

In John 8:3-4 certain (Zealot) scribes and Pharisees bring to Jesus in the Jerusalem Temple a woman just caught in the act of adultery. Yet her male counterpart, the adulterer, is missing and is nowhere mentioned in the narrative. The usual explanation for this on the part of the commentators is simply that he escaped.[98] D. Carson states that

> one wonders why the man was not brought with her. Either he was fleeter of foot than she, and escaped, leaving her to face hostile accusers on her own; or the accusers themselves were sufficiently chauvinistic to focus exclusively on the woman. The inequity of the situation arouses our feelings of compassion, however guilty she herself was.[99]

J. Derrett proposes a way out of this dilemma by suggesting that the adulteress was caught in a trap which her own husband had set in order to get rid of her. He hired and paid witnesses to testify against her. The male (Jewish) adulterer then bought his own life by paying off the witnesses.[100] Yet this makes no sense in the context. John 8:3-4 has certain scribes and Pharisees bring the adulteress to Jesus. They are Zealots, as Derrett himself implies.[1] Rigorists, intent on maintaining the ritual and

---

[97] According to Mark 3:18 par. (cf. also Acts 1:13), he even had a disciple who was a Zealot: Simon. Jesus was certainly well aware of what the Zealots were legally allowed, and not allowed, to do. According to Kohler, art. "Zealots" 641, Sepphoris near Jesus' home town of Nazareth was a Zealot stronghold. See Josephus, *Ant.* 14.413, where Herod goes there first; and 17.271.

[98] Cf. Sus 39, as well as H. Meyer in *Evangelium des Johannes* (1834) 110; M.-J. Lagrange, *Évangile selon Saint Jean* (Ebib; Paris: Gabalda, 1936[5]) 225; R. Brown, *The Gospel According to John (i-xii)* (AB 29; Garden City, NY: Doubleday, 1966) 333; and B. Lindars, *The Gospel of John* (NCB; London: Oliphants, 1977) 309.

[99] *The Gospel According to John* (Grand Rapids, MI: Eerdmans, 1991) 334.

[100] Cf. his art. "Law" 5-7. On p. 6, n. 4, he cites *b. Ketub.* 46a (Soncino 262) on a husband's hiring witnesses, yet they testify regarding his wife as having committed adultery *before* she married her husband (see notes 5 and 12). L. Morris in *The Gospel According to John* (NICNT 4; Grand Rapids, MI: Eerdmans, 1971) 885, states: "if the whole thing was engineered provision would have been made for the man to escape."

[1] Cf. his "Law" 9, "a few young zealots, keen to purify the people of sinners, can certainly be expected" (among those who brought the adulteress to Jesus), and 12, with references to the narrative of Phinehas. In n. 6 of the latter page Derrett

moral purity of the Jewish people, especially in Jerusalem, they would never have taken a bribe nor have assented to letting a Jewish adulterer go free, while wanting to stone the adulteress. Then the adulterer would even have been free to repeat the performance with other victims.

I propose instead that the man with whom the Jewish adulteress had sexual intercourse was a Roman and a heathen. Therefore he was not (and could not be) killed by Zealots for the crime of adultery. Before buttressing this suggestion, I first would like to call attention to the fact that in *b. Sanh.* 82a on *m.* 9:6, as noted above, the Court of the Hasmoneans had already decreed that a Jewish man who had sexual intercourse with a heathen woman is liable to punishment on four accounts, the last being that she is considered a married woman.[2] H. Freedman comments on this: "The troublous times of the Maccabees would seem to have led to licentiousness and a lowering of moral standards, and consequent liaisons with heathens."[3] This was true not only for Jewish men, but also for women (although probably to a much lesser extent) in the period of Greek occupation of Palestine.

The next major challenge to Jewish marital fidelity began when the Roman Pompey occupied Judea in 63 BCE. The "Psalms of Solomon," written originally in Hebrew in Jerusalem probably shortly after this,[4] mention in 2:11 that the Romans "set up the sons of Jerusalem for derision because of her prostitutes."[5] In fact, "the daughters of Jerusalem were available to all..." (2:13). "Everyone committed adultery with his neighbor's wife..." (8:10), and "the children of the covenant (living) among the gentile rabble adopted these (practices)" (17:15).[6] Reminiscent of Jesus' statement in John 8:7 are the words concerning a member of the Sanhedrin: "he is harsh in words in condemning (κατακρῖναι) sinners at judgment. And his hand is the first one against him (the sinner) as if in zeal (ὡς ἐν ζήλει), yet he himself is guilty of a variety of sins and

---

mentions *m. Sanh.* 9:6, yet he draws other conclusions than I do from this for John 8.

[2] Soncino 544-545; a parallel is found in *b. 'Avoda Zara* 36b (Soncino 176-177).

[3] *Sanhedrin* (Soncino 544, n. 8). M. Hengel in *Die Zeloten* 192 calls attention here to Jub 30:7-17. The "adulteress" of v 8 was certainly meant in regard to a heathen. See *OTP* 2.112-113, and 43-45 for the writing as originally in Hebrew, from Palestine, sometime between 161-140 BCE.

[4] Cf. R. Wright in *OTP* 2.640-641.

[5] *OTP* 2.652. As later noted for Tiberias, Jerusalem like other major cities most probably had its "whores' lane." Cf. Str-B 3.67.

[6] *OTP* 2.652, 659 and 666. Even if the author in part exaggerates, many of his assertions will have been true.

intemperance. His eyes are on every woman indiscriminately...," and "with his eyes he speaks to every woman of illicit affairs" (4:2-5).[7] The Roman occupation, as in Greek times, unfortunately also led to marital infidelity. If the daughters of Jerusalem were available to "all," this certainly included at least some Romans.

In the next century matters even deteriorated in this respect, with the consolidation of Roman power. A Pharisee in Jesus' parable could stand for example in the Temple and thank God in prayer that he is not like other men, including the adulterers (of his time – Luke 18:11). According to Mark 8:38, Jesus considered his to be an "adulterous and sinful generation," which was certainly not only meant metaphorically.

R. Yoḥanan b. Zakkai, a first generation Tanna, escaped from Zealot-held Jerusalem during the Jewish-Roman War of 66-70 CE.[8] The Mishnah tractate *Soṭah* on the suspected adulteress of Num 5:11-31 states at 9:9 that he caused the rite of the bitter water drunk by the suspected adulteress in Jerusalem to cease "when adulterers became many."[9] The context makes it very probable that this was before 66 CE.[10] It is also recorded that at least one daughter of a priest (still in her father's home) was burnt to death before 66 CE because of committing adultery (in Jerusalem).[11] If the daughter of a priest was caught while engaging in such behavior, it is very probable that those further down the social scale of priests / Levites / Israelites did so also, and certainly more frequently.

I therefore suggest that the man with whom the Jewish adulteress was caught *in flagranti* was a Roman, a member of the occupying military power. Matters had intensified even more since the conditions indicated in *Pss. Sol.* 17:15 above. The Roman may have been a soldier, who was not allowed to marry while in service.[12] As of 6 CE, for example, a Roman

---

[7] *Ibid.*, 2.655.

[8] Strack and Stemberger, *Introduction* 74-75. A contemporary appears to be Neḥunya "ben ha-Qanah" (*ibid.*), probably "the son of the Zealot."

[9] Albeck 3.258; Danby 305; Neusner 464.

[10] The Tosefta notes regarding this at 14:2 (Neusner 3.204): "But now there are many who see [their lovers] in public."

[11] Cf. *m. Sanh.* 7:2 in Albeck 4.190; Danby 391; Neusner 596. Literally "playing the whore," this is correct if she was already betrothed, as is probably meant. Jastrow 406 on זני, זנה has both "to run about as a prostitute, to be faithless, be unchaste," and "commit adultery." See also *b. Sanh.* 52b on this, where the R. Eleazar b. Zadok of the Mishnah remembers seeing such an execution as a child, and the similar case of Imarta the daughter of the priest Tali (Soncino 353 and 352).

[12] Even children sired from a soldier's wife when he was in military service were considered illegitimate. During his service he was not to have contact with his wife. Cf. the art. "Das Eherecht der römischen Soldaten" by J. Jung in *Aufstieg und*

military unit had its permanent quarters in the Antonia Fortress at the NW corner of the Temple Mount in Jerusalem. Josephus' term τάγμα for this unit in *Bell*. 5.244 literally corresponds to the Latin *legio*, a legion,[13] which was "divided into 10 cohorts, the number of men varying between 4,200 and 6,000."[14] Yet the native of Jerusalem may mean simply a cohort, as implied in *Ant*. 20.122. Here L. Feldman estimates that each cohort "had a strength of 500 to 600 men."[15] The number of Roman soldiers in Jerusalem increased at the Jewish pilgrimage festivals, when Pontius Pilate came from Caesarea Maritima with his *cohors praetoria*.[16]

It is also known that the Jewess Berenice, sister of Agrippa II,[17] in Rome in 75 CE "continued the love affair with Titus which had started in Palestine." She even hoped to marry the general, yet under Roman pressure he had to break up the relationship.[18] Berenice, although no longer married, was certainly not the only Jewess who fell in love or had an affair with a Roman military man. This also applied to the period before the outbreak of the Jewish-Roman War in 66 CE.

If not a soldier, the Roman may have been a lonely civil servant stationed in Jerusalem, a merchant, or of any other occupation. This explains why the scribes and Pharisees of John 8:3-5 only drag the Jewish adulteress to Jesus. They correctly state that in the (oral) *halakhah* given to Moses (at Sinai), he commanded them, the Zealots, to stone such persons (v 5). The *halakhah* of *m. Sanh*. 9:6 states that the Jewish man who has sexual intercourse with a heathen woman, the Zealots may / can / should strike down (killing him, at the moment of the act). This applied, of course, also to a Jewish woman.

Yet the Zealots did not dare to spontaneously arrest the Roman adulterer. In the first place he was a citizen of the world power presently occupying Palestine. Great care was to be taken in such a flammable situation, in which the lives of other, innocent Jews could be endangered.

Niedergang der römischen Welt. Principat, II.14, ed. H. Temporini (Berlin and New York: de Gruyter, 1982) 302-346.

[13] LSJ 1752.

[14] W. Smith and J. Lockwood, *latin-english Dictionary* 395. On "cohors," see p. 122.

[15] Cf. his n. "h" on this passage in the LCL. See also Acts 21:31.

[16] Cf. Str-B 1.1035-1036, which should be corrected by the articles on "Antonia" and "Jerusalem, Herod's Palace" in *Jesus & His World*, ed. J. Rousseau and R. Arav 12-14 and 151-152.

[17] Cf. Acts 25-26 for their encounter with Paul in Caesarea.

[18] Cf. Schürer, *The history* 1.479, with the sources cited in notes 39-41. She is called "as bigoted as she was dissolute" on p. 475.

Secondly, even the *lex Juliana de adulteriis,* passed by Augustus ca. 17 BCE in part because his daughter Julia was publicly promiscuous, no longer allowed a Roman husband to kill his Roman wife if she was caught in the act of adultery. Yet he could kill the Roman adulterer "if he was an actor, a freedman of any one in the immediate family, (or) a pimp, condemned by a public court..."[19] The (Roman) adulterer of John 8 certainly did not belong to one of the latter categories, nor is a (Jewish) husband mentioned at all. Most importantly, the Roman law only applied to *two* Roman citizens, and not to a Roman man and a non-Roman, Jewish woman. The same was true for the tradition still found in *m. Sanh.* 9:6, where Zealots may kill the *Jewish* person having sexual intercourse with a heathen. No mention is made (in contrast to Numbers 25, with Cozbi) of their right to also kill the heathen involved.

Without taking the time to notify the Jewish husband, the Zealots hastily drag off his adulterous wife in John 8. They wish to stone her very soon because of the legal stipulation that their behavior is valid only if done spontaneously and forthwith. The above discussion explains why the husband is lacking in John 7:53 – 8:11, as well as the (Roman) adulterer.

Finally, *m. Sanh.* 9:6 speaks of a Jewish man having sexual intercourse with an אֲרָמִית, literally an Aramean / Syrian woman. This term meant, however, not only a "heathen" in general, but also a "Roman." The terms אֲרָמִי and רוֹמִי were so similar that the first was often meant as "Roman."[20] This certainly encouraged the Zealots, vehemently opposed to Roman military occupation of their homeland, to strike down and kill a married Jewish woman in Jerusalem who had sexual intercourse with a Roman.

It was not only adultery, however, which was at stake here. The possible issue from such an immoral union was a *mamzēr*, a bastard, who was greatly looked down upon and who had major disadvantages in Jewish society.[21] In addition, a Jewish woman who had sexual intercourse with a heathen was considered to be in great danger of being

---

[19] Cf. L. Raditsa, "Augustus' Legislation Concerning Marriage, Procreation, Love Affairs and Adultery" in *Aufstieg und Niedergang der römischen Welt,* Principat, II.13, ed. H. Temporini (Berlin and New York: de Gruyter, 1980) 312. See also p. 292: "the law did not provide for the death penalty, except in the instance when a father came upon his daughter and her lover and killed them both." This was not the case for the married adulteress of John 8. See also the art. "Adultery" by A. Berger and B. Nicolas in *The Oxford Classical Dictionary* (Oxford: Clarendon, 1970²) 10-11, and the art. "Adulterium" by L. Hartmann in *PW* 1.432-435.

[20] Cf. Krauss, *Sanhedrin-Makkot* 262; Jastrow 122-123; and Levy 1.168.

[21] Cf. the extensive discussion in Jeremias, *Jerusalem* 337-342.

"drawn after him," i.e. to idolatry.[22] This was one of the worst sins in Judaism because it denied the exclusive rights of the zealous / jealous God, the LORD, and called into question the very existence of His chosen people, the Jews.

VII. Jesus' Writing in the Ground.

After certain Zealot scribes and Pharisees dragged a woman caught in the act of adultery to Jesus and asked him to give them his opinion on the matter (whether she should be stoned to death or not), John 8:6 states that he (sitting) bent down and wrote (καταγράφω) with his finger in the earth / ground. When they continued to question him (about the matter),[23] he straightened up and said to them: "Let him who is without sin among you be the first to throw a stone at her" (v 7). Then he again bent down and wrote (γράφω) in the earth (v 8).

There is no difference between καταγράφω and γράφω in Hebrew. Both are expressed simply by כָּתַב.[24] The Hellenistic Jewish Christian translator or a later editor of the narrative simply wanted to vary his style and added κατα-. Both verses (6 and 8) speak of Jesus' writing εἰς τὴν γῆν, literally "into the earth." However, εἰς here should properly be ἐν, for Jesus wrote "in" the earth. This error in Greek was typical of the time.[25] The original was most probably בָּאָרֶץ, with a ב, as in Jer 17:13, the only instance in the Hebrew Bible of "writing (being written) 'in the earth.'"[26]

---

[22] Cf. for example *b. 'Avoda Zara* 36b (Soncino 177) in connection with *m. Sanh.* 9:6. *Mek.* Baḥodesh 8 (Lauterbach 2.262-263) has R. Ḥananya b. Gamaliel, a second generation Tanna (Strack and Stemberger, *Introduction* 82), demonstrate how worshiping idols is the same as committing adultery (the second and sixth Commandments).

[23] The imperfect of ἐπιμένω implies several times, that is, their persistence. As Zealots, they wanted to trap Jesus too.

[24] Cf. the Hebrew New Testament of the United Bible Societies (p. 258). The imperfect tense employed for both Greek terms does not imply here extended behavior. This is shown by the simple perfect in Hebrew.

[25] Cf. BDF § 205 (pp. 110-111).

[26] The verb כתב occurs 218 times, but only here with "in the earth." The LXX has ἐπὶ τῆς γῆς. Jesus could in fact write something "in the earth / ground" in the "new" Temple of Herod the Great, for "The construction of the courts was completed only in 63 CE under Agrippa II (*Antiq.* 2,9.7 / 219). Obviously, the [outer] Court of the Gentiles was the last one to be completed. Circa 30 CE, it was not yet paved, and its surface was made of hardened earth." Cf. the art. "Stone, Stoning" in *Jesus & His World*, ed. Rousseau and Arav, 266.

The most various suggestions have been made in the course of the centuries as to what, if anything, Jesus wrote in the ground. Was he only doodling, in order to gain more time to think? Was his behavior "simply a studied refusal to pronounce judgment," as C. Barrett maintains, noting John 8:15?[27] Did Jesus write down the specific sins of the accusers, found as a variant in v 8? Did the writing indicate "that he does not wish to be involved in the matter..."?[28] Did Jesus write down "the words He later spoke"?[29] R. Brown believes that "if the matter were of major importance, the content of the writing would have been reported."[30] U. Becker in his monograph thinks the two occurrences of Jesus' writing in the earth are due to the narrator or author and do not belong to the original narrative at all.[31] Others, following Ambrose, Augustine and Jerome, have proposed Jer 17:13, noted above.[32] More recently J. Derrett has argued for Exod 23:1b and 7a.[33]

I would now like to propose two other specific texts from the Hebrew Bible, the beginnings of which Jesus wrote in the earth. Even in printed midrashim today, often only the beginning of a biblical verse is cited. The reader is assumed to know Scripture so well that he or she can continue the quotation. This was even more so the case at the time of Jesus. The narrative in John 8 does not state that the crowd of normal Jewish people whom Jesus had been teaching in the Temple recognized

---

[27] Cf. his *The Gospel According to St. John* (London: SPCK, 1962) 6.

[28] Cf. B. Lindars, *The Gospel of John* 310.

[29] Cf. L. Morris, *The Gospel According to John* 888.

[30] *The Gospel According to John (i-xii)* 334. He summarizes other opinions on pp. 333-334, as do R. Schnackenburg, *Das Johannesevangelium, II. Teil* 228-229; W. Barclay, *The Gospel of John* (Philadelphia: Westminster, 1956) 3-4; and U. Becker, *Jesus und die Ehebrecherin* 85-86. Becker emphasizes the non-permanency of what is written, as in *m. Šabb.* 12:5 (Str-B 2.521). Writing with dust from the roads, however, has nothing whatsoever to do with writing in the earth so that what is written can be read.

[31] *Jesus und die Ehebrecherin* 87.

[32] Cf. the texts in Becker, *op. cit.,* 61-62. This is also maintained by O. Schwarz, "Jer. 17,13 als möglicher alttestamentlicher Hintergrund zu Jo. 8,6.8" in *Von Kanaan bis Kerala.* Festschrift J. P. M. van der Ploeg, ed. W. Delsman et al. (Neukirchen-Vluyn: Neukirchener; Kevelaer: Butzon and Bercker, 1982) 239-256.

[33] Cf. his "Law" 19 and 23. His suggestion that the husband brings false charges against his wife in order to divorce her is already found in Philo, *Spec. Leg.* 3.79-81. In "Jesus schreibt mit dem Finger auf die Erde: Joh 8,6b.8" in *BZ* 40 (1996) 91-93, H. Schöndorf thinks of Exod 31:18. The contrast is between the old law (Moses) and the new (in Jesus). That is Johannine theology, but not what Jesus wrote in the earth.

the source of his writing in the earth. Yet the thoroughly trained scribes, experts in the written and oral law, often knew the entire Bible by heart, especially those passages which they and their colleagues used to buttress definite legal teachings.[34] The Zealot Pharisees mentioned in John 8:3 together with the scribes certainly also knew both the Scriptures long associated with the oral *halakhah* now found in *m. Sanh.* 9:6, and with the rite of testing a suspected adulteress (Num 5:11-31). Thus if Jesus bent down and wrote only the beginning of each verse, they would immediately have recognized its association with the theme of fornication / adultery in general, and its relevance to the situation of the adulteress caught in the act, with which they now were testing Jesus. Since not all the scribes and Pharisees could stand in the front row and read what Jesus wrote on the ground, those in front are pictured as informing the ones behind them of the contents. Thus John 8:9 says: "Now when they 'heard' it (thus not Jesus' statement of v 7), they departed, one by one...." This also implies that the two verses written by Jesus in the earth, with cumulative effect, caused them to become ashamed of their Zealot behavior in regard to the adulteress and thus to depart. The following two verses from the Hebrew Bible fulfill these criteria.

1) *Mal 2:11.*

The section Mal 2:10-16 deals with God's demanding faithfulness in the marriage covenant. Verse 11 reads:

Judah has been faithless (בָּגְדָה יְהוּדָה),
and abomination has been committed in Israel and Jerusalem;
for Judah has profaned the sanctuary of the LORD, which He loves,
and has married the daughter of a foreign god.

Verse 12 then states: "May the LORD cut off from the tents of Jacob anyone who does this...." The prophet castigates him who is faithless to the wife of his youth (v 14). The addressees should take heed to themselves, and not let anyone be faithless to the wife of his youth (v 15). Verse 16 repeats that they should take heed to themselves, and not be faithless.

---

[34] Cf. for example *t. Meg.* 2:5, which relates that R. Meir, a third generation Tanna (Strack and Stemberger, *Introduction* 84), went to a certain town and found no copy of the Scroll of Esther in Hebrew, so he simply wrote one out from memory (Neusner 2.284-285). This is quoted in *y. Meg.* 4:1, 74d (Neusner 19.145), where it is followed by statements by two other rabbis: one could "write out the entire Scripture from memory," the other "the entire Torah" (p. 146).

Targum Jonathan, certainly reflecting popular Palestinian interpretation, broadens the meaning of the individual "Judah" in 2:11 by expanding this twice to "the people of the house of Judah."[35] All Jews are now addressed. It also interprets "and has married the daughter of a foreign god" as "they have chosen to marry wives from the daughters of the nations."[36] Instead of repeating the Hebrew in v 15, literally "take heed (pl.) to your spirit,"[37] the Targum has: "take heed to 'yourselves.'"[38] As in the Hebrew, an appeal is made here to self-scrutiny on the part of those who have been unfaithful to their own wives. This corresponds in content to Jesus' statement in John 8:7, "Let 'anyone among you who is without sin' be the first to throw a stone at her (the adulteress)."

The faithless behavior (בגד)[39] of Judah, after whom all Jews were named (יְהוּדָה / יְהוּדִים), consisted in Mal 2:11 in his marrying the daughter of the Canaanite Shua, who bore him three sons. That is, he married a heathen. *Gen. Rab.* Vayesheb 85/1 on Gen 38:1, "It happened at that time that Judah went down from his brothers...," applies Mal 2:11 to Judah in his "going down," i.e. degrading himself by marrying a heathen woman.[40] Judah's seeking out a prostitute (Gen 38:16), from the viewpoint of later Jews, was certainly also a part of his being "faithless."[41]

In *b. Meg.* 15a a baraitha has R. Yehoshua b. Qorha, a third generation Tanna,[42] state that "'Malachi is the same as Ezra,' and the Sages say that Malachi was his proper name." R. Naḥman, probably a

---

[35] English in Cathcart and Gordon 233, Aramaic in Sperber, *The Bible in Aramaic* 3.502.

[36] *Ibid.*

[37] Cf. BDB 1037 on שמר, niph., 1.

[38] Sperber 3.503.

[39] BDB 93: "act or deal treacherously, faithlessly, deceitfully, in the marriage relation...."

[40] Cf. Theodor and Albeck 1029, and Soncino 2.787, with n. 1. See also *Tanḥ.* B Vayesheb 9 on Gen 38:1 (Buber 182, Bietenhard 1.207), which specifically refers to Gen 38:2. In *Eliyyahu Zuṭa* 3 (Friedmann, p. 177), Mal 2:11 also refers to Judah's forsaking Israelite seed and cleaving "to those to whom it was not fitting for them to marry" (Braude and Kapstein 418).

[41] The prostitute was Tamar, his own daughter-in-law, to whom Judah had not given his son Shelah in marriage although he had grown up since the deaths of his brothers Er and Onan. This was also a lack of faithfulness (cf. Gen 38:11).

[42] Strack and Stemberger, *Introduction* 85.

third generation Babylonian Amora,[43] then employs Mal 2:11 to prove this, also citing Ezra 10:2, "We have broken faith with our God and have married foreign women...," to show that it was Malachi / Ezra who put away the foreign women.[44]

The above Judaic materials help to understand *b. Sanh.* 82b better, which comments on *m.* 9:6, "he who has sexual intercourse with an Aramean (heathen) woman – Zealots may / can / should strike him down (killing him, at the moment of the act)." R. Kahana, a second generation Palestinian Amora and student of Rab, a first generation Babylonian Amora who studied under Rabbi in Palestine,[45] asked his teacher what would happen if Zealots did *not* strike down such a person. Since Rab could not remember the traditional answer to this, R. Kahana "was made to read in his dream" Mal 2:11. He then recited the entire teaching to Rab. Verse 11a, "Judah has been faithless," refers to idolatry, as in Jer 3:20. Verse 11b refers to pederasty, as in Lev 18:22. Verse 11c, "for Judah has profaned the sanctuary of the LORD," refers to harlotry, as in Deut 23:18. And verse 11d, "and 'has been intimate with' the daughter of a foreign god," refers to intimacy with a heathen woman.

The latter term, "has been intimate with" (בעל), in biblical Hebrew means "to marry."[46] In rabbinic Hebrew, however, it means "to have sexual intercourse (both legal or illicit), to embrace a woman." In fact, a בּוֹעֵל is a lover or adulterer in contrast to a בַּעַל, a "husband."[47] This explains why the rabbis interpreted Mal 2:11d not as Judah's having married, but as having illicit sexual intercourse with the daughter of a foreign god.

The conclusion of the above teaching recalled by R. Kahana is that the punishment for the behavior indicated in Mal 2:11 is found in v 12, "The LORD will cut off the man who does this...," which is then elaborated for the (later, post 70 CE) scholar and the priest. They will have no offspring to follow in their footsteps.[48] The term "cut off" (כרת) in rabbinic Hebrew means not receiving capital punishment by the hand of man, but "divine punishment through premature or sudden death."[49]

---

[43] *Ibid.*, 101.

[44] Soncino 87.

[45] Cf. Strack and Stemberger, *Introduction* 95 and 93 respectively.

[46] BDB 127.

[47] Jastrow 182.

[48] Soncino 543-544. It is also found in part in Targum Jonathan on the verse (Cathcart and Gordon 233-234), as well as in *Eliyyahu Zuṭa* 3 (see n. 40).

[49] Cf. Jastrow 674 on the verb, but especially the noun כָּרֵת.

This is a later watering down of the original meaning, "to cut off" by killing. Before 70 CE the latter was certainly also the meaning of the verse as applied to a Jew having sexual intercourse with a heathen woman. By allowing the Zealots to do such killing, the LORD cuts off such a person.

* * *

The above interpretation of Mal 2:11 is definitely Tannaitic, as indicated by Rab's having forgotten it. Since it is employed to explain *m. Sanh.* 9:6, I suggest that it is the first scriptural passage Jesus wrote in the earth in John 8:6. The first two Hebrew words, בגדה יהודה, sufficed for the scribes and Zealot Pharisees since this is the only occurrence in the Hebrew Bible of בגד with Judah. The admonition in the context, Mal 2:15-16, "take heed to yourselves," because of husbands' being unfaithful to their own wives, unfortunately did not have the desired effect on Jesus' opponents. Nor did Mal 2:12 impress them: "The LORD (and not the Zealots) should cut off...." They persisted in questioning Jesus about the matter of the married woman caught in the act of adultery. This led him to tell them: "Let him who is without sin among you be the first to throw a stone at her" (John 8:7). Then, to reinforce this statement, Jesus again bent down and wrote the beginning of a second biblical verse in the earth.

2) Hos 4:14.

The phrase in John 8:7, ὁ ἀναμάρτητος ὑμῶν, "him who is without sin among you," is somewhat clumsy translation Greek, literally meaning "your (pl.) sinless one." This is the only occurrence in the NT of ἀναμάρτητος.[50] In Hebrew this expression could be: הָאִישׁ מִכֶּם נָקִי מֵעָוֹן,[51] literally "the man among you (pl., who is) free of sin." These words, especially "free of sin," were a clear hint to Jesus' opponents of what he now, having again bent down, would write in the earth (John 8:8). In early Judaic tradition, the phrase "not free of sin" was interpreted by Hos 4:14.

The rite employed in the Jerusalem Temple to determine whether a man's wife had "gone astray" by having sexual intercourse with another man is described in Num 5:11-31. From the verb שטה in vv 12,19-20 and 29

---

[50] In the LXX it paraphrases a Hebrew expression in Deut 29:19, and is also found without a Hebrew equivalent in 2 Macc 8:4 and 12:42.

[51] Cf. the Hebrew New Testament of the United Bible Societies (258), which has מִי מִכֶּם נָקִי מֵחֵטְא. See also the Hatch-Redpath concordance (1.62) for עָוֹן behind ἁμαρτία in numerous LXX references.

derived the name of the later Mishnah tractate סוֹטָה.[52] As noted in section
I. above, the only occurrence of תפש in connection with adultery in the
Hebrew Bible is Num 5:13, "she was not taken (in the act)." The scribes
and Zealot Pharisees themselves employed this verb of the adulteress
"caught" in the act in John 8:4. Acting in light of the legal principle still
found in *m. Sanh.* 9:6 with its קַנָּאִין, "Zealots," they may also have thought
of Numbers 5 because the husband's "jealousy," in various phrases,
occurs here in concentrated form ten times: vv 14-15,18,25 and 29-30. It is
the same Hebrew root as "zeal."

After the husband's having subjected his wife suspected of adultery
to this rite, the final verse of the unit (31) states: "'The man shall be free
from sin' (נִקָּה הָאִישׁ מֵעָוֹן), but the woman shall bear her sin."[53] I suggest
that Jesus derived his own phrase, "he who is without sin" in John 8:7,
from this Hebrew phrase. The adjective נָקִי means "clear, *free from,*
exempt," "innocent."[54]

Human nature being what it is, very early Judaic tradition in fairness
questioned whether it was only a married woman who could commit
adultery. The Tannaitic midrash *Sifre* Num. Naso 21 on Num 5:31 asks
for example why it is stated: "And the man is free of sin." (This is only
true) "when the man (himself) is free of sin, 'the woman shall bear her
sin.'" But not in accordance with what Scripture says:[55]

> I will not punish your daughters when they play the whore,
> nor your daughters-in-law when they commit adultery;
> for the men themselves go aside with whores, and sacrifice with cult
>   prostitutes;
> thus a people without understanding comes to ruin (Hos 4:14, NRSV).

He (Hosea) says to the men: Since you (m. pl.) run after whores, the
waters (of bitterness) will not put the woman to the test. Thus it is stated:
"The man who is free of sin." (It is) this sin (which is meant).[56]

---

[52] Cf. Jastrow 963 on this noun.

[53] Cf. BDB 730-731 on עָוֹן as iniquity, Jastrow 1053 as perversion, wrong, "sin."
The LXX has ἁμαρτία here, with ἀθῷος (free from, guiltless: LSJ 34).

[54] BDB 667.

[55] That is, the contents of the following citation, Hos 4:14, apply when the man is
not free of sin. The terminology (ולא כענין) is difficult to express in English. A
minor strand of interpretation in the Babylonian Talmud assumes that if a
husband sleeps with his wife even though he knows she is unclean through
intercourse with another man, the husband is "not free of iniquity." See *Yebam.*
58a (Soncino 389); *Soṭa* 28a (Soncino 137-138); *Qidd.* 27b (Soncino 132); and *Šebu.*
5a (Soncino 15).

[56] Horowitz 25. I follow the interpretation proposed by Kuhn 68, who in n. 11
refers to John 8:7. Neusner in *Sifre to Numbers* 1.125 interprets differently.

This text from Hosea is already found in *m. Soṭa* 9:9, which states: "When adulterers became many, (the rite of) the bitter water (Numbers 5) ceased. And Rabban Yoḥanan ben Zakkai caused it to cease, for it is written: (Hos 4:14)."[57] As noted above, I believe Yoḥanan b. Zakkai canceled this rite before 66 CE because of a general degeneration in morals. It was caused for the most part by the Roman occupation.

In *b. Soṭa* 47b, which comments on the above statement of the Mishnah, "Our Rabbis taught" the following concerning Num 5:31a: "at the time when the man is free from iniquity, the water proves his wife; but when the man is not free from iniquity, the water does not prove his wife." Then the rabbis explain why Hos 4:14 was quoted in the Mishnah to support this, and they comment on each of its statements. Sinning by men with either a married or an unmarried woman, for example, is included in the verse. R. Eleazar[58] concludes the unit by maintaining that Hosea spoke to Israel (Jewish men): "If you are scrupulous with yourselves, the water will prove your wives; otherwise the water will not prove your wives."[59]

Targum Jonathan on Hos 4:14 reflects the same direction of interpretation found in the above Judaic sources. It castigates men with a double standard. The Hebrew of v 14b says "the men themselves (הֵם) go aside with whores, and sacrifice with cult prostitutes." Transporting this to its own age, the Targum renders: "they (m.) keep company with harlots, and they eat and drink with prostitutes."[60]

In light of the above analysis of Judaic interpretation of Num 5:31 and Hos 4:14, connected to the case of an adulteress, I suggest that Jesus wrote the beginning of the latter verse in the earth in John 8:8 – לֹא אֶפְקוֹד עַל בְּנוֹתֵכֶם, "I (God) will not punish your daughters." Since Jer 5:9, 29 and 9:8 also contain the verb "I will not punish," the addition of "your

---

[57] Albeck 3.258-259; Danby 305; Neusner 464. J. Lightfoot had already called attention to this text and to *b. Soṭa* 47a in 1859. Cf. his *A Commentary on the New Testament from the Talmud and Hebraica* (Oxford: Oxford University Press, 1859; reprint Peabody, MASS: Hendrickson, 1989) 3.327. See also D. Amram, art. "Adultery" in *JE* (1891) 1.217, who refers to John 8:7. They are followed by others. Yet none of them notes the significance of "free from sin" in Num 5:31 and of Hos 4:14 as the second verse Jesus wrote in the earth.

[58] Cf. Strack and Stemberger, *Introduction* 98, for him as possibly Eleazar ben Pedat, a third generation Palestinian Amora. The Munich MS here, however, has Eliezer (ben Hyrcanus), a second generation Tanna.

[59] Soncino *Soṭa* 251-252. Part of this is also found in *y. Soṭa* 9:9, 24a (Neusner 27.251). Cf. also *Num. Rab.* Naso 9/44 on Num 5:31 (Mirqin 9.219-220, Soncino 5.318).

[60] Sperber 3.392; Cathcart and Gordon 38.

daughters" was necessary here for the sake of clarity. Only Hos 4:14, however, begins so in the Bible, and only it has as its object "your daughters." The scribes and Zealot Pharisees, well acquainted with the rite of the suspected adulteress, would have recognized the verse immediately. Jesus had already prepared them for it in his phrase "free of sin" in John 8:7, derived from Num 5:31, traditionally associated with Hos 4:14.

This biblical verse emphasized that *God* would not punish young Jewish women who played the harlot, nor married women who committed adultery. It was thus definitely not the task of Zealots to do so. The prophet Hosea stated that this was because the men themselves went aside with whores. Yoḥanan b. Zakkai's decision to cancel the rite of the suspected adulteress substantiated this: adultery had unfortunately increased so much that the ordeal had become meaningless.

Jesus certainly did not accuse the highly venerated scribes and Pharisees assembled before him of personally committing adultery with another man's wife, (although such behavior cannot be excluded completely for a particular individual).[61] Yet as a man himself, he knew that it was possible to view a woman lustfully, which meant already committing adultery with her in one's heart (Matt 5:27-28; cf. 15:19 with a parallel in Mark 7:21). Later leading rabbis honestly admitted to such adulterous thoughts.[62]

Shamed by Hos 4:14 into admitting to themselves as men that they too had committed fornication or adultery with their eyes / hearts, the scribes and Zealot Pharisees now departed from the scene, one by one, beginning with the oldest. More mature and experienced in life, the latter could honestly concede that they too did not have a pure conscience in this regard.[63] The younger men followed their example, leaving the accused adulteress alone with Jesus in the middle of the crowd.

---

[61] Cf. Jer 23:14, "the prophets of Jerusalem...commit adultery and walk in lies." Targum Jonathan on the "prophet" of v 11 has "scribe." See Sperber 3.316, and Cathcart and Gordon 112, with the discussion on pp. 32-33. It is often difficult to differentiate between the literal and metaphorical meaning of "committing adultery" (for example, as "practicing idolatry").

[62] Cf. Aqiva, Meir and others cited by Str-B 3.109-111, as well as examples of committing adultery with one's eyes in 1.299-301.

[63] A (later) variant in 8:9 even adds: "and convicted by their conscience, they departed...."

VIII. The Punishment of Stoning.

In John 8:5 the scribes and Zealot Pharisees who brought a Jewish woman just caught in the act of adultery to Jesus state: "In the (oral) *halakhah* Moses commanded us (Zealots) to stone such women." As pointed out above, there are no indications that a betrothed virgin is meant here. According to Deut 22:21 and 24 she may be stoned.

No specific method of capital punishment is prescribed in the Hebrew Bible for an adulteress who is already properly married to her husband (Deut 22:22; Lev 20:10), the case assumed here. Tannaitic interpretation of the latter verses required strangulation.[64] It was considered to be the least severe mode of capital punishment, followed by beheading, burning and stoning, the harshest.[65] There is no reason to believe strangulation was not the usual punishment for a properly married adulteress also before 70 CE.[66] The reason for the exceptional stoning of the adulteress of John 8:5 is found in the scriptural justification for the original zealots' behavior in Numbers 25. In *m. Sanh.* 9:6 the Zealots may / can / should strike down (and kill) a Jewish man who has sexual intercourse with a heathen woman. (The same was true for a properly married Jewish woman.) The method of killing such a person is not stated. It was, however, stoning, which was derived from Num 25:4-5, just before the prototype Zealot Phinehas' killing of Zimri and Cozbi, whom he caught in the act.

Because of the Israelite men's fornicating with the heathen daughters of Moab, even bowing down to their gods, including Baal Peor (Num 25:1-3), the LORD told Moses: "Take all the chiefs of the people, and hang them in the sun before the LORD, that the fierce anger of the LORD may turn away from Israel" (v 4). Thus "Moses said to the judges of Israel: 'Every one of you put to death his men who have yoked themselves to Baal Peor'" (v 5).

The verb translated here in 25:4 as "hang," הוֹקַע, is the hiphil singular imperative of the very rare יָקַע.[67] It is not found in rabbinic Hebrew. This is one reason Judaic commentators felt it necessary to spell out what was meant by it. In addition, it was not clear for them to whom the object of

---

[64] Cf. *Sifre* and *Sifra ad loc.*, translated in Str-B 1.295-296.

[65] Cf. *m. Sanh.* 7:1 (Albeck 4.189; Danby 391, with n. 5; and Neusner 595-596).

[66] Against Blinzler, "Die Strafe" 38-39 and 45, and others who surmise that after 70 CE the in general more lenient Pharisees, now in the absolute majority, changed stoning to strangulation. No texts attest such a change at that time.

[67] BDB 429: be dislocated, alienated. Here "of some solemn form of execution, but mng. uncertain." The versions have impale, expose, crucify.

the verb, "them," referred: to the heads of the people, or to the Israelites who had fornicated with the daughters of Moab and bowed down to their heathen gods. In *Num. Rab.* Balak 20/23 on v 4, R. Yudan, (the same as Yehudah bar Ilai,) a third generation Tanna,[68] preferred the first option "because they had not checked the people." His frequent interlocutor, R. Nehemya, also a third generation Tanna,[69] disagreed, maintaining that God told Moses: "Appoint for them heads of Sanhedrins who shall judge everyone who had (fornicated and) gone to Peor." God will point out the transgressor by removing the cloud above him and causing the sun to shine on him "so that all will know who it is that has gone astray, and they will hang (תלה) him." This is then proved from 25:5: "And Moses said to the judges of Israel: 'Every one of you put to death his men,'" etc.[70]

In *b. Sanh.* 34b the term הוֹקַע of Num 25:4 is interpreted in light of the same verb in 2 Sam 21:6 as "hanging" (תְּלִיָּיה). This verse from Numbers is also employed to explain *m. Sanh.* 4:1, "capital charges must be tried by day and concluded by day." Then, in 35a, the question is asked: "If the people had sinned (in Num 25:2-3), wherein had the chiefs sinned?" Rab, a first generation Babylonian Amora who studied with Rabbi in Palestine,[71] then states that God told Moses: "Divide them (the heads of the people) into (many) courts." As J. Schachter notes, this was to try the offenders. Rab thus interprets just as R. Nehemya does.[72]

The Tannaitic midrash *Sifre* Num. Balak 131 on Num 25:4 explains the verse similarly. God tells Moses: "Install the heads of the people as judges, and let them hang (צלב) the sinners before the sun."[73] In *y. Sanh.* 10:2, 28d this line of interpretation is also followed. A calculation is made that since there were 78,600 judges of Israel, each killing two offenders, a total of 157,200 Israelites were put to death.[74]

---

[68] Strack and Stemberger, *Introduction* 84-85. See Str-B 5/6.175 for the identity of the names.

[69] *Introduction* 85.

[70] Mirqin 10.273; Soncino 6.822-823, which I slightly modify. A parallel is found in *Tanh.* B Balak 28 on Num 25:4 (Buber 2.148, Bietenhard 2.382-383).

[71] Cf. n. 63, p. 12.

[72] Soncino 220-221, with Schachter's notes on the latter page.

[73] Horowitz 172; Kuhn 518, with notes 110-112. See also for the first part Targum Onqelos (Grossfeld 140), and for both parts the Palestinian Targum (Rieder 2.232, Etheridge 433), Fragment Targum (Klein 1.106 and 204; 2.78 and 163), and Neofiti 1 (Díez Macho 4.243 and 601) on Num 25:4.

[74] Neusner 31.339-340. For the number of 78,600 judges, cf. also *b. Sanh.* 18a (Soncino 90), something "our rabbis taught" in regard to Exod 18:21.

In all these Judaic sources, just before the incident of Phinehas' killing Zimri and Cozbi when he catches them *in flagranti*, special, very small courts are set up to try those Israelites who fornicated with heathen women and bowed down to their gods. Here Moses commands (literally, "says to")[75] the judges of Israel: Let each man "kill" (הרג) his men who have joined themselves to Baal Peor (Num 25:5). Judaic tradition, as described above, interprets this to mean that the heads of the people "hang" (v 4) those who offended in regard to sexuality and idolatry. The term "hang" in *Num. Rab.* 20/23 cited above in this regard is תָּלָה.[76] Early Jewish commentators thought of the hanging done here as automatically preceded by "stoning" (סָקַל),[77] and thus associated Num 25:4-5 with the description of the procedure of stoning still found in *m. Sanh.* 6:4.

Here in the Mishnah Deut 17:7 is quoted ("stoning" is found in v 5): "The hand of the witness shall be 'first' (בָּרִאשֹׁנָה) against him to put him to death." I suggest that this strongly influenced Jesus' term "first" (πρῶτος) in John 8:7, "Let him who is without sin be the 'first' to throw a stone at her." Jesus addresses this to the "witnesses" who had caught the adulteress in the very act, the scribes and Pharisees.

After this quotation from Deuteronomy, R. Eliezer (b. Hyrcanus), an older second generation Tanna known for his only repeating what he himself had heard,[78] states: "All that have been stoned (סקל) must be hanged (תלה)." The majority opinion of the Sages, however, disagreed: "None is hanged except the blasphemer and the idolator." A description of hanging is then given, with Deut 21:23 quoted to buttress the assertion that the body is taken down the same day.[79]

---

[75] Cf. BDB 56,4. for this meaning of אמר. It, and not צוה (Jastrow 1267), may thus be behind the ἐνετείλατο of John 8:5.

[76] Jastrow 1671. He translates *m. Sanh.* 6:4, for example, as: "how is the hanging (of the convict stoned to death) done?" Such "hanging" after stoning was most probably the fate of Jesus' brother James, whom the Sadducean high priest Ananus had killed in 62 CE for transgressing the Law. See Josephus, *Ant.* 20.200.

[77] Jastrow 1020.

[78] Cf. Strack and Stemberger, *Introduction* 77, and W. Bacher, *Die Agada der Tannaiten* (Strassburg: Trübner, 1903) 1.96 – "seine Anhänglichkeit an Überliefertes."

[79] Albeck 4.187; Danby 390; Neusner 594-595. See also *b. Sanh.* 45b-46a (Soncino 300-301) on this. In *m. Sanh.* 7:5 on the idolator, it is stated that "if a man excretes to Baal Peor, (he is to be stoned, because) this is how it is worshiped" (Danby 392, in n. 11 referring to Num 25:3 and 5 and other passages). As indicated by *b. Sanh.* 64a (Soncino 436-437), it appears that Baal Peor was still worshiped in later centuries.

The above complex of traditions, now still found in *m. Sanh.* 6:4, explains why in Judaic tradition the "idolator" Israelites of Num 25:1-3 and 5, to be put to death by hanging (v 4), were first thought to be "stoned." This is paraphrased well by L. Ginzberg in regard to the judges and executioners of the offenders as follows: "These carried out Moses' command and stoned the sinners, whose corpses then hung upon the gallows for a few minutes."[80] This recalls the Zealots' statement in John 8:5, "In the *halakhah* Moses 'commanded' us (Zealots) to 'stone' such women." This oral *halakhah* was thus not only that now found in *m. Sanh.* 9:6, but also in early Judaic interpretation of "stoning" those to be hanged in Num 25:4. The woman caught in adultery in John 8, however, was only to be stoned, not also to be hanged. The majority of the Sages rejected the latter for women.[81] As indicated above, her adultery with a Roman male was thought of by the Zealots not only as a sexual offense against the husband, but also as idolatrous. She was in grave danger of being drawn after the heathen and his gods, and of then contaminating her whole people.[82] In such a situation drastic measures were needed, and the Zealots took them, wanting to stone her. For the reasons cited above she was not strangled, the customary punishment for a married woman caught in adultery.

IX. Sin No More.

Jesus tells the adulteress in John 8:11 that, like the scribes and Pharisees who have now departed, "Nor do I condemn you." Then he adds, however: "Go, (and) from now on sin no more." In regard to the latter R. Brown states: "The 'no more' is somewhat tautological after 'from now on.'"[83] Since "sin no more" occurs in 5:14, B. Lindars asks whether it is a later ecclesiastical addition.[84] U. Becker considers "from now on" to be a later expansion, "perhaps in the style of a formula of absolution from the early church."[85] Finally, J. Sanders and B. Martin think: "The difficulty of this verse (11) certainly favours the authenticity of the incident recorded."[86]

---

[80] *Legends* 3.383, dependent on the sources he refers to in n. 790.

[81] Cf. *m. Sanh.* 6:4, as in n. 79.

[82] Cf. again *b. 'Avoda Zara* 36b, with *m. Sanh.* 9:6 quoted (Soncino 177, with n. 3).

[83] *The Gospel According to John (i-xii)* 334.

[84] *The Gospel of John* 312.

[85] *Jesus und die Ehebrecherin* 68.

[86] *The Gospel According to St. John* (Blacks; London: Black, 1968) 466.

I suggest that the entire sentence is original, and that its apparently tautological character is due to Jesus' awareness of an already traditional interpretation of Jer 17:13. As remarked above, his "writing in the earth" twice (John 8:6 and 8) recalls this Jeremiah verse, the only occurrence of the phrase in the Hebrew Bible.

The prophet Hosea was told by God to take a wife of harlotry, "for the land commits great harlotry by forsaking the LORD" (1:2). She is encouraged to put away her harlotry and adultery (2:4, Eng. 2), and Hosea forgives her, as God does with Israel. In the Palestinian triennial lectionary system, Hos 14:2-10 was the haftarah or prophetic reading for the Sabbath of Repentance, located between New Year's Day and the Day of Atonement. This is because of "Repent / return" in v 2. The twenty-fourth section of *Pesiqta de Rav Kahana* is based on the latter verse.[87]

In 24/2 R. Eliezer (b. Hyrcanus), an older second generation Tanna,[88] interprets the first phrase of Jer 17:13, "The LORD is Israel's pool of hope (מִקְוֵה)," as God's telling Israel they are to pray in the synagogue of their city. If this is not possible, in other places, ending with Ps 4:5 (Eng. 4): "Commune with your heart upon your bed, be still." Commenting on the latter, R. Yudan, also called Yehudah b. Ilai, a third generation Tanna,[89] says this means that you must restrain yourself and "refrain from the sin you might commit": דום מאותה העבירה שיש בידך.[90] This interprets the phrases אַל-תֶּחֱטָאוּ, "do not sin," and דֹמּוּ סֶלָה, "be silent. *Selah*" (RSV). The verb דמם in the Hebrew Bible means "to be silent,"[91] but in rabbinic Hebrew, as here, it can also mean "to leave off," "to refrain."[92] A baraitha in *b. 'Erub.* 54a states that "Selah" refers to a process which

---

[87] Cf. Braude and Kapstein 365, with n. 1, as well as Braude's *Pesikta Rabbati* 2.770, n. 1, and the table on p. 910. See also the art. "Triennial Cycle" by J. Jacobs in *JE* (1906) 12.254-257, and "Triennial Cycle" in *EJ* (1971) 15.1386-1389, but especially the art. "Sabbath, Special" in *EJ* (1971) 14.572-573 on the Sabbath of Repentance and Hos 14:2.

[88] Cf. n. 78.

[89] Cf. n. 68. If not, he is a fourth generation Palestinian Amora (Strack and Stemberger, *Introduction* 103).

[90] Mandelbaum 352, Braude and Kapstein 367. A parallel is found in *Midr. Pss.* 4/9 on Ps 4:5 (Buber 46 or 23b, Braude 73). It has R. Eliezer b. Jacob, either a first or third generation Tanna (Strack and Stemberger, *Introduction* 75 and 85, respectively).

[91] BDB 198-199.

[92] Jastrow 314, citing this passage as in *Midrash Psalms*.

never ceases.[93] Therefore it means "forever."[94] The phrase דמו סלה can then be interpreted as "refrain forever."

I suggest that Jesus was aware of early Judaic interpretation of Jer 17:13 in light of Ps 4:5. He then borrowed elements from the latter to say: מֵעַתָּה אַל־תֶּחֱטָאִי ,עַד עוֹלָם,[95] "From now on do not sin / refrain from sinning – forever!" The Hellenistic Jewish Christian translator correctly rendered "from now on" as ἀπὸ τοῦ νῦν. Feeling theologically uncomfortable with the element of refraining from sinning "forever," however, he with less felicity translated this as μηκέτι, "no longer," with ἁμάρτανε: "sin no more." Perhaps he was influenced by the עד of עד עולם. He may have combined it as עד with אל to produce μη ... ἐτι, μηκέτι.[96] This explains why the Greek appears to be tautological.

X. The Extent, Content and Setting of the Narrative.

In regard to John 7:53 – 8:11, J. McDonald states: "The narrative is a unity." "In terms of narrativity... there is no case for holding that the pericope as it stands is composite."[97] Others, however, do maintain the latter. In regard to the form of the narrative found in the comment on Sirach 7 by Didymus the Blind, a fourth century CE Alexandrian, B. Ehrman asks whether an older version of the pericope is not preserved by Didymus. He omits, for example, John 8:6b and 8–11. This leads Ehrman to believe that two stories were later conflated to produce what is now in John.[98] D. Lührmann considers the Didymus version of the story not to be a "Vorlage," but an earlier, simpler form of the narrative. Greatly changed, it evolved into what is now John 8:3-11.[99]

---

[93] Soncino 376-377, with Ps 48:9 (Eng. 8) as the proof text.

[94] See Jastrow 993. Targ. Pss. 4:8 has לעלמין, "forever" (Merino 80).

[95] On this phrase cf. Jastrow 1129, עתה. It is also found in connection with ועד עולם, "from now on 'and forever,'" as in the table blessing cited in b. Ber. 46a (Soncino 279 – "from now and for all time").

[96] Cf. Delitzsch's translation in his Hebrew New Testament (181): אַל־תֶּחֱטָאִי עוֹד. Instead of "from now on," however, he renders "go 'your way.'" Delitzsch too sensed the difficulties in the Greek text. The United Bible Societies' Hebrew New Testament (259) has here: "Go, and do not continue to sin any more," the latter also with עוד.

[97] "The So-Called 'Pericope de Adultera'" 423.

[98] "Jesus and the Adulteress" in NTS 34 (1988) 32 and 36-37.

[99] "Die Geschichte von einer Sünderin und andere apokryphe Jesus-überlieferungen bei Didymos von Alexandrien" in NovT 32 (1990) 302. For him, the problems of a second repentance and the rigorism of the Montanists in the

In his monograph on the *pericope de adultera*, U. Becker considers the following to be secondary elements: the mention of Jesus' typical opponents, the scribes and Pharisees in John 8:3; their intention of putting Jesus to the test (v 6a); the writing in the earth (vv 6b and 8); the extensiveness of the conversation between Jesus and the adulteress in vv 10-11; and the command "From now on sin no more" (v 11). In addition, details in 7:53 – 8:2 regarding the situation of the narrative are secondary for Becker, and the insertion of the non-Johannine pericope at this point in the Fourth Gospel.[100]

I agree with Becker's last point completely, with all other commentators. In addition, the narrative may originally have begun: "Jesus entered the Temple, and all the people...," as of 8:2. The section 7:53 to 8:2a ("Early in the morning, again") may have been added by the redactor who inserted the pericope at this point in John. It now means that on the last day of the pilgrimage feast of Booths (Sukkoth: 7:2,8,10,14 [Jesus' teaching in the Temple, and 28], 37), Jesus is pictured as retiring to the Mount of Olives to his quarters and returning early the next morning to continue his teaching in the Temple.

Yet the latter note on the situation of the pericope applies equally well to the pilgrim festival of Passover. In the Synoptics, Jesus is described as staying in Bethany on the east slope of the Mount of Olives, and from there entering the city of Jerusalem and the Temple numerous times.[1] Thus 7:53 – 8:2 could even be original, belonging, however, to a different context. The setting of the Temple for the chief priests, scribes and elders' question of by whose authority Jesus does "these things" (Mark 11:27-28); the Pharisees' and Herodians' attempt to entrap Jesus in his talk by asking whether or not it is lawful to pay taxes to Caesar (12:13-14); the Sadducees' trick question regarding the resurrection (12:18); and a scribe's asking Jesus which is the greatest commandment (12:28; Matt 22:35 and Luke 10:25 have "to test" Jesus), admirably fits John 7:53 – 8:11.[2] Here too some scribes and (Zealot) Pharisees try to put

---

second century CE caused the new version, an example for repentant sinners (*ibid.*).

[100] *Jesus und die Ehebrecherin* 173. He argues for these at various points in his book, for example on pp. 57 and 87-90.

[1] Cf. Mark 11:11-12,15,19-20 (in the morning), 27; 13:3; 14:3,13, as well as the art. "Bethany" by K. Clark in *IDB* 1.387-388.

[2] Many other commentators also favor this setting. See for example C. Barrett, *The Gospel According to St. John* 491; J. Schneider, *Das Evangelium nach Johannes* (ThHNT, Sonderband; Berlin: Evangelische Verlagsanstalt, 1978[2]) 339; W. Grundmann, *Das Evangelium nach Markus* (ThHNT 2; Berlin: Evangelische Verlagsanstalt, 1977[7]) 329, who posits a position between Mark 12:17 and 18; and

Jesus to the test (v 6) by making him oppose Moses (v 5), or agree with them that the adulteress caught in the act should be stoned. The latter would have made Jesus very unpopular with the great majority of the crowd, who would have considered a punishment less than death (for example, a divorce and the loss of her marriage settlement, the *kethubah*)[3] more appropriate. In addition, if as seems probable (John 18:31), only the Romans could now pronounce a sentence of capital punishment in Palestine, Jesus by agreeing with the Zealots would have openly joined the growing opposition to Rome, a very dangerous act. The Roman governor and judge, Pontius Pilate, having come from Caesarea Maritima to Jerusalem for the Passover festival, was very near and could immediately have him arrested.

As in all the other situations in which particular Jewish leaders attempted to entrap him, Jesus also solved the trick question put to him in regard to the adulteress. He cleverly threw the responsibility for stoning her, a deed legitimate for Zealots, back upon them by stating: (Only) "he who is without sin should throw the first stone at her." This silenced them, as reported for similar encounters.[4]

For the above reasons, including the discussion of the individual verses in other sections above, I believe the *pericope de adultera* is a unit as it now stands (at least from 8:2 on, "[Jesus] entered the Temple..." to v 11). In spite of the many variants found in the apparatus of the Nestle-Aland Greek text, the narrative makes very good sense as it is. According to the proposal I have made in this study, there is no reason to believe the story is composite, nor that it was enlarged from an earlier narrative, nor that individual details such as the mention of "scribes and Pharisees" and writing in the earth are secondary. The opposite is true. Jesus is portrayed as countering an attempt by such Zealots to entrap him by his appealing to Judaic traditions on the Scriptures already known to them.

G. Macgregor, *The Gospel of John* (Moffatts; London: Hodder and Stoughton, 1959) 211. It is probable, however, that all the events now described as occurring in "Holy Week" before Jesus' crucifixion in Jerusalem originally took place over a more extended period of time, perhaps even on separate visits to Jerusalem. Liturgical practice, before the Gospel of Mark, may have telescoped them together as specific readings for the various days of Passion Week.

[3] Cf. Jastrow 680, and the Mishnah tractate of this name (*Ketubot*), with later comment on it.

[4] Cf. Mark 11:31-33; 12:17, with Luke 20:26; 12:24-27; and 12:34 – "And after that no one dared to ask him any question."

XI. The Original Language.

Most sentences in Mark are simply connected by καί, corresponding to the Semitic *waw*. The *pericope de adultera* also has such sentences, yet in addition eleven instances of δέ after the first word of a sentence (nine if the two occurrences in 8:1 and 2a are from a secondary introduction). U. Becker calls the latter "good Greek" and thinks it should be especially considered in regard to the question of the original language.[5] Yet he does not even consider the possibility of *de* as having been introduced by the Hellenistic Jewish Christian who translated the pericope from a Semitic original.

Becker also asks whether either the Hebrew אֶחָד אֶחָד or the Aramaic חַד חַד is behind the expression εἷς καθ᾽ εἷς in 8:9,[6] which I consider to be the case.[7] Employing additional arguments, he argues *in toto* for a "spoken Jewish Greek."[8] This seems strange since he believes the pericope derives from Jesus.[9] Therefore it must originally have been either in Aramaic or Hebrew.

Throughout this study I have argued for the background of the legal issue involved in the narrative as deriving from what is still found in *m. Sanh.* 9:6, in Hebrew. Based on this legal principle, the Tannaitic midrash *Sifre* on Numbers 25 contains one of the very few instances of an Israelite / Jewish person fornicating / committing adultery (זנה for both) with a heathen, where both are caught "in the act" (בשעת מעשה). This is the background of the expression ἐπ᾽ αὐτοφώρῳ in John 8:4. It also explains how Zealots can say to Jesus in v 5: "In the (oral) *halakhah* (in *m. Sanh.* 9:6 and in regard to Num 25:5), Moses commanded (only) us (Zealots) to stone such women." Judaic interpretations of Mal 2:11, the beginning of which Jesus wrote in the earth in John 8:6, are also connected to *m. Sanh.* 9:6. Those on Hos 4:14, the beginning of which Jesus then wrote in the earth in John 8:8, deal with the closely related topic of the adulteress in Numbers 5 (with "taken [in the act]" in v 13). Above, I have also proposed a Semitic background for the term ἀναμάρτητος in John 8:7 as found in Judaic interpretation of Num 5:31. Finally, I suggested that "from now on sin no more" in John 8:11 is ultimately based on Ps 4:5 (Eng. 4), connected in early Judaic tradition with Jer 17:13. The latter is

---

[5] *Jesus und die Ehebrecherin* 71.

[6] *Ibid.*, p. 63.

[7] Cf. the Hebrew New Testaments of Delitzsch (181) and the United Bible Societies (258) for the Hebrew form.

[8] *Jesus und die Ehebrecherin* 71.

[9] *Ibid.* 174, with three arguments.

the only occurrence in the Hebrew Bible with the phrase "to write in the earth."

With the exception of the targums, all of the Judaic materials I have cited in this study, especially those related to *m. Sanh.* 9:6, Numbers 25 and 5, are in Hebrew. They cause me to believe that the first follower of Jesus who formed this episode into a narrative did so in that language, even if at least Jesus' dialogue with the adulteress in John 8:10-11 was more probably originally in Aramaic.[10] Even if the whole story was first narrated and later written down in Aramaic, my main point is that this was done in a Semitic language. Only later, as with all the other original Gospel pericopes, did a Hellenistic Jewish Christian translate the narrative into Greek, its present form.

XII. The Historicity and Genre.

1. *The Historicity*.

H. Köster believes the pericope John 7:53 – 8:11 is quite old, but not from the life of Jesus. Its life setting is rather later congregational debates on whether or not adultery, a mortal sin, may be forgiven. It "authorizes a positive answer to this question through a narrative which was projected back into the life of Jesus."[11] J. Becker also calls it an "ideal and constructed scene."[12]

Yet the overwhelming majority of commentators on the narrative consider it historical, in part for very different reasons. U. Becker correctly observes, for example, that there are no preconditions, such as repentance, to be fulfilled by the adulteress before Jesus says he too does not condemn her. She is simply to sin no more (8:11).[13] One would expect at least one such precondition in a story later invented to show that adultery may indeed be forgiven, but not by "cheap grace." First, the offender should at least confess his or her sin, thus repenting. None of this is even hinted at in the narrative.

---

[10] The scribes and Pharisees may have spoken Hebrew to Jesus in vv 4-5, with his answer only to them in v 7 also in Hebrew. The scribes certainly employed this language in legal situations. These particular Zealotic Pharisees, dependent also on the oral *halakhah* for the legitimacy of their stoning the adulteress, probably also knew Hebrew well enough to speak it. However, we simply do not know how much Hebrew Jesus could speak.

[11] "Die ausserkanonischen Herrenworte als Produkte der christlichen Gemeinde" in ZNW 48 (1957) 233.

[12] *Das Evangelium nach Johannes. Kapitel 1-10*, 334.

[13] *Jesus und die Ehebrecherin* 174 and 154.

One possible reason the pericope was not taken up by one of the four Evangelists, states G. Macgregor, is "because it offended the taste of the early Church and seemed subversive of moral discipline...."[14] The church father Augustine, in contrast, thought that the narrative was indeed originally in one of the Gospels, but was later removed because "some were of slight faith" and "to avoid scandal."[15] Macgregor's view is much more probable. The implicit danger to marriage morals in the earliest Jewish Christian communities prevented the narrative from being inserted into a Gospel. Such apparently "cheap grace," even if from Jesus, could too easily be misused. Therefore for a long time the story was only circulated orally, perhaps later entering the non-canonical, Jewish Christian "Gospel According to the Hebrews."[16]

H. Meyer had already remarked in 1834 that the strange manner in which Jesus countered the question designed to put him to the test, i.e. his writing in the earth twice, "bears the stamp of originality and not fabrication."[17] R. Eisler agreed, noting that the story cannot have been made up later because the writing in the earth was very clear to the deeply shamed scribes and Pharisees who were trained in the Scriptures. Yet it was "no longer understandable to the Christian or Gentile Christian community not so steeped in the Bible."[18]

This is an important argument for the historicity of the narrative. A later writer would hardly have invented such a strange gesture. As I have proposed above, Jesus was not simply doodling or seeking to gain time for thinking. Instead, he wrote the beginnings of two biblical verses, Mal 2:11 and Hos 4:14, which were closely connected in early Judaic tradition to what became *m. Sanh.* 9:6, and to the rite of testing the suspected adulteress by the bitter waters, Numbers 5. These two verses, especially as known from their contexts in Judaic tradition, caused the scribes and Pharisees to feel ashamed and to abandon their condemnation of the woman caught *in flagranti.*

---

[14] *The Gospel of John* 211.

[15] Quoted by Barclay in *The Gospel of John* 2.336, without the sources. U. Becker in *Jesus und die Ehebrecherin* 183-184 lists numerous passages in Augustine which deal with the pericope.

[16] Cf. U. Becker, *Jesus und die Ehebrecherin* 99-100. In *Eccl. Hist.* III.39.17 (LCL 298-299) Eusebius maintains that Papias "expounded another story about a woman who was accused before the Lord of many sins, which the Gospel according to the Hebrews contains." Translation by K. Lake. The long oral circulation of the pericope helps to explain the large number of variants.

[17] *Evangelium des Johannes* 112.

[18] "Jesus und die ungetreue Braut" 306.

Gentile Christians and even Hellenistic Jewish Christians were not aware of Palestinian Jewish interpretation, including Mal 2:11 and Hos 4:14, of the *halakhah* now still found in *m. Sanh.* 9:6, and of Numbers 5, in Hebrew and / or Aramaic. Therefore knowledge of what Jesus wrote in the earth was lost at the latest when the narrative of the adulteress was translated into Greek. Only in Palestinian Jewish Christian circles, with Aramaic (or less probably, Hebrew) as their main language, was such knowledge preserved, at least at the beginning. This explains why, if Papias is correct, the *pericope de adultera* was only found in the Jewish Christian, non-canonical "Gospel According to the Hebrews." Such Christians very soon became only a very small minority in the larger, Gentile dominated church. Indeed, they were even considered heretical for certain of their views, such as on the virgin birth. It is something of a miracle that the narrative of the adulteress survived at all.

Finally, another major factor contributed to the story's not being incorporated into one of the canonical Gospels, all completed by the end of the first century CE. I proposed above that the adulterer did not simply "escape," as maintained by almost all the commentators. The Zealots who caught him committing adultery with a Jewish woman in Jerusalem were, according to *m. Sanh.* 9:6, only allowed to strike down (and kill) the Jewish person fornicating with a heathen. If the adulterer was a Roman, as I have suggested, they would not be interested in him according to the stipulation of their own oral *halakhah*. Just as importantly, as a citizen and representative of the occupational power Rome, he would not be tried for such an offense in a Jewish court, but in a Roman court, perhaps under Pontius Pilate in Jerusalem. It in turn according to current Roman law would by no means demand capital punishment for him in such a case. The scribes and Zealot Pharisees were not interested in taking the two persons caught in adultery to a Roman court, or the Jewish adulteress to a Jewish court, the Great Sanhedrin in Jerusalem. In their zeal they wanted to stone the adulteress. This they were only legally allowed to do if they did it immediately – בשעת מעשה, in the moment of the act. On the way out of Jerusalem to stone her, they encountered Jesus teaching in the Temple and seized what they considered a very auspicious occasion on which to entrap him. Yet, as with his answer to the similar question regarding whether or not it is proper to pay taxes to Caesar (Mark 12:17), Jesus here too foiled his opponents. They thus failed in both their endeavors.

For the above reasons I agree with almost all the commentators that the *pericope de adultera* is historical.

2. The Genre.

H. Köster believed that John 7:53 – 8:11 was later invented within the context of congregational debates on whether or not adultery may be forgiven.[19] R. Bultmann considered it an apocryphal apophthegm.[20] R. Schnackenburg labels it a biographical apophthegm. The life setting for the congregation was catechesis, demonstrating Jesus' attitude to a sinner and to the people who prosecute her.[21] J. Becker follows Schnackenburg in calling the pericope a biographical apophthegm. The hearer should know that under the condition of 8:11c, adultery can be forgiven. Thus it seeks to missionize. "The life of the sinner does not have to end with death. With Jesus' forgiveness, presented through baptism, it may begin as new life."[22] Yet baptism would then have to be connected to this narrative from the outside. There is no hint of it whatsoever within the story.

John 7:53 – 8:11 can best be labeled an "entrapment narrative," as I indicated above at the end of the discussion of its historicity.[23] It is most like the narrative of whether or not it is lawful to pay taxes to Caesar (Mark 12:13-17 par.). This also seeks to trap Jesus into either issuing an anti-Roman statement, sympathetic to the Zealots, or into making himself very unpopular with the majority of his fellow Jews assembled in

---

[19] Cf. n. 11. See now also H. Leroy, "Jesus und die Ehebrecherin (Joh 7,53 – 8,11)" in E. Ehrlich and B. Klappert, eds., *Wie gut sind deine Zelte, Jaakov*, Festschrift R. Mayer (Gerlingen: Bleicher, 1986) 145-149: it is a story created for a learned dispute in regard to the Law and mercy.

[20] *The History of the Synoptic Tradition* (New York and Evanston: Harper & Row, 1963) 63.

[21] *Das Johannesevangelium, II. Teil* 233. He believes the discipline of doing penance is at the most in the background of the narrative. On biographical apophthegms, see Bultmann, *The History* 27-37 and 55-61.

[22] *Das Evangelium nach Johannes. Kapitel 1-10*, 334, quotation p. 335. J. Gnilka in *Johannesevangelium* (Die neue Echter-Bibel; Würzburg: Echter-Verlag, 1983) 65 also states: "Since it demonstrates the change in life made possible by Jesus, one can imagine that it was used as an effective story in missionizing."

[23] Cf. also J. McDonald, "The So-Called 'Pericope de Adultera'" 420, for the term "entrapment narrative," as well as B. Lindars, *The Gospel of John* 308 on "not falling into the trap of publicly refuting the Law." He believes the pericope, like the question of paying taxes to Caesar, belongs to such "controversy stories." U. Becker in *Jesus und die Ehebrecherin* 91 and 83 considers the narrative to be a strongly reworked or expanded form of a Synoptic controversy story. Yet since Bultmann (*The History* 40) contends that "controversy dialogues are all of them imaginary scenes," which is not true for John 7:53 – 8:11, I hesitate to employ this term.

the Temple by asserting a seemingly pro-Roman stance: Pay the tax. His answer, "Render to Caesar the things that are Caesar's, and to God the things that are God's" (v 17), cleverly threw the responsibility back onto the questioners.

The same is true for the *pericope de adultera*. Zealots tried to put Jesus to the test by challenging him to respond to their statement: "In the (oral) *halakhah* Moses commanded us (Zealots) to stone such women. What therefore do *you* say about this?" (John 8:5) If he agreed with the Zealots, Jesus could get into deep and immediate trouble with the Romans, especially if the Jews had already lost to Rome the right of capital punishment. If he disagreed with the Zealots, he would actively question the validity of the oral *halakhah* given to Moses at Sinai. As in the question of paying taxes to Caesar, Jesus cleverly avoided the trap set for him by causing the scribes and Pharisees to drop their accusation. Shamed, they departed from the scene. The term "entrapment narrative" describes this situation best.

* * *

While the narrative of the woman caught in adultery has had a very complicated textual history, Christians throughout the centuries have been grateful that it was finally inserted at the end of chapter seven of John's Gospel. It is truly a "lost pearl," which not only warns them of judging / condemning others hypocritically and with great zeal when they themselves are not free of the same behavior (Matt 7:1-5; Luke 6:37-38,41-42). It also encourages them to be merciful, as God Himself is merciful (Luke 6:36), giving even major sinners a second chance.[24] That indeed is amazing grace, which is very Jesus-like.

---

[24] Contrast the situations described in Philo, *Spec. Leg.* 1.55 and 2.253: merciless, pitiless.

"Christ Walking on the Waves." Reproduced in O. Benesch, *The Drawings of Rembrandt* (London: The Phaidon Press, 1954) 1.23; Cat. No. 70, figure 74. Ca. 1632-1633.

Chapter Two

Walking on the Sea

The Crossing of the Reed Sea in Exodus 14-15, and Jesus as Second Moses and Messiah in Mark 6:45-52, Matt 14:22-33, and John 6:16-21

The narrative of Jesus' walking on the Sea of Galilee to the disciples in a boat is now found in Mark 6:45-52, Matt 14:22-33, and John 6:16-21. Luke omits it. A. Edersheim considered it a "weird scene,"[1] while M. Hooker notes that "This short narrative bristles with difficulties for the modern reader."[2] There are indeed major difficulties and incongruities in the episode. The following indicate several of them.

---

[1] *The Life and Times of Jesus the Messiah* (original 1886; reprinted Grand Rapids, Michigan: Eerdmans, 1942) 1.691. Recent bibliography on the Markan pericope, on which I concentrate, is found in R. Gundry, *Mark. A Commentary on His Apology for the Cross* (Grand Rapids, Michigan: Eerdmans, 1993) 335-344. See also J. Heil, *Jesus Walking on the Sea. Meaning and Gospel Functions of Matt 14:22-33, Mark 6:45-52 and John 6:15b-21* (AnBib 87; Rome: Biblical Institute, 1981) 1 and 175-181, as well as W. Berg, *Die Rezeption alttestamentlicher Motive im Neuen Testament – dargestellt an den Seewandelerzählungen* (Hochschulsammlung Theologie, Exegese, Band 1; Freiburg: Hochschul Verlag, 1979) 344-361.

[2] *The Gospel According to St. Mark* (Black's; London: Black, 1991) 168. She also mentions the apparent "uselessness" of the miracle (169). After removing what she considers Mark's editorial activity in Mark 6:45 and 52, A. Yarbro Collins

Mark 6:45 states that Jesus made his disciples go by boat before him (from somewhere on the western shore, the site of the feeding of the 5000) to Bethsaida, located in Jesus' time either at the NE end of the Sea of Galilee or on the former course of the Jordan River slightly above the Sea, but probably with its own harbor.[3] Yet 6:53 notes that after the incident of Jesus' walking on the Sea and their "crossing over, they came to land at Gennesaret," which was located on the NW side of the Sea, some 5 km (3 miles) north of Magdala or 8 km (5 miles) north of Tiberias.[4] In addition, Jesus from a mountain can see the disciples rowing very hard "in the middle of the Sea" (Mark 6:47-48; RSV and NRSV wrongly "out on the sea," implying only somewhere off shore). The hearer / reader of the narrative must think he has super vision. Also, why does Jesus ostensibly first intend to "pass by" the disciples in the boat in 6:48? Doesn't the wind's ceasing when Jesus enters the boat indicate that this narrative is somehow connected to the stilling of the storm in 4:35-41? Is the special material concerning Peter's walking on and sinking in the water (Matt 14:28-31) due to the Evangelist himself, or did he appropriate it from a source? Finally, is the entire episode historical, or is it a transplanted Resurrection account,[5] an optical

---

speaks of "the deceptively simple narrative which the evangelist found in one of his sources." See her "Rulers, Divine Men, and Walking on the Water (Mark 6:45-52)" in *Religious Propaganda and Missionary Competition in the New Testament World*. Essays honoring Dieter Georgi, ed. L. Bormann et al. (NovTSup 74; Leiden: Brill, 1994) 207-227, quotation p. 211. On p. 218, n. 41, Yarbro Collins notes the 1991 University of Toronto, St. Michael's College, dissertation by W. Cotter, "The Markan Sea Miracles: Their History, Formation and Function," unavailable to me.

[3] Cf. the art. "Bethsaida" in *Jesus & His World*, ed. J. Rousseau and R. Arav, 19-24. It is now identified with et-Tell, some 1800 meters NNE of the present entrance of the Jordan into the Sea / Lake. According to John 1:44, three of the disciples, Philip, Andrew and Peter were from Bethsaida, literally "House of Fishing." Matthew in 14:22 omitted "Bethsaida" from Mark's account, probably because he sensed the geographical difficulties which followed.

[4] See the art. "Gennesareth" in *Jesus & His World* 109-110, as well as the map of the Sea on p. 23. John complicates the matter by having the disciples originally start for Capernaum (6:17). Yet he wanted Jesus there, for in its synagogue Jesus could hold his discourse on the bread of life (6:24-25, 59). "Boats from Tiberias" on the SW side of the Sea, which "came near the place where they ate the bread" (6:23 – the feeding of the 5000 in vv 1-15), indicate John's opinion that the disciples started their boat journey from somewhere in the NW of the Sea.

[5] See most recently P. Madden, *Jesus' Walking on the Sea*. An Investigation of the Origin of the Narrative Account (BZNW 81; Berlin: de Gruyter, 1997). I only know of this as announced by de Gruyter, and from Professor J. Fitzmyer, the dissertation advisor.

illusion,[6] simply due to Jesus' "wading through the surf near the hidden shore,"[7] to his floating out to the disciples on a large, invisible beam,[8] or to something else?

In the following essay I shall propose new solutions to a number of the difficulties sensed in the pericope of Jesus' walking on the Sea. My major thesis is that the narrative is based on a Palestinian Jewish Christian reinterpretation of Judaic traditions concerning the dividing of the Reed Sea in Exodus 14-15, combined with an interpretation of Jesus the Messiah as hovering or walking over the water in Gen 1:2.

Section I, the core of the study, first analyzes sixteen aspects of Judaic interpretation of Exodus 14-15 as reflected in Mark 6:45-51, and then eight more as reflected in the special Petrine material of Matt 14:28-31 and 33. Section II describes Judaic traditions concerning the Messiah as "hovering" over the water in Gen 1:2. Section III defines the extent of the original, pre-Markan narrative. Section IV proposes a concrete cause for its origin and date. Section V deals with the original language and provenance of the narrative. Finally, section VI addresses its historicity and purpose.

I. The Israelites' Crossing the Reed Sea,
and the Disciples' Crossing the Sea of Galilee

Introduction

The main salvific event in the history of Israel was that of the exodus from Egypt, especially the description of the actual event in Exodus 14 and the Song of Moses in chapter 15. It later "formed the center of the Israelite confessions of faith and cultic worship."[9] Each spring, for example, the Passover pilgrimage festival at the time of Jesus vividly recalled this event.[10] Even for those who could not journey to Jerusalem,

---

[6] Cf. P. Lapide, *Er wandelte nicht auf dem Meer* (Gütersloh: Gütersloher Verlagshaus, 1984) 16-50, reference from p. 21.

[7] V. Taylor in *The Gospel According to St. Mark* (New York: St. Martin's Press, 1966) 327.

[8] K. Barhdt, cited with numerous other proposals in H. van der Loos, *The Miracles of Jesus* (NovTSup 9; Leiden: Brill, 1965) 658-661.

[9] Cf. G. Wright, art. "Exodus, Book of" in *IDB* 2.188-197, quotation p. 195.

[10] An excellent description and analysis of biblical and Judaic sources on the Passover pilgrimage is offered by S. Safrai, *Die Wallfahrt im Zeitalter des Zweiten Tempels* (Forschungen zum jüdisch-christlichen Dialog 3; Neukirchen: Neukirchener Verlag, 1981).

the reciting of an early form of the Passover haggadah in the synagogue and / or the family recalled the essentials of the exodus narrative.[11] The statement now still found in *m. Pesaḥ.* 10:5 was probably also typical of Palestinian Judaism in the first half of the first century CE: "In every generation a person is duty-bound to regard himself as if he personally has gone forth from Egypt, since it is said, 'And you shall tell your son in that day saying, It is because of that which the Lord did for me when I came forth out of Egypt' (Exod 13:8)."[12] The emphasis here is on "for me" (לִי), personally.

Finally, the dividing of the Reed / Red Sea in Exodus 14-15 was connected to the daily recital of the *Shema'* in the morning and the evening. This is shown for example in *Exod. Rab.* Beshallaḥ 22/3 on Exod 14:31, which states: "Our Rabbis taught: He who recites the *Shema'* must mention the division of the Red Sea...."[13] The events described in Exodus 14-15 were thus a part of every devout Palestinian Jew's daily life.

It is therefore easily understandable that exodus motifs and imagery are also found in other sections of the Hebrew Bible, including a plea for God's aid from the Babylonian captivity described as a second exodus in Isaiah.[14] The appropriation of such motifs and imagery continued not only in the Pseudepigrapha,[15] but also in the NT. The Jewish Christian Paul, for example, could speak of Christ as "our paschal lamb," which has been sacrificed (1 Cor 5:7; cf. Exod 12:21). One instance in the Gospels

---

[11] One critical treatment of this topic is that of B. Bokser, *The Origins of the Seder. The Passover Rite and Early Rabbinic Judaism* (Berkeley: University of California Press, 1984). P. von der Osten-Sacken kindly calls my attention to the article by G. Stemberger, "Pessachhaggada und Abendmahlsberichte des Neuen Testaments" in *Kairos* 29 (1987) 147-158. While I share some of Stemberger's skepsis about the early dating of particular sections of *m. Pesaḥ.* 10, I disagree with his complete "agnosticism," for example on p. 156: "We cannot say how the Jewish rural population which could not travel to Jerusalem celebrated the festival."

[12] J. Neusner, *The Mishnah* 250. See also H. Danby, *The Mishnah* 151, as well as the Hebrew in Albeck 2.178.

[13] Mirqin 5.258; Soncino 3.276. See also *t. Ber.* 2:1 (Zuckermandel and Liebermann 3; Neusner 1.6), cited in *y. Ber.* 1:5 (Neusner / Zahavy 1.57). On Jesus' great respect for the *Shema'*, Deut 6:4 (-9), see Mark 12:28-34 par. See also *Mek. R. Ish.* Pisḥa 16 on Exod 13:3 (Lauterbach 1.135, with n. 3), as well as the fact that the phylacteries contained Exod 13:1-10; 13:11-16; Deut 6:4-9; and 11:13-20 (Pisḥa 17 on Exod 13:9 in Lauterbach 1.150, with n. 6).

[14] Cf. Isa 51:10-11 for the latter, as well as other references in the Psalms cited by G. Wright in his art. "Exodus, Book of" 196.

[15] See the passages noted in the index under the entry "Exodus, the" in *OTP* 2.948, as well as "Moses, as leader of Jews out of bondage" in 2.979.

is the narrative of the disciples' crossing the Sea of Galilee in a boat, and Jesus' walking towards them.[16] The following analysis corroborates this proposal. It relies primarily on Palestinian Judaic interpretation of Exodus 14-15.

1. *The Sea of Galilee, and the Reed (or Red) Sea.*

The earliest Palestinian Jewish Christians, perhaps even Galileans living near the Sea of Galilee or Tiberias, could easily create a narrative of the disciples rowing tortuously against a head wind on that Sea in light of motifs and terminology from the Israelites' crossing the Reed Sea after a strong east wind was against them. In part this was possible because the same Hebrew word (יָם) was employed in both cases. It means both "sea" and "lake."[17]

a) Mark 6:47,48 and 49 all mention the "sea" (θάλασσα), which in 1:16 and 7:31 is called the Sea of Galilee. Of the eighteen occurrences of the noun

---

[16] Others have already made general statements concerning the exodus background of the narrative. Cf. for example M. Hooker's statement that the episode is "a symbolic repetition of the crossing of the sea by Moses and the Israelites..." in *The Gospel According to St. Mark* 170. See also A. Guilding, *The Fourth Gospel and Jewish Worship. A Study of the Relation of St. John's Gospel to the Ancient Jewish Lectionary System* (Oxford: Clarendon Press, 1960) 66: "The Miracle of the walking on the water seems to reflect the crossing of the Red Sea (Exodus 15)," as well as B. Gärtner, *John 6 and the Jewish Passover* (ConNT 17; Lund: Gleerup, 1959) 17-18, and R. Brown, *The Gospel According to John, I-XII* 255-256. I will call attention to the work of W. Berg below in regard to the "fourth watch," and to that of O. Betz in regard to Peter and Naḥshon. Only after finishing this essay did the article by W. Stegner become available to me, "Jesus' Walking on the Water: Mark 6:45-52," in *The Gospels and the Scriptures of Israel*, ed. C. Evans and W. Stegner (JSNTSup 104 / Studies in Early Judaism and Christianity 3; Sheffield, United Kingdom: Sheffield Academic Press, 1994) 212-234. Stegner, who does not deal with the question of historicity as I do, calls attention to a number of the motifs and expressions I analyze below, yet he only deals with "the familiar story (of the exodus) from the Septuagint" (p. 215) and cites very few Semitic Judaic sources. In addition, Stegner is not aware of Judaic interpretation of the Messiah's "hovering" over the water in Gen 1:2. My many disagreements with his proposal, while sound in its general direction, will be apparent throughout. Above all, the narrative does not deal with "the defeat of the chaotic and the demonic forces associated with the sea..." (p. 234; see also the quotation from E. Malbon on p. 218, and pp. 228-230).

[17] Cf. BDB 410-411 and Jastrow 579. The Aramaic has the same meanings. In *Mek.* Beshallaḥ 4 on Exod 14:15, "to the sea," the Mediterranean is interpreted as the Reed Sea (Lauterbach 1.217, with n. 2). This is another example of equating one sea with another because of the same term, יָם. In *Exod. Rab.* Beshallaḥ 21/8 on Exod 14:15 (Mirqin 5.253; Soncino 3.271), this is said by R. Aqiva, a second generation Tanna (Strack and Stemberger, *Introduction* 79).

in Mark, sixteen refer to this Sea. John 21:1 calls it the Sea of Tiberias, and in 6:1 he explains the Sea of Galilee as the Sea of Tiberias.

However, Luke is technically correct in labeling this body of fresh, non-saline water in Greek a "lake" (λίμνη – 5:2; 8:22-23,33), and he calls it Lake Gennesaret (5:1). The term "sea" elsewhere in the Gospels derives from usage in the Hebrew Bible, which was taken over by the LXX.

b) The Sea through which the Israelites passed and in which their Egyptian pursuers drowned was the Reed Sea (יַם-סוּף),[18] translated in the LXX as the Red Sea (θάλασσα ἐρυθρά). Of the seventeen occurrences of the full name in the MT, all but three refer directly to the exodus event.[19] All fourteen are translated by θάλασσα in the LXX.

The Reed Sea is explicitly named in regard to the actual exodus event in Exod 13:18, 15:4 and 22. Yet it usually is referred to in this context simply as Sea (יָם). In chapters 14-15 it occurs twenty-five times alone. I suggest that this heavy concentration of occurrences forms the thought background for the narrative of Jesus' walking on the "sea." As noted above, it employs θάλασσα, sea, in Mark 6:47,48 and 49.

The Sea of Galilee is called by the earlier name, the Sea of Chinnereth, in Num 34:11 and Josh 13:27 (Chinneroth in 12:3). Yet Deut 33:23 simply refers to it as the "Sea," as in Mark 6. This too may have encouraged the Palestinian Jewish Christian author of Mark 6:45-51, whose mother tongue may have been Aramaic, but in my opinion wrote his account in Hebrew, to refer to the Sea of Galilee in vv 47-49 simply as the Sea.

2. Crossing the Sea of Galilee, and Crossing the Reed Sea.

a) Jesus' home town was Nazareth, but at the time of his public ministry he appears to have made Capernaum on the north shore of the Sea of Galilee his home (Mark 1:21; 2:1; 3:19; and 9:33). Located on the Via Maris, it was some 3 km or 2 miles west of where the Jordan River flowed into the Sea.[20] While still located within the tetrarchy of Herod Antipas, whose new capital was at Tiberias on the SW side of the Sea, Capernaum offered Jesus the opportunity, if necessary, of quickly escaping "that fox" (who at least once wanted to kill him – Luke 13:31-

---

[18] Cf. BDB 693 for the term "reed."

[19] This is reduced by one if the locust plague in Exod 10:19 is considered a preliminary stage, leading up to the exodus. Then only Num 33:10-11 remain. Cf. also Acts 7:36 and Heb 11:29 for the Red Sea and the exodus.

[20] Cf. the art. "Capernaum" in *Jesus & His World* 39-47.

32) by traveling by boat eastward to the safe territory of Philip.[21] Jesus not only preached at times to the large crowds on the shore from a boat (Mark 4:1). Because of his great popularity, he also employed it to escape being crushed by them (3:7-9). In addition, Mark reports numerous occasions on which Jesus went off with his disciples by boat or "crossed over" to the other side of the Sea.[22]

I suggest that Jesus' frequent boat trips, especially his "crossing over" to the other side of the Sea, provided the background with which a Palestinian Jewish Christian described Jesus as walking on the Sea at night towards his disciples, who were crossing over to the other side.

Mark 6:45 states that Jesus urged his disciples to get into the boat and "go before" (προάγω) him to the other side, to Bethsaida. After the incident of Jesus' walking on the Sea, Mark in 6:53 provides a transitional sentence: "And when they had 'crossed over' (διαπεράω)...." In his Hebrew New Testament, F. Delitzsch employs forms of the Hebrew verb עבר for the above two Greek verbs. He also uses the same term for Jesus' wanting to "pass by" (παρέρχομαι) the disciples in the boat in v 48.[23]

The incident of Jesus' walking on the Sea while his disciples "cross over" to the other shore is, I propose, based on the Israelites' "crossing over" to the other shore of the Reed Sea at their exodus from Egypt, especially as described in Judaic tradition.[24]

b) Exodus 14-15 provides the biblical description of how the Israelites actually passed through or crossed the Reed Sea at their exodus from Egypt. While a number of Hebrew verbs are employed for the motion involved, only 15:16 employs עבר twice. *Mek.* Shirata 9 on this verse

---

[21] This is described well by P. Lapide in *Er wandelte nicht auf dem Meer* 32-42.

[22] Cf. 4:35 (διέρχομαι); 5:1-2,21 (διαπεράω); 6:31-32; and 8:10 and 13. This does not mean, however, that I consider all these data, for example 4:35, to be historical. In part they are from the Evangelist or the sources he employed.

[23] Cf. pp. 73-74, as well as the United Bible Societies' New Testament on 6:48 and 53 (p. 107). Both Delitzsch (p. 175) and the UBS (p. 250) also employ the term עבר in John 6:17. If Delitzsch's term for "shore" or "side" in Mark 6:45, עֵבֶר (Jastrow 1040), is correct, this may be an intentional word play. The same may be true for עֶרֶב, "And when 'evening' came..." in Mark 6:47.

[24] O. Betz in "The Concept of the So-called 'Divine Man' in Mark's Christology" in *Studies in New Testament and Early Christian Literature.* Essays in Honor of Allen P. Wikgren, ed. D. Aune (NovTSup 33; Leiden: Brill, 1972) 229-240, also maintains that Mark 6:45-52 has its background in "the Red Sea event," with "crossing over." He considers it only a variant of the stilling of the storm in 4:35-41 (p. 239; cf. also p. 235). Yet that narrative is independent, based primarily on Palestinian Jonah traditions.

interprets the object of the first phrase, "Till Your people pass over," as "the sea."[25]

In other sections of the Bible the verb עבר was frequently applied to the Israelites' crossing or passing through the Reed Sea. Two examples from the Psalms are 78:13 ("He divided the sea and let them 'pass through' it") and 136:14. In the latter the psalmist says it is appropriate to give thanks to God, "who divided the Reed Sea in sunder" (v 13), and who "made Israel 'pass through' the midst of it" (v 14). An example from the prophets is Isa 51:10, where the Lord made "the depths of the sea for the redeemed to 'pass over.'"[26] Wisd 19:8 also speaks of those protected by God's hand at the Reed Sea as "passing through" (διέρχομαι) as one nation.

Early Judaic comment on Exodus 14-15 employs similar terminology. Philo of Alexandria, born ca. 20 BCE,[27] states in *Mos.* 2.247 of the Israelites: "They could not 'cross' (περαιόω[28]) the sea for want of boats." He uses the same verb in 1.179, where he notes that "They 'crossed' in the early dawn." The Jewish Christian Paul writes in 1 Cor 10:1 that "our fathers were all under the cloud, and all 'passed through' (διέρχομαι) the sea...." The author of Hebrews, most probably a diaspora Jew also converted to Christianity, states in 11:29, "By faith they 'crossed' (διαβαίνω) the Red Sea as if on dry land." *Pseudo-Philo*, originally written in Hebrew, probably in Palestine "at about the time of Jesus,"[29] retells the crossing of the Reed Sea in 10:6 by inserting the verb "passed / crossed" into its quotation of Exod 14:22, "And Israel 'passed' (*pertransivit*) through the middle of the sea on high ground."[30] In *Exod. Rab.* Beshallaḥ 22/7 on Exod 15:1, R. Yoḥanan, a second generation Palestinian Amora,[31] states that "When the angels desired to chant Song before God on that night when Israel 'crossed' (עָבְרוּ) the Sea, the Holy One, blessed be He,

---

[25] Lauterbach 2.75. Historically, the Arnon, Jordan and Jabbok are of course meant, as seen in the interpretation of the second "pass over," and in the targums. It is significant that the Tannaite commentator felt compelled to apply the first occurrence of the verb to the Israelites' passing over or crossing the Reed Sea.

[26] This is quoted in *Mek.* Beshallaḥ on Exod 14:15 (Lauterbach 1.217).

[27] Cf. the LCL edition, translated by F. Colson and G. Whitaker, 1.ix.

[28] LSJ 1364. The cognate noun is used to express the same thought in *Mos.* 1.172.

[29] Cf. D. Harrington in *OTP* 2.298-300.

[30] *OTP* 2.317. The Latin is found in Harrington, *SC* 229, 1.116.

[31] Strack and Stemberger, *Introduction* 94-95.

prevented them...."[32] *'Avot R. Nat.* A 33 has Moses repeatedly tell the Israelites at the Reed Sea: "Rise, go across (עברו)!" Yet they make one stipulation after another before crossing over.[33] Finally, both *Pseudo-Jonathan* and the *Fragment Targum* have the Israelites say, after witnessing the miracles and wonders God did for them at the Reed Sea: "Come, let us place a crown upon the head of the Redeemer, who 'causes (us) to pass over' (מעבר), but who does not (Himself) 'pass away.'"[34]

All these Judaic (and Jewish Christian) sources, from the Bible itself to the later Aramaic paraphrases of it, show how a Palestinian Jewish Christian describing the disciples in a boat crossing the Sea of Galilee, could easily describe this event in terms of *the* crossing of water in the Bible, that of the Reed Sea at the exodus. This general statement is buttressed by the following points.

3. *Jesus' Praying at a Mountain, and Moses' Praying Before a Mountain.*

a) The Gospel of Mark notes that at certain times Jesus withdrew to a lonely place, sometimes to pray.[35] He also is described as going up a mountain.[36] Certainly aware of this basic motif already found in early oral tradition, the Palestinian Jewish Christian author of what is now Mark 6:45-51 was reminded of similar Judaic tradition on Moses' praying in connection with a mountain before the Israelites in danger at the Reed Sea. One factor which may have encouraged him to do so was the fact that already in early Judaic sources the Messiah is thought of as the redeemer of Israel. Rabbinic traditions also speak of Moses as the first

---

[32] Mirqin 5.263, with parallels in n. a; Soncino 3.285.

[33] Schechter 96-97; Goldin 133-135.

[34] Cf. Rieder 1.105 for *Pseudo-Jonathan*. I modify Etheridge's translation here (p. 495), preferring it to that of Maher (*Targum Pseudo-Jonathan: Exodus* 205). The same applies to the *Fragment Targum* (Klein 1.172 for MS "V"; English in 2.130). MS "P" of the latter has an acrostic poem after 14:29 in which Moses is to tell the sea at the letter Gimmel: "the redeemed of the Lord 'will pass through' your midst." The letter Taw ends the poem by stating: "The sea returned from its waves, and the Israelites 'passed through' its midst" (Klein 1.77, Eng. 2.43-44).

[35] Cf. 1:36, with prayer; 6:31-32; and Gethsemane in 14:32,35.

[36] Cf. 3:13, to which Luke 6:12 adds that he prayed; 9:2, to which Luke 9:28 also adds that he prayed; as well as John 6:3 and 15, and Matt 5:1 (and 8:1) and 15:29. The Greek ὄρος means both mountain and hill (LSJ 1255, BAGD 582), which is also true for the Hebrew הַר (BDB 249, Jastrow 365). Near the N shore of the Sea of Galilee there are only some hills, yet no steep mountains, as for example on the W shore of Tiberias.

redeemer, and the Messiah as the final or great redeemer.[37] The Palestinian Jewish Christian then appropriated imagery from Judaic tradition on Moses to describe Jesus as "going off to the mountain / hill to pray" in Mark 6:46 while the disciples were already in the Sea. It should be noted that both the RSV and the NRSV have "he 'went up' on the mountain" here. Yet the verb employed, ἀπέρχομαι, simply means that Jesus "went off" or "departed" to the mountain.[38] He can thus be pictured as praying upon the mountain / hill, but just as well as before a mountain, as in the Garden of Gethsemane at the base of the Mount of Olives. This is important to note because of the position at which Moses prayed in Judaic tradition on the crossing of the Reed Sea.

b) Josephus, born ca. 37-38 CE and a native of Jerusalem whose mother tongue was Aramaic, finished his *Antiquities* in 93-94 CE.[39] In 2.320-349 (2.15.3-6) he retells the story of the crossing of the Reed Sea with many embellishments, most of them certainly from Palestinian haggadah already known to him. He notes that the pursuing Egyptians confined the Israelites "between inaccessible cliffs and the sea; for it was the sea in which terminated a 'mountain' (ὄρος)...." Where "'the mountain' (τοῦ ὄρους) abuts upon the sea, they (the Egyptians) blocked the passage of the Hebrews, pitching camp at its mouth..." (2.325). Moses also says to God in this situation: "thine is the sea, thine the 'mountain' (ὄρος) that encompasseth us..." (337).[40] The "mouth" of the mountain here is haggadic interpretation of "*Pi ha-ḥiroth*," the site at the Sea where the Israelites encamped (Exod 14:2 and 9), only possible in Hebrew or Aramaic.[41] Josephus continues by stating that the Israelites were "under

---

[37] Cf. the references to the pre-Christian Psalms of Solomon and to rabbinic traditions in Str-B 1.67-70.

[38] BAGD 84. Matt 14:23 has, however, "to go up" (ἀναβαίνω). Cf. already John 6:3 with ἀνέρχομαι. In v 15, at the end of the narrative of the feeding of the 5000, Jesus again goes off to the mountain by himself. Therefore John omits the mountain of Mark 6:46 and the notice that Jesus was alone on the land in v 47, which were probably also known to him. I leave the question of whether or not he knew the Gospel of Mark open.

[39] Cf. the LCL edition by H. Thackeray and L. Feldman, 1.vii, and *Ant.* 20.267. The first draft of his *Jewish War* was written in Aramaic (1.xi).

[40] Cf. also "hemmed in by mountains" in 328 and "the mountains behind you" in 333. Philo in *Mos.* 1.169 states that "'high on the hill' appeared the enemy's forces, armed and drawn up for battle."

[41] The form פִּי is the construct of פֶּה, "mouth" (BDB 804). The LXX, unable to decipher the unknown place name (BDB 809), has here ἔπαυλις, an encampment or military quarters (LSJ 611).

the eyes of the Egyptians" at the Sea (334), which interprets the Israelites' "lifting up" their eyes to see the Egyptians in Exod 14:10, just after Pi ha-hiroth is mentioned in v 9. Exhausted, the Egyptians decide to remain overnight (on the mountain overlooking the Sea), and to engage in battle only the next morning. In this very difficult situation Moses "makes supplication" (ἱκετεύω)[42] to God, i.e. he prays to Him (334).

I suggest that Judaic tradition on Moses' praying to God at a mountain[43] before the Sea provided the general background for the Palestinian Jewish Christian author of Mark 6:45-51. He too had Jesus, for him the second Moses or great redeemer of Israel, pray at a mountain (v 46) while the disciples had grave difficulties in the Sea.[44]

Moses' prayer is commented upon extensively in rabbinic sources.[45] It is based on Exod 14:15, where the Lord asks Moses: "Why do you 'cry out' to Me? Tell the people of Israel to go forward." The Hebrew צָעַק means to cry or cry out, usually for help, to the Lord.[46] It is a form of prayer request. *Pseudo-Philo* 10:4 for example inserts *exclamavit*, Moses "cried out" to the Lord, into a biblical quotation just before citing Exod 14:15.[47] Another example is *Mek.* Beshallaḥ 4 on the verse, where R. Eliezer (b. Hyrcanus), a second generation Tanna,[48] has God ask Moses: "Moses, My children are in distress, the Sea forming a bar and the enemy pursuing, and you stand there 'reciting long prayers' (מרבה בתפלה). Why

---

[42] LSJ 826.

[43] The Hebrew על ההר can mean either "upon the mountain" or "at the mountain." When Jesus is described as "seeing" the disciples' tortuous rowing in the middle of the Sea of Galilee in Mark 6:48, he is of course thought of as being "upon" the mountain, looking down at the Sea.

[44] Against Stegner, "Jesus' Walking" 222, who thinks Jesus sees the disciples' distress from the mountain or hill as derived from the Lord's "looking down" from the "pillar of fire and of cloud" in Exod 14:24 and His seeing the Israelites' distress. This verse rather deals with the Lord's looking down upon the *Egyptians* in the Sea.

[45] Cf. also Philo, *Mos.* 1.173, where Moses "silently 'interceded' with God to save them (the Israelites) from their desperate afflictions...."

[46] BDB 858, Jastrow 1294. For Moses' crying out in Exod 15:25 and prayer, cf. *Mek.* Vayassaʻ 1 on the verse in Lauterbach 2.91-92.

[47] *OTP* 2.317; the Latin is in Harrington, *SC* 229, 1.116.

[48] Strack and Stemberger, *Introduction* 77.

do you cry out to Me?" R. Eliezer then adds: "There is a time to be brief (in prayer) and a time to be lengthy."[49] The Hebrew תְּפִלָּה is "prayer."[50]

The above examples suffice to illustrate Moses' praying before a mountain while the Israelites were in great distress at the Sea. It provided the background for Jesus' praying at or on a mountain in Mark 6:46 while the disciples were in difficulties in the Sea.

4. *Twelve Disciples, and Twelve Tribes.*

a) According to Mark 3:14 Jesus appointed twelve men to associate with him in his ministry. This number is frequently mentioned.[51] In a Q tradition found in Matt 19:28 and Luke 22:30, Jesus promised his disciples that in the future they would "sit on (twelve) thrones judging the twelve tribes of Israel." When Jesus urges his disciples to enter the boat and go before him to Bethsaida on the other side of the Sea of Galilee, and they encounter great difficulties in rowing there, all twelve may be assumed to be in the boat "in the middle of the Sea" (6:47). Here too Jesus and the twelve in the middle of the Sea of Galilee recall Moses and the twelve tribes of Israel in the middle of the Reed Sea.

b) In *Pirq. R. El.* 42, which deals with the exodus, R. Eliezer (b. Hyrcanus)[52] is quoted as saying:

> On the day when He said, "Let the waters be gathered together" (Gen 1:9), on that very day (the third day of Creation – Tuesday) were the waters congealed (at the Reed Sea), and they were made into twelve valleys, corresponding to the twelve tribes, and they were made into walls of water, between each path, and (the people) could see one another, and they saw the Holy One, blessed be He, walking before them....[53]

While the attribution to early rabbis of particular sayings in this work is often considered doubtful, the content of the above tradition of twelve valleys in the Reed Sea, corresponding to the twelve tribes, appears to be very early. *Mek.* Beshallah 5 on Exod 14:16 says, for example, that the Sea's being divided into twelve parts was the second of

---

[49] I slightly modify the English in Lauterbach 1.216. The whole section deals repeatedly with the theme of Moses' praying too long. A parallel tradition is found in *Exod. Rab.* Beshallah 21/8 on Exod 14:15 (Mirqin 5.253; Soncino 3.270).

[50] Jastrow 1686-1687.

[51] Cf. Mark 4:10; 6:7; 9:35; 10:32; 11:11; and 14:10, 17, 20 and 43.

[52] Cf. n. 48.

[53] Friedlander 330, with notes; Eshkol 161.

the ten miracles done for Israel there.[54] This is also found with variants, including the twelve tribes, in '*Avot R. Nat.* A 33,[55] B 38,[56] *Exod. Rab.* Beshallaḥ 24/1 on Exod 15:22,[57] *Deut. Rab.* Vezot ha-Berakhah 11/10,[58] *Midr. Pss.* 114/7 and 136/7,[59] and *Targ. Ps.-Jon.* Exod 14:21.[60]

The above Judaic sources show that a Palestinian Jewish Christian describing Jesus' walking towards his twelve disciples in the boat in the middle of the Sea of Galilee, was encouraged to have all twelve disciples there because the Reed Sea was divided into twelve divisions for the twelve tribes of Israel.

5. *In the Middle of the Sea.*

a) Both the RSV and the NRSV read in Mark 6:47, "And when evening came, the boat was out on the sea...." This is an inadequate translation, for it implies that the boat with the disciples could be anywhere in the Sea of Galilee, even just off the shore. Yet the Greek ἐν μέσῳ τῆς θαλάσσης should be taken literally: "in the middle of the Sea." Corroboration of this is found in John 6:19, which has: "When they had rowed about 25 or 30 stadia, they saw Jesus walking on the water and coming near the boat...." Since a *stadion* is 185 meters or 607 feet,[61] these distances are 4,625 meters or 15,175 feet, and 5,550 meters or 18,210 feet, respectively.

The present Sea of Galilee is shaped like a harp, which probably gave it its name in antiquity (Chinnereth). Its greatest width is ca. 13 km or 8 miles, its length being ca. 21 km or 13 miles.[62] John's only approximate

---

[54] This is found in the Friedmann edition (p. 30a). Lauterbach (1.223) has "two" in his main text, but "twelve" in his footnote (siglum ד for the agreement of the Constantinople, Venice and Leghorn editions: 1.1).

[55] Schechter 96; Goldin 134, with n. 27 on p. 206: "I.e., 12 paths were cut through the waters for the 12 tribes."

[56] Schechter 99; Saldarini 227.

[57] Mirqin 5.270; Soncino 3.294.

[58] Mirqin 11.158; Soncino 7.185.

[59] Cf. respectively Buber 474 and Braude 2.219-220, and Buber 520-521 and Braude 2.327.

[60] Rieder 1.103 and Maher 201, with other references, including church fathers, in his n. 28.

[61] BAGD 764. Matt 14:24 simply has "many stadia" here.

[62] Josephus in *Bell.* 3.506 says at his time the Sea was 40 stadia wide and 140 long. Thackeray in his n. "a" plausibly proposes that he wanted to give the average or shorter width. In the first century CE the Sea was longer, however, because the

notice of the disciples' having rowed 25 or 30 stadia thus corresponds roughly to "the middle of the Sea" in Mark 6:47. Both mean the same place. The middle of the northern section, where most of the Jewish population lived, is most probably intended.[63]

b) The Hebrew New Testament of F. Delitzsch translates "in the middle of the Sea" in Mark 6:47 as בְּתוֹךְ הַיָּם.[64] Precisely this phrase occurs in Exod 14:16,22,27,29 and 15:19. Closely related to it is אֶל־תּוֹךְ הַיָּם in 14:23. All six instances relate to the Israelites' walking through or in the middle of the Reed Sea on dry ground, with the one exception of 14:27, which also deals with the Lord's subsequent destruction of the Egyptians, also in the middle of the Sea. The LXX translates בתוך הים in Exod 14:29 and 15:19 with ἐν μέσῳ τῆς θαλάσσης, exactly as in Mark 6:47.[65]

For the above reasons I suggest that the Palestinian Jewish Christian author of Mark 6:45-51 borrowed the phrase "in the middle of the Sea" from the biblical account of the Israelites' walking "in the middle of the Sea" when the Lord divided the waters for them there.

6. A Head Wind.

a) Mark 6:48 says Jesus saw the disciples in their boat in the middle of the Sea "straining at the oars against an adverse wind" (NRSV). The RSV has for the latter: "for the wind was against them." The Greek is ἦν γὰρ ὁ ἄνεμος ἐναντίος αὐτοῖς, to which important MSS add σφόδρα, "extremely" or "greatly." In spite of its weaker attestation, the latter may be the original reading because the parallel tradition in John 6:18 speaks of a "strong wind" (ἄνεμος μέγας).

The term ἐναντίος in regard to a wind means "opposite, against, contrary."[66] In the NT it is only found here, in the parallel tradition at

---

Jordan River had not yet pushed so much sediment down towards the Sea. Cf. the art. "Sea of Galilee" in *Jesus & His World* 246, as well as the map on p. 23, showing ancient harbors.

[63] Cf. the statement by R. Riesner: "Die 25 bis 30 Stadien (5 bis 6 km) in Joh 6,19 bezeichnen wohl für den Nordteil richtig die Mitte des Sees." See his art. "Genezareth, See" in *Das Grosse Bibellexikon*, ed. H. Burkhardt *et al.* (Wuppertal: Brockhaus; Giessen: Brunnen, 1987) 1.440. Professor Riesner kindly provided me with this reference.

[64] P. 73.

[65] It has εἰς μέσον τῆς θαλάσσης in 14:16, 22 and 23, and simply μέσον τῆς θαλάσσης in 14:28.

[66] BAGD 262. It is probably לְנֶגֶד in Hebrew. See BDB 617, 2.b., and the Hebrew New Testament of Delitzsch (p. 73).

Matt 14:24, and in Acts 27:4. I have translated it above as "head wind," for the disciples were indeed "straining at the oars" against it.

In section 5. above on "in the middle of the Sea," I noted that the disciples' boat is most probably thought to be in the northern part of the Sea of Galilee. In addition to arguments from b) below for the strong wind coming from the east, geography and present-day fishermen support the assertion that the disciples were battling a severe wind from the east.

There are a number of deep ravines or gorges bordering on the NE section of the Sea of Galilee. They lead down from the Golan Heights, from which sudden winds sweep through them across the Sea.[67] Very high waves are produced, in part because they cannot roll out elsewhere. Present-day fishermen especially fear the dangerous winds which, without warning, drop down within a matter of minutes from the direction of Gamla on the Golan Heights. They regularly observe that direction because some fishermen have not returned alive from such sudden storms.[68] They especially fear the so-called *sharkiyeh*, an eastern wind which appears especially in periods of weather transition such as Passover.[69]

John 6:4 mentions that the feast of Passover was near. It was also the time of the feeding of the 5000 and Jesus' walking on the Sea (vv 1-15 and 16-21). Jesus had first gone to the "other side" of the Sea of Galilee (6:1), where the feeding took place. This is considered by almost all commentators to be on the NW side of the Sea, from which the disciples started (eastward) to Capernaum (6:17). As noted above, John apparently changed this place name from Bethsaida, as still found in Mark 6:45, in order to get Jesus to Capernaum, where he held his "bread of life" discourse in the synagogue (6:24,59).

The above leads me to think the feeding of the 5000 at the "lonely place" to which Jesus and the disciples went by boat (Mark 6:32) was also on the NW shore of the Sea, from which the disciples are represented as leaving for the "other side," for Bethsaida (in the northeast; v 45). Here too almost all the commentators consider this to be the direction envisaged: from west to east.[70] If the notice of time in John (near

---

[67] Cf. Luke 8:23, where a storm wind "comes down" on the Lake.

[68] Cf. the statement of the fisherman Albert Kubi cited by U. Sahm in his art. "Die Stürme kommen ohne jede Warnung" in the Berlin "Tagesspiegel" of April 19, 1987, p. 3.

[69] Riesner, "Genezareth, See" 440. See also the art. "Sea of Galilee" in *Jesus & His World* 246, bottom right page.

[70] Cf. for example M.-J. Lagrange, *Évangile selon Saint Marc* (Ebib; Paris: Gabalda, 1966) 173: "The wind thus blew from the northeast, which is often the case in that northern part of the lake"; M. Hooker, *The Gospel According to St. Mark* 170; V.

Passover) is also correct, it helps to explain the sudden storm wind from the east, especially typical of that time of year. The disciples headed into it in their boat, yet it caused them to get way off their course, to the middle of the Sea.

The main reason for the disciples' straining at the oars because of a strong eastern wind, however, derives from the east wind at the crossing of the Reed Sea.

b) Exod 14:21 states that "the Lord drove the sea back by 'a strong east wind' all night, and made the sea dry land, and the waters were divided" for the Israelites to cross from the western to the eastern shore of the Reed Sea. The "strong east wind" in Hebrew is רוּחַ קָדִים עַזָּה. Together with רוּחַ, the term קָדִים, "east," means "east wind."[71] The same wind is referred to in Exod 15:8 and 10. According to the earliest Judaic chronology, *Seder 'Olam* 5, Israel departed from Egypt on the fifteenth of Nisan and entered the Reed Sea on the evening of the seventh day after that. The next morning, when they sang the "Song" of Exodus 15 on the eastern shore, was also the seventh day, the "last festival day of Passover."[72]

Mek. Beshallaḥ 5 on Exod 14:21 states that this east wind is the strongest of all the winds. It was used by God not only on the evil Egyptians at the Reed Sea, but also to punish the generation of the flood, the people of Sodom, of the tower of Babel, and many others.[73]

The source of this strong or mighty wind was the east. Transferred by the Palestinian Jewish Christian narrator from the Reed Sea to the Sea of Galilee, it explains why the disciples had to strain so much at their oars in order to head towards Bethsaida in the NE of the Sea. It also fit the strong storm winds which suddenly can come from the east or northeast, especially at the time around Passover. It should be noted that this east wind has nothing to do with the great wind which caused a "mighty tempest" on the sea in Jonah 1:4. That wind in rabbinic tradition is considered to be the one which proceeded on three occasions "to

---

Taylor, *The Gospel According to St. Mark* 329 (N or NE wind); he is followed by W. Lane, *The Gospel According to Mark* (NICCNT 2; Grand Rapids, Michigan: Eerdmans, 1974) 235, and C. Mann, *Mark* (AB 27; New York: Doubleday, 1986) 305.

[71] Cf. BDB 870 and Jastrow 1315. It appears twice in Exod 10:13 of the locust plague brought to the Egyptians by the east wind. The LXX at Exod 14:21 has instead the south wind. Philo follows it in *Mos.* 1.176, where the wind is of "tremendous violence" (βιαιότατος).

[72] See Milikowsky 244-245 and 463. In Judaic thinking the day extends from sunset to sunset.

[73] Lauterbach 1.229-230.

destroy the whole world with its inhabitants."[74] It does form, however, part of the background of the narrative of the stilling of the storm in Mark 4:35-41 par.

Finally, the fact that רוּחַ, "wind," can also mean "spirit" or "ghost," is relevant to the disciples' thinking Jesus, walking on the Sea, was a spirit or ghost (φάντασμα) in Mark 6:49. I shall comment more extensively on this in section 9. below.

7. *Rowing with Difficulty or Tortuous Rowing.*

a) Because of the (strong) head wind, Jesus' twelve disciples in their boat on the Sea of Galilee "were straining at the oars" (NRSV) or "were distressed in rowing" (RSV of 1957[2]): βασανιζομένους ἐν τῷ ἐλαύνειν (Mark 6:48).

The Greek of this verse begins with the participle "And having seen," which depends on the verb ἔρχεται, "he comes" to them walking on the Sea. Preceding "he comes" is a notice of time: "about the fourth watch of the night." The NRSV correctly has all of this in one sentence. By dividing it up, the RSV makes it appear that there is a time interval between Jesus' seeing the disciples rowing hard, and his coming to them, which is not the case.

The verb ἐλαύνω in the sense of "row" occurs in the NT only here and in the parallel tradition of John 6:19.[75] In the LXX it is employed of mariners' rowing in 3 Kgdms 9:27.[76] Isa 33:21 mentions a "rowboat" (πλοῖον ἐλαῦνον). Here it translates the Hebrew אֳנִי-שַׁיִט. Delitzsch employs this root in his Hebrew New Testament, "in their rowing," at Mark 6:48: בְּשׁוּטָם.[77] I suggest that Matthew, whom I consider to be bilingual,[78] knew not only the Markan version of this narrative, but also the Hebrew or

---

[74] See the haggadah by R. Huna in *Gen. Rab.* Bereshith 24/4 (Soncino 1.200-201), with parallels in *Lev. Rab.* Thazria 15/1 on Lev 13:2 (Soncino 4.188-189), and *Eccl. Rab.* 1:6 § 1 (Soncino 8.18-19). The other two occasions deal with Job and Elijah.

[75] BAGD 248.

[76] Cf. LSJ 529 for other instances with "row." In *Bell.* 2.635 Josephus relates that he "sailed" at full speed for Tiberias on the Sea of Galilee.

[77] P. 73. The noun שַׁיִט is only found in Isa 33:21; the verb שׁוּט, "to row," occurs only in Ezek 27:8 and 26 of rowers. See also Jastrow 1531.

[78] Cf. my essay "The Magi at the Birth of Cyrus, and the Magi at Jesus' Birth in Matt 2:1-12" in *New Perspectives on Ancient Judaism*, 2, ed. J. Neusner et al. (Howard Clark Kee Festschrift; Lanham, Maryland: University Press of America, 1987) 99-114, now reprinted in my *Barabbas and Esther and Other Studies in the Judaic Illumination of Earliest Christianity* (USFSHJ 54; Atlanta: Scholars Press, 1992) 95-111.

Aramaic version with שׁוֹם. Since the same verb can also mean "to strike,"[79] he omitted Mark's ἐν τῷ ἐλαύνειν and changed the sentence to: "the boat was beaten (struck) by the waves" (RSV), for which the NRSV has "battered" (14:24).

The term ἐλαύνω, however, can also frequently mean "to drive," like a chariot or a horse, both in the transitive and intransitive senses.[80] I suggest that the Hellenistic Jewish Christian who translated the Semitic original of Mark 6:45-51 into Greek employed ἐλαύνω not only because it could also mean "to row" in the LXX. He was also aware of the background of most of the narrative in Exodus 14, which speaks of the Egyptian chariots "driving" heavily.[81] Philo even employs the verb ἐλαύνω in Mos. 1.169 for the Egyptians, with their "cavalry, javelineers, slingers, mounted archers," "light armed troops" and 600 chariots (168) "driving" at fullspeed toward the Israelites at the Reed Sea. Exod 14:25 most probably also provided the background for the term βασανιζομένους in Mark 6:48.

b) Exod 14:7 says Pharaoh took "600 picked chariots and all the other chariots of Egypt with officers over all of them" to pursue the Israelites at the Reed Sea. The Egyptians, "all Pharaoh's horses, his chariots, and his horsemen" then entered the Sea after them (v 23). Yet the Lord "discomfited them" (v 24), "removing their chariot wheels so that 'they drove heavily'" (v 25). The NRSV has here: "so that they turned with difficulty." The latter in Hebrew is וַיְנַהֲגֵהוּ בִּכְבֵדֻת, with the verb נהג, "drive, conduct."[82]

Haggadic interpretation of Exod 14:25 commenced at a very early time. This is shown in Ezekiel the Tragedian's drama "Exagōgē" 232-233, which notes of the Egyptians at this point: "then all at once, as if with chains our chariot wheels were bound." Perhaps from the early second century BCE, and from Alexandria, it was originally written in Greek.[83]

---

[79] Jastrow 1531, with the noun שׁוֹט as "rod, scourge." The latter is also biblical (BDB 1002): "scourge, whip."

[80] LSJ 529.

[81] Cf. also ἐλαύνω in 2 Macc 9:4 of a charioteer's "driving" without stopping, as well as Josephus, Bell. 7.152 (Vespasian), Ant. 2.90 (Joseph), and 19:6 (Gaius Caligula), and Philo, Mut. 149, for driving a chariot.

[82] Cf. BDB 624. Literally, the phrase is "He made it (the chariot) drive with difficulty," with the piel. 2 Kgs 9:20 also employs this verb of Jehu's "driving" his chariot (v 16).

[83] OTP 2.817 for the quotation, and pp. 803-804 for the rest.

In *Mek.* Beshallaḥ 6 on the verse, R. Judah (b. Ilai), a third generation Tanna,[84] says the chariot wheels below were burned by the fire from above. "Nevertheless, the yokes and the chariots kept on running ahead in spite of the drivers."[85] R. Nehemiah, also a third generation Tanna,[86] maintained that "the pins of the wheels flew off." "Nevertheless, the yokes and the chariots kept on running ahead by themselves even in spite of the animals. Before, the mules pulled the chariots, but now the chariots pulled the mules."[87] The latter phenomenon is also noted in *Frag. Targ., Ps.-Jon.* and *Neof.* Exod 14:25.[88]

I suggest that Pharaoh's chariot, hardly able to proceed in the middle of the Reed Sea after the Lord divided it by a strong east wind, is the model for the disciples' boat in the Sea of Galilee, struggling against the eastern head wind. Literally, the Hebrew is singular: "and He caused it (the chariot) to drive with difficulty." As noted above, the verb ἐλαύνω in Mark 6:48 is employed not only for rowing, but also for "driving" a chariot.

The next phrase in Exod 14:25 is בִּכְבֵדֻת. The term כְּבֵדֻת occurs only here in the MT. Literally "heaviness," it is meant here as "difficulty."[89] R. Judah (b. Ilai) interprets it in *Mek.* Beshallaḥ 6 as just retaliation for the Egyptians' making the Israelites do even "heavier work" in Exod 5:9.[90] "With difficulty" is also the interpretation of *Targ. Ps.-Jon.* Exod 14:25: בקשיו, from קְשִׁיוּ, "hardness, severity."[91] The LXX here has: "He made them go μετὰ βίας." The term βία means "bodily strength, force."[92] This interpretation is also reflected in *Targum Onqelos:* בתקוף.[93] The term תְּקוֹף means "strength, power,"[94] so the difficulty envisaged both in the LXX and in *Targum Onqelos* entails much physical exertion.

---

[84] Strack and Stemberger, *Introduction* 84-85.

[85] Lauterbach 1.241.

[86] Strack and Stemberger, *Introduction* 85.

[87] See n. 85.

[88] Cf. Klein 1.76 and 169-170, and 2.42-43, 128; Rieder 1.103, and Maher 61-62; and Díez Macho 2.93 and 448, respectively.

[89] BDB 459. It is not found in rabbinic Hebrew or Aramaic.

[90] Lauterbach 1.241-242.

[91] Jastrow 1431. See Rieder 1.103 and Maher 202.

[92] LSJ 314.

[93] Drazin 147.

[94] Jastrow 1690. Drazin 146, n. 29, has "with difficulty," but in his text "with anger," which must be a typing mistake.

This is exactly the situation portrayed in Mark 6:48, where Jesus sees his disciples βασανιζομένους in their rowing across the Sea of Galilee. Since they have been rowing the boat[95] between "evening" (v 47) and early morning (see the next section, 8.), they have been at this for at least eight hours.[96] They are pictured as physically exhausted.

The term βασανίζω means to torture or torment. The translation "strain" in the known occurrences is only used metaphorically of style: a forced, unnatural, strained style. Nowhere is the verb meant as actual physical strain.[97] I therefore suggest that βασανιζομένους is translation Greek, intended in part to render something like the disciples' rowing בקשיו or בתקוף, "with (great physical) difficulty" or "with (the expenditure of much physical) strength." It was based in part on the same phrase in Judaic interpretation of Exod 14:25, "with difficulty."

Another closely related factor, however, also influenced the Hellenistic Jewish Christian translator's choice of βασανιζομένους for the Semitic original. Judaic comment on the fate of the Egyptians in their chariots in the Reed Sea emphasizes how they were justly punished, tormented and tortured there for their previous evil treatment of the Israelites. Philo for example in *Mos.* 2.256 states that the Israelites there "behold their enemies fallen under a 'chastisement' (κολασθέντες) which no words can express, through the power of God and not of man." This chastisement or punishment is also described by Josephus in terms of natural phenomena. At the Sea there were windswept billows as well as thunder and lightning, and thunderbolts were hurled (at the Egyptians). In fact, "there was not one of those destructive forces which in token of God's wrath combine to smite (ἐπ' ἀπωλείᾳ) mankind that failed to assemble then..." (*Ant.* 2.344). The ministering angels' hurling arrows, great hailstones, fire and brimstone (Ezek 38:22) at the Egyptians is also

---

[95] A wooden boat from 40 BCE to 80 CE was discovered in 1986 somewhat south of Kibbutz Ginosar on the NW shore of the Sea of Galilee. It is 8.2 by 2.3 meters. "The boat was most likely used for fishing and transport of people and cargo. It could have been sailed, or rowed by a crew consisting of four oarsmen and a helmsman." See the brochure "An Ancient Boat Discovered in the Sea of Galilee" (Jerusalem: Israel Department of Antiquities and Museums, 1988) 9. A first century CE mosaic from Migdal (Hebrew, p. 8) shows a boat with six oars (three visible on one side). Josephus in *Bell.* 2.635 states that at the beginning of the Jewish-Roman War (66-70 CE) he found 230 boats on the Sea of Galilee, with no more than four sailors on each.

[96] Cf. E. Gould, *The Gospel According to St. Mark* (ICC 32; Edinburgh: Clark, 1955) 121. See also J. Schniewind, *Das Evangelium nach Markus* (NTD 1; Göttingen: Vandenhoeck & Ruprecht, 1960) 65: "almost all night."

[97] LSJ 308, II.2.3.

emphasized in *Mek.* Beshallaḥ 7 on Exod 14:27.[98] Indeed, the *Mekilta* notes on "And the Lord overthrew / routed / shook off the Egyptians" in the same verse that "He delivered them into the hands of youthful angels," who were "cruel" (אכזרים).[99] So that the Egyptians could receive this "punishment" (פּוּרְעָנוּת), the Lord even rejuvenated them.[100] They suffered "all sorts of cruel and strange deaths."[1] The Lord "punished" (דִּין) them "with the same device with which they planned to destroy Israel...."[2]

Finally, R. Yose, (probably the Galilean, a second generation Tanna),[3] maintained on Exod 14:25 that one can prove that the Egyptians who stayed in Egypt were "smitten" (לקוּן) with the same "plagues" (מַכּוֹת) as those with which the Egyptians at the Sea were "smitten," and each group saw the other in that condition. He buttresses this by quoting that part of v 25 where the Egyptians in the Sea say: "Let us flee from before Israel, for the Lord (also) fights for them in Egypt (במצרים)."[4] The noun מַכָּה means a wound, plague, stroke or blow.[5] The verb translated "smitten" above, לקה,לקי, means to suffer, be smitten, be struck, or be punished (with lashes).[6] It should be noted that this early Judaic

---

[98] Lauterbach 1.245. In *Pesiq. R.* 21/9 (Braude 1.430) and *Midr. Pss.* 18/17 on Ps 18:13 (Braude 1.246), God rejects such help from the angels and requites the Egyptians Himself.

[99] Lauterbach 1.246. See Jastrow 62 on the adjective.

[100] *Ibid.* See Jastrow 1148 on the noun. The verb פרע (Jastrow 1235) is employed of the Lord's "punishing" Pharaoh personally at the Sea in *'Avot R. Nat.* A 27 (Schechter 83; Goldin 113). A parallel is found in *Num. Rab.* Naso 8/3 with 1 Sam 2:30 (Soncino 5.207). Wisd 19:4 speaks of the Egyptians' filling up at the Reed Sea the "punishment" (κόλασις) which their torments still lacked.

[1] Beshallaḥ 7 on Exod 14:31 (Lauterbach 1.251). On this, see also Shirata 6 on Exod 15:8 (Lauterbach 2.50-51).

[2] Also Beshallaḥ 7 on Exod 14:26 (Lauterbach 1.243). On the verb, see Jastrow 300-301.

[3] Strack and Stemberger, *Introduction* 81. He is called so in a similar saying in *Mek.* Beshallaḥ 7 on Exod 14:31 (Lauterbach 1.251). If he is Yose (b. Ḥalafta), however, he was a third generation Tanna (Strack and Stemberger, *Introduction* 84).

[4] Beshallaḥ 6 (Lauterbach 1.242). I modify Lauterbach's translation.

[5] Jastrow 781. Cf. the Mishnah tractate Makkoth, "Punishments." See already Jub 48:17 for God's "smiting" the Egyptians by throwing them into the midst of the Sea (*OTP* 2.140). This writing is from Palestine, originally in Hebrew, and composed ca. 161-140 BCE (2.43-45).

[6] Jastrow 718.

comment is made on Exod 14:25, which also contains the phrase "driving with difficulty" discussed above.

The verb βασανίζω in Mark 6:48 basically means torture, torment, with severe physical distress.[7] In its occurrences in the LXX it never has a Hebrew equivalent. I therefore suggest that the Hellenistic Jewish Christian who translated the Semitic original of βασανιζομένους ἐν τῷ ἐλαύνειν was aware not only of the background of the imagery in the Egyptian chariots' "driving with difficulty" in the Sea in Exod 14:25, but also in the fact that the Egyptians in Judaic tradition on the very same verse were tortured or tormented there. This encouraged him to choose the somewhat unusual term βασανιζομένους, lit. "tormented" or "tortured."[8] A modern translation could be: "And when he (Jesus) saw them in their tortuous rowing...." That is, the cruelly painful rowing lasting all night caused the disciples to be physically exhausted.[9] Another corroboration of Judaic tradition on Exod 14:25 as the background for this imagery is found in the phrase "about the fourth watch" in Mark 6:48. It derives from the neighboring verse, Exod 14:24.

8. *Evening, All Night, and the Morning Watch.*

a) Mark 6:45 states that after the feeding of the 5000, Jesus "immediately" urged his disciples to enter the boat and precede him to the other side (of the Sea of Galilee), to Bethsaida, while he dismissed the crowd (of the 5000). Then he went to a mountain to pray (v 46). "And when evening came," the boat was in the middle of the Sea and he was alone on the land (v 47).

This notice of time is illogical after what is supposed to have happened at the immediately preceding feeding of the 5000. Mark 6:35 first notes that "the hour is already very late," and then repeats this by the disciples' telling Jesus "the hour is already late." This is a clear sign that the two narratives were originally independent. However, as John

---

[7] LSJ 308 and BAGD 134.

[8] Cf. also other sources cited by Ginzberg, *The Legends* 3.25-31, with the relevant notes in 6.8-11. Ginzberg notes not only the general punishment of the Egyptians in the Sea, but also their "anguish," "torture," "excruciating pain" and "torment" (3.27).

[9] Again, "rowing with difficulty" in Mark 6:48 has nothing to do with the stilling of the storm episode in 4:35-41, nor with Jonah 1:13. There the men's rowing to bring the ship back to land is expressed by חתר, "dig, row (as digging into the water)" (BDB 369.2, only found here). The addition of "hard" in the RSV and NRSV is not in the Hebrew term (oars have to dig into the water!), but is derived from the context. The Jonah narrative in Judaic tradition, however, does form the major background to the stilling of the storm narrative.

6:1-15 and 16-21 also show, they were already together in the pre-Gospel tradition. Since John omits any notice of its becoming late or evening in the narrative of the feeding of the 5000, his time notice in v 16 ("When evening came...") does not contradict it, as in Mark. He then relates in v 17, "It had already become 'dark,'[10] and Jesus had not yet come to them." The term "dark" here is the noun σκοτία, which may reflect the חֹשֶׁךְ of Exod 14:20, translated in the LXX as σκότος.[11]

The next section of v 20 states in the Hebrew that "it illuminated the night, and neither (the Egyptians nor the Israelites at the Sea) approached each other all night." The LXX found the first phrase difficult and paraphrased it by saying: "The night passed (διῆλθεν), and they did not mingle with each other all night." This time notice may also have contributed to the fact that the original Palestinian Jewish Christian narrator of Mark 6:45-51 has Jesus walk towards the disciples in the boat on the Sea of Galilee only "about the fourth watch of the night" (v 48 – περὶ τετάρτην φυλακὴν τῆς νυκτός).

Mark 13:35 has Jesus list the four periods of the night: evening, midnight, cockcrow and the fourth, morning. In OT times the night was divided into three watches. After the Roman conquest of Palestine by Pompey in 63 BCE, however, the Roman system soon prevailed.[12] This means that Jesus came walking on the Sea towards his disciples sometime between 3 and 6 a.m. It also means that they had now been rowing for some eight hours, ever since "evening." The rowing was understandably more "tortuous" for them now, especially because of the (strong) head wind.

The time notices of "evening" until the "fourth watch," and thus "all night," also derive from Judaic tradition on Exodus 14.

b) Philo in *Mos.* 1.176 states that "at sunset," that is, when it becomes evening, "a south wind of tremendous violence arose" (Exod 14:21), and "the murkiness of the night struck terror into the pursuers." Then the Hebrews crossed on a dry road "at about dim (morning) twilight" (περὶ βαθὺν ὄρθρον).[13] Here περί, "about," occurs just as in Mark 6:48. The same

---

[10] The MSS ℵ and D have here: "Now the darkness overtook them...."

[11] The LXX appears to reverse the order of cloud and darkness in the MT. It employs γνόφος, which means both darkness and "storm cloud" (LSJ 354), for the Hebrew עֲנָן (BDB 777-778).

[12] Cf. Acts 12:4 with four squads of Herod Agrippa's soldiers guarding Peter in prison, one squad for each watch. See also the other sources cited in Str-B 1.688-691.

[13] Cf. LSJ 302 on βαθύς, 5. F. Colson in the LCL translates "in the early dawn."

three notices of time are found here as in vv 47-48: sunset / evening, night and the earliest morning.

Exod 14:20 speaks of "the darkness" at the Reed Sea, before "night." That is, evening is envisaged. Then "all night" is mentioned. In v 21 "the Lord drove the sea back by a strong east wind 'all night' and made the sea dry land, and the waters were divided." Following this the Israelites went into "the middle of the sea" on dry ground, followed by the Egyptians (vv 22-23). Then, "in the morning watch" the Lord discomfited / engaged in battle with the Egyptians (v 24), removing their chariot wheels, causing them to drive "with difficulty" (v 25). Finally, Moses stretched forth his hand over the Sea (from the eastern shore), and the Sea returned to its wonted flow "when the morning appeared" (לִפְנוֹת בֹּקֶר – v 27).[14] The Egyptians then perished in the Sea.

Here too the same general time pattern prevails as in Philo and Mark 6:47-48.[15]

The closest philological parallel in the story of Jesus' walking on the Sea to the narrative of the Israelites' crossing of the Reed Sea is found in the phrase "about the fourth watch of the night" in Mark 6:48 and "in the morning watch" in Exod 14:24. The latter is בְּאַשְׁמֹרֶת הַבֹּקֶר in Hebrew, for which the LXX has ἐν τῇ φυλακῇ τῇ ἑωθινῇ. While Neofiti 1 and the Fragment Targum on this expression have "at morning time,"[16] both Onqelos and Pseudo-Jonathan retain "in the morning watch."[17] Mek. Beshallaḥ 6 on the phrase notes: "This was at the blossoming of the sun," i.e. at the break of day.[18]

The author of Mark 6:45-51 transferred the phrase "in the morning watch" from Exod 14:24 to his own time, influenced by the Roman system of four night watches. He described Jesus as walking on the Sea, wanting to pass by the disciples (Mark 6:48). That is, he was still at some distance from the boat. Seeing him, they thought he was an apparition / spirit / ghost and reacted by screaming / crying out (v 49). That is, the

---

[14] Cf. BDB 133 on בֹּקֶר,1.b: "at the turn of the morning." The NRSV has "at dawn."

[15] Again, while the stilling of the storm incident also begins at evening (Mark 4:35), there is no time progression. All takes place on the same evening. In the model for the story, Jonah 1:1-16, there is no notice of time at all. This is another indication that Mark 6:45-51 is independent of the stilling of the storm narrative.

[16] Cf. Díez Macho 93 and 448, and Klein 1.76 and 2.42, as well as 1.169 and 2.128, respectively.

[17] Cf. Drazin 146-147, and Rieder 1.103, respectively. Maher (61) wrongly has "at morning time," or he employs a different textual basis. See Jastrow 770 on מטרא for "watch."

[18] Lauterbach 1.239, who has "sunrise."

time notice of its being "about" the fourth watch of the night means that the disciples could make out a figure on the Sea, but not well enough to recognize it as Jesus. This fits the time just before daybreak, the end of the fourth watch of the night, very well.

9. *Walking on the Sea and an Apparition / Phantom / Spirit.*

a) About the fourth watch of the night, i.e. in the twilight before daybreak, Jesus went from his position on the shore of the Sea of Galilee towards his disciples in the boat, "walking upon the Sea, and he wanted to overtake them" (Mark 6:8 – περιπατῶν ἐπὶ τῆς θαλάσσης καὶ ἤθελεν παρελθεῖν αὐτούς). When they saw him "walking on the Sea" (ἐπὶ τῆς θαλάσσης περιπατοῦντα), they thought it was an "apparition" (φάντασμα), and they cried out (v 49). All the disciples had seen "it" and were terrified (v 50).

Here too the motifs of an apparition appearing at night in the Sea, walking on the Sea, and perhaps Jesus' "wanting to overtake" the disciples in the Sea of Galilee derive from Judaic interpretation of the narrative of the Israelites and Egyptians at the Reed Sea in Exodus 14-15.

b) 1) *The Prince or Guardian Angel of Egypt Hovering / Flying in the Air.*

In *y. Sanh.* 7:13, 25d R. Eliezer, R. Joshua and R. Aqiva are described as bathing in a public bathhouse (employing the hot springs) of Tiberias on the Sea of Galilee. After a heretic performed some magic on them there, R. Joshua suggested they all go down to the Sea. Arriving there, the heretic spoke an incantation and the Sea divided itself. He then asked them: "Didn't your teacher Moses also do so at the (Reed) Sea?" They replied to him: "Don't you agree with us that our teacher Moses walked in it?" He answered yes. Then they said to him: "Then walk into it!" He walked into it. R. Joshua thereupon pronounced a decree over the "prince of the Sea" (שרה דימא), and it swallowed him up.[19]

Here, in a legendary account, the Sea of Galilee is represented as having its own שׂר, prince or guardian angel,[20] just as all the nations do.[21] In addition, Moses' walking into the midst of the Reed Sea is associated with (the impossibility of) walking in the Sea of Galilee. This incident shows how a Palestinian Jewish Christian, perhaps himself from Galilee,

---

[19] I paraphrase the incident. Cf. the English translation in Neusner 31.259, and the German by Wewers 209, who numbers it 7:19(11), 25d.

[20] Jastrow 1627. The prince of (all the evil) spirits (the pl. of רוּחַ) is referred to in *Lev. Rab.* Vayyiqra 5/1 on Lev 4:3 (Soncino 4.61).

[21] Cf. for example *Lev. Rab.* Emor 29/2 on Lev 23:24 (Soncino 4.370) for those of Babylon, Media, Greece and Rome.

could also transfer motifs and expressions from the Israelites' crossing the Reed Sea to the Sea of Galilee. Judaic tradition on the activity of the prince or guardian angel of Egypt at the Reed Sea encouraged him to do so.

One early example of the latter is found in *Mek.* Shirata 2 on Exod 15:1, "the horse and his rider (or its chariot) 'He has thrown' into the Sea": "When Israel observed the 'prince' (שרה) of the (Egyptian) kingdom falling down (into the Sea), they began to render praise."[22] *Exod. Rab.* Beshallaḥ 22/2 on Exod 14:26 also has R. Abbahu, a third generation Palestinian Amora,[23] state regarding the Egyptian: "God first drowned their 'guardian angel' (שׁר) in the Sea, and then all of them went down after him. For this reason it says: 'that the waters may come back upon *miṣraim* (first), and after that 'upon his chariot and his horsemen' (v 26)."[24] Here מִצְרַיִם is considered singular, therefore it is held to be the name of the prince or guardian angel of "Egypt."

R. Eleazar b. Pedat, also a third generation Palestinian Amora,[25] commented on Cant 2:14, "O My dove, in the cleft of the rock," as relating to the situation of the Israelites at the Reed Sea in *Exod Rab.* Beshallaḥ 21/5 on Exod 14:15, "Why do you cry to Me?"

> When Israel departed from Egypt, they lifted up their eyes (cf. Exod 14:10) and saw the Egyptians pursuing after them, as it says: "When Pharaoh drew near" (*ibid.*). Now, it does not say "were marching" (נֹסְעִים, pl.), but "was marching" (נֹסֵעַ, sing.), because when Pharaoh and the Egyptians began to pursue them, they raised their eyes heavenwards and saw the "guardian angel" (שׁר) of Egypt hovering in the air and were in great fear, as it says, "And they were in great fear" (*ibid.*). What then is the meaning of "and behold, *miṣraim* was marching after them"? Because the name of their guardian angel was Miṣraim, and God does not cast down a nation before He destroys their guardian angel.[26]

---

[22] Lauterbach 2.20, which I slightly modify.

[23] Strack and Stemberger, *Introduction* 98.

[24] Mirqin 5.257, and Soncino 3.276, slightly modified by me.

[25] Strack and Stemberger, *Introduction* 98. Both he and Abbahu were students of Yoḥanan (bar Nappaḥa), a second generation Palestinian Amora who first taught in Sepphoris and then in Tiberias on the Sea of Galilee (Strack and Stemberger, *Introduction* 94-95).

[26] Mirqin 5.249; Soncino 3.264-265. A partial parallel is found in *Deut. Rab.* Debarim 1/22 on Deut 2:31, in part in the name of "the rabbis" (Soncino 7.24-25).

The verb נסע in Exod 14:10 means in biblical Hebrew to set out, journey, march,[27] and in rabbinic Hebrew to move, march.[28] The guardian angel of Egypt is thus pictured as "moving" towards the Israelites at the Reed Sea. This movement is described as "hovering in the air" (פּוֹרֵחַ בָּאֲוִיר). The verb פרח is only found in rabbinic Hebrew in the meaning "to fly, fly off."[29]

I suggest that the Palestinian Jewish Christian author of Mark 6:45-51 was aware of the above Judaic tradition in an earlier form. The fearful guardian angel of Egypt, moving towards the Israelites in order to destroy them, and "hovering / flying" through the air, formed part of the basis for his remark that the disciples in the boat in the Sea of Galilee saw an "apparition" (φάντασμα) moving towards them. They also reacted by "crying out" (v 49), and they were "terrified," "being afraid" (v 50). It is precisely the last term which is found in the above rabbinic narrative, based on the verbal expression "to be of great fear" in Exod 14:10. This verse also has the Israelites' "crying out," the same verb employed in 14:15, the base verse commented on in the above midrash.

"Flying / moving in the air" is not the same, of course, as walking on the Sea or on the water. One further step in that direction, however, is the emphasis in Judaic comment on Exodus 14-15 on the Lord as flying on the wind and walking on the water.

2) The Lord as Flying, Appearing and Walking at / on the Reed Sea.

R. Eleazar b. Pedat's interpretation of Cant 2:14 cited above in section 1) is based on very early material. This is shown, for example, in the Tannaitic *Mek.* Beshallaḥ 3 on Exod 14:13. The Israelites at the Reed Sea were like a dove fleeing from a hawk. It wanted to escape by entering a cleft in the rock, but could not because a hissing serpent was within. The situation of being between the Egyptians and the Sea was similar for the Israelites.[30] R. Eliezer (b. Hyrcanus), an older second generation Tanna,[31] maintained that the phrase in Cant 2:14, "Let me see Your countenance," refers to the (precarious) occasion at the Reed Sea, as interpreted by Exod 14:13.[32]

---

[27] BDB 652.

[28] Jastrow 918.

[29] Jastrow 1223, 2). For the Aramaic cognate, Jastrow has 2) to move swiftly, fly.

[30] Lauterbach 1.211. Traditional Judaic interpretation of the Song of Songs has it as a dialogue between God and Israel. Cf. Donsqi 29-30.

[31] Strack and Stemberger, *Introduction* 77-78.

[32] Cf. *Mek.* Baḥodesh 3 on Exod 19:17 in Lauterbach 2.220.

The above narrative of the dove and hawk is also related in *Cant. Rab.* 2:14 § 2, which begins: "It was taught in the school of R. Ishmael," who was also a second generation Tanna.[33] It notes that when the dove tried to turn back from the cleft, "it could not because the hawk was 'hovering' outside."[34] The term "hovering" here is literally "standing" (עוֹמֵד). M. Simon's translation is correct, however, for a bird which cannot enter a cleft in the rocks because a snake is inside does not "stand" on the rock to be easily attacked. It "hovers" before the entrance, just out of reach. I shall comment below in section II. on the relevance of this "hovering" to Jesus' walking on the Sea.

The above narrative continues by stating that the endangered dove "began to 'cry' and beat its wings" to attract its owner's attention. This is how Exod 14:10, "And they were in great fear, and the Israelites 'cried out' to the Lord," is then interpreted, resulting in the Lord's saving them (v 30).[35] As noted above, these two expressions are also found in Mark 6:49-50 when Jesus walks towards the disciples in their boat on the Sea of Galilee.

The Lord also "appeared" in various forms, including flying and on the wings of the wind, to aid the Israelites at the Reed Sea. In *Cant. Rab.* 1:9 § 6 on "I compare you, my love, to a mare of Pharaoh's chariots," the Rabbis say: "(The expression 'mares' is used) because the Israelites appeared like mares, and the wicked Egyptians who pursued them were like stallions eager with desire, and they ran after them until they were sunk in the sea."[36]

R. Aqiva, a younger second generation Tanna,[37] comments in *Cant. Rab.* 1:9 § 4 on this verse by stating that "Pharaoh rode first on a stallion and, if one may say so, the Holy One, blessed be He, 'appeared' (נִגְלָה) on a stallion, as it says: 'He rode upon a cherub, and flew (וַיָּעֹף); He came swiftly upon the wings of the wind (רוּחַ)' (Ps 18:11, Eng. 10). Pharaoh then said: 'Surely this stallion kills its rider in battle. I will therefore ride on a mare.' Thus it is written, 'to my mare among the chariots of

---

[33] Strack and Stemberger, *Introduction* 79. Cf. the fact that R. Ishmael comments on Exod 14:27 in *Cant. Rab.* 1:9 § 6 (Soncino 9.71).

[34] Donsqi 72-73; Soncino 9.129.

[35] *Ibid.*

[36] Donsqi 40; Soncino 9.71.

[37] Strack and Stemberger, *Introduction* 79.

Pharaoh' (Cant 1:9)." Then Pharaoh changed to horses of various colors, as Hab 3:15 is interpreted.[38]

This narrative continues by having R. Samuel b. Naḥman, a third generation Palestinian Amora active in Tiberias,[39] say that when Pharaoh had used up all his weapons of war, God triumphed over him, asking him if he had winds, a cherub and wings. R. Ḥanina b. Papa, a student of Samuel,[40] buttressed this by maintaining that God "carries His chariot and rides on something which is not tangible," as Ps 18:11 (quoted above) is interpreted. He notes that in the Psalm verse it says the Lord "came swiftly" (וַיֵּדֶא), yet the parallel in 2 Sam 22:11 says "He was seen" (וַיֵּרָא) upon the wings of the wind."[41]

The rabbis were well aware of the minor differences between Psalm 18 and 2 Samuel 22, including the frequent scribal mistaking of ר and ד.[42] It is important to note here that the Lord is "seen" (ירא) on the wings of the wind (רוּחַ) at the Reed Sea, just as Jesus appears as a "spectacle" to the disciples when a (strong) head "wind" (ἄνεμος) makes their rowing tortuous on the Sea of Galilee. The latter is רוּחַ in Hebrew, רוּחָא in Aramaic. Since it can also mean "(evil) spirit" or "demon,"[43] it may in part stand behind φάντασμα in Mark 6:49.[44]

It should also be noted that the Lord is pictured as "flying" (עוּף)[45] through the air at the Reed Sea in order to come to the aid of the endangered Israelites. He took the cherub with which He flew "from between the wheels of the chariot" (in Ezekiel 1, with its throne

---

[38] Donsqi 39; Soncino 9.69. There are parallels, with variants, in *Mek.* Beshallaḥ 7 on Exod 14:29 (Lauterbach 1. 247-248); *Exod. Rab.* Beshallaḥ 23/14 on Exod 15:1 (Mirqin 5.268; Soncino 3.291); *'Avot R. Nat.* A 27 (Schechter 83; Goldin 113-114, Neusner 167); and *Midr. Pss.* 18/14 on Ps 18:11 (Buber 142-143; Braude 1.243-245, who speaks of a "phantom stallion" and a "phantom mare" – p. 243).

[39] Strack and Stemberger, *Introduction* 97.

[40] He was also a third generation Palestinian Amora and colleague of Abbahu (Strack and Stemberger, *Introduction* 100).

[41] Donsqi 39-40; Soncino 9.70.

[42] Cf. *Soferim* 8.1, 38b for all the variants (Soncino, *Minor Tractates* 247-249).

[43] See Jastrow 1458, 4), and other examples in the Aramaic form.

[44] In his Hebrew New Testament (p. 74), Delitzsch for example employs a double term: מַרְאֵה-רוּחַ.

[45] BDB 733 (l.b. notes the Lord's "hovering" like a bird in Isa 31:5), and Jastrow 1055. See also the art. "Angel," in regard to cherubim, by T. Gaster in *IDB* 1.131-132. For 2 Sam 22:9-11 as referring to Pharaoh and the Reed Sea event, see *Targum-Jonathan* on these verses (Harrington-Saldarini 201; Sperber 2.202-203).

chariot).[46] Ps 18:11 probably provided the basis for other passages where the Lord "flies" to the aid of the endangered Israelites.

The notice of the Lord's "appearing" (נגלה) at the Reed Sea, also to help the Israelites, occurs frequently in similar passages.[47] It can also be expressed by נראה.[48] In other passages the Lord is described as "walking" on or through the Sea, usually based on verses from the Hebrew Bible. Three of them are the following:

A) *Ps 77:20 (Eng. 19)* states of God:

> Your way was through the sea (בַּיָּם דַּרְכֶּךָ),
> Your path (שְׁבִילְךָ בְּ') through the mighty waters;
> yet Your footprints were unseen (NRSV).

This is interpreted of God's activity at the Reed Sea in *Exod. Rab.* Bo 18/5 on Exod 12:29;[49] Beshallaḥ 25/6 on Exod 16:4, where it is noted that no human can so carve out a way in the sea;[50] *Tanḥ.* B Vayyesheb 11 on Gen 38:1;[51] and *Pirq. R. El.* 42.[52]

B) *Ps 68:25 (Eng. 24)* relates:

> Your ways are seen (רָאוּ הֲלִיכוֹתֶיךָ), O God,
> the ways (הֲלִיכוֹת) of my God, my King, into the sanctuary....

---

[46] *Midr. Pss.* 18/15 on Ps 18:11 (Buber 144, Braude 1.244). Cf. also R. Judah (b. Ilai's) remark in 18/14 on the wind as proceeding from between the wings of the heavenly creatures (in Ezekiel 1; Braude 2.447, n. 47).

[47] Cf. for example *Mek.* Beshallaḥ 5 on Exod 14:21 (Lauterbach 1.228); Shirata 3 on 15:2 (Lauterbach 2.25); 4 on 15:3 (Lauterbach 2.30); and 7 on 15:10 (Lauterbach 2.58-59).

[48] Cf. *Pirq. R. El.* 42 (Eshkol 161-162, with "He appeared in the water"; Friedlander 331) in connection with Cant 1:9. See also *Eliyyahu Zuṭa* 19 (Friedmann 28; Braude and Kapstein 495).

[49] Mirqin 5.216; Soncino 3.223. In 17/5 on Exod 12:23, God in a parable is represented as saying: "I will cross over (עבר) the waves of the sea" (Mirqin 5.209; Soncino 3.215). The Reed Sea is also meant.

[50] Mirqin 5.279; Soncino 3.306. On this motif, cf. also *Lev. Rab.* Kedoshim 25/3 on Lev 19:23 (Mirqin 8.64; Soncino 4.316); *Midr. Pss.* 25/11 on Ps 25:10 (Buber 213, Braude 1.353); and *Tanḥ.* B Vayyesheb 11 on Gen 38:1 (Buber 182, Bietenhard 1.208).

[51] Cf. the end of the preceding note.

[52] Eshkol 161, Friedlander 330.

This is interpreted of God's activity at the Reed Sea in *Midr. Pss.* 68/13 on Ps 68:25[53] and in *Pirq. R. El.* 42.[54]

C) *Isa 43:16-17* states:

> Thus says the Lord, who makes a way in the sea (בְּיָם דָּרֶךְ),
> a path (נְתִיבָה) in the mighty waters,
>
> 17) Who brings out chariot and horse, army and warrior....

The first verse is related to the Reed Sea event in *Exod. Rab.* Bo 15/15 on Exod 15:15;[55] *Cant. Rab.* 2:15 § 2;[56] *Eliyyahu Zuṭa* 19;[57] and *Tanḥ.* B Vayyesheb 11 on Gen 38:11.[58]

The Lord thus not only "flew," "hovered" and "appeared" on the wings of the wind at the Reed Sea (Ps 18:11 and 2 Sam 22:11). The passages cited above, in Judaic tradition, also maintain that His way, His path, was in the Reed Sea. *Pirq. R. El.* 42 even says the Israelites saw God there "walking before them" (מְהַלֵּךְ לִפְנֵיהֶם).[59]

This imagery was employed of the LORD at the Reed Sea. It definitely encouraged the Palestinian Jewish Christian author of Mark 6:45-51 to describe his Lord, Jesus, in similar terms at the Sea of Galilee. There Jesus "walks" upon the Sea in vv 48-49. The major background for Jesus' walking or "hovering" over the Sea, however, derives from Judaic interpretation of God's Spirit as "moving" or "hovering" over the face of the waters at the Creation in Gen 1:2. There he is the Messiah. I shall analyze this in section II. below.

3) *An Apparition.*

In section 2) above I noted that in *Mek.* Baḥodesh 3 on Exod 19:17, R. Eliezer (b. Hyrcanus), an older second generation Tanna, maintained that

---

[53] Buber 319, Braude 1.547.

[54] Eshkol 161. Friedlander 330 translates the A. Epstein MS (xiv), but remarks in n. 10 that the first editions have Ps 68:25. Cf. also the fact that Ps 68:26 is interpreted of the Reed Sea event in *Exod. Rab.* Beshallaḥ 23/7 on Exod 15:1 (Mirqin 5.263; Soncino 3.285-286).

[55] Mirqin 5.178; Soncino 3.178.

[56] Donsqi 76; Soncino 9.136, with n. 2.

[57] Friedmann 28; Braude and Kapstein 495.

[58] Buber 182, Bietenhard 1.208. *Targum Jonathan* also relates v 17 to the Reed Sea. This is shown by its employment of the verb "swallow" from Exod 15:12. See Stenning 146-147.

[59] Eshkol 161, with Ps 68:25 and 77:20; Friedlander 330.

the phrase "Let me see Your countenance" in Cant 2:14 referred to God at the Reed Sea event, as interpreted by Exod 14:13.[60] This is buttressed by *Cant. Rab.* 2:14 § 3, which also cites Exod 14:13 on this phrase. It then interprets "your voice" in Cant 2:14 as the Song of the Israelites, beginning with Exod 15:1; "sweet is your voice" also as the Song; and "your countenance is comely" as Exod 15:2.[61]

The above sentence from Cant 2:14 in Hebrew is: הַרְאִינִי אֶת־מַרְאַיִךְ. Both verb and noun here have the same root, "seeing" (ראה). A מַרְאֶה can be a sight, phenomenon or "spectacle."[62] Exod 3:2 for example states that an angel of the Lord "appeared" (וַיֵּרָא) to Moses in a flame of fire out of the midst of a bush. Moses then turned aside to "see" this great "spectacle" (מַרְאֶה). In his retelling of this incident in *Ant.* 3.62, Josephus, a native of Jerusalem whose mother tongue was Aramaic, labeled this spectacle a φάντασμα, the same term employed in Mark 6:49.[63]

Gen 32:22-32 relates the incident of a man's wrestling with Jacob until the breaking of the day (vv 24, 26 and 31). It tells him he has striven with God (v 28). Jacob is astonished that he is still alive after having seen God face to face (v 30). Josephus retells this episode in *Ant.* 1.331-334 and calls Jacob's wrestler opponent a "phantom" or "apparition" (φάντασμα) in 331 (twice) and 333, who at the end simply "vanished" (ἀφανὲς γίνεται – 333). Josephus' identification of him as an "angel of God" (333) agrees with rabbinic sources here.[64] A similar incident occurs in Judg 6:11-24, where an angel of the Lord "appeared" (וַיֵּרָא) to Gideon in v 12.

---

[60] See notes 31-32.

[61] Donsqi 63; Soncino 9.130. There is a word play in the latter between "your countenance" (מַרְאֵךְ) and "they pointed" (מַרְאִין). These are the interpretations of R. Eleazar (ben Pedath), who also explained Exod 14:10 in light of Cant 2:14 in *Exod. Rab.* Beshallaḥ 21/5 (Soncino 3.264). It may also be noted that R. Eliezer in *Mek.* Shirata 3 on Exod 15:2 (Lauterbach 2.24) maintained that even a (simple) maidservant "saw at the Sea what Isaiah and Ezekiel and all the prophets never saw" (God Himself). He undergirds this with Ezek 1:1, with מַרְאוֹת of God.

[62] BDB 909, 1.a; Jastrow 834.

[63] In 2.267 he labels it an ὄψις, "vision" or "sight." Both מַרְאֶה and מַרְאָה can mean this (BDB 909). Josephus' text of the Hebrew Bible was probably unvocalized, so both interpretations were possible.

[64] Cf. *Gen. Rab.* Vayyishlaḥ 78/1 on Gen 32:27 for Michael or Gabriel, and 77/3 on Gen 32:25 and 78/3 on Gen 32:29 for Esau's guardian angel (Theodor and Albeck 916, 912 and 921; Soncino 2.714, 711 and 717 respectively). *Targ. Ps.-Jon.* Gen 32:25 has Michael (Rieder 1.51; Maher 114), and *Neofiti 1* on the same verse Sariel (Díez Macho 1.217 and 588).

Josephus in *Ant.* 5.213 calls him a "spectre" (φάντασμα) in the form of a young man.[65]

The above examples from Josephus, especially *Ant.* 3.62, where מַרְאֶה is rendered φάντασμα, make it probable that the Semitic background of φάντασμα in Mark 6:49 was also מַרְאֶה, which has no Aramaic cognate.[66] The Palestinian Jewish Christian who created the narrative of Mark 6:45-51 knew of the central association of Cant 2:14 ("Let me see Your מַרְאֶה") with Exod 14:10, from which he borrowed other imagery as well. He therefore employed it of the "apparition / spectre / phantom" which walked on the Sea towards the disciples. For him, of course, the phantom was in reality Jesus, the Son of God.

When a Hellenistic Jewish Christian translated this narrative from the Semitic into Greek, he employed the same term Josephus did for מַרְאֶה: φάντασμα.

10. *Wanting to Overtake Them.*

a) Just before his disciples see Jesus walking on the Sea, considering him an "apparition / phantom," Mark 6:48 remarks concerning him: "and he wanted to overtake them" (καὶ ἤθελεν παρελθεῖν αὐτούς). This Greek phrase puzzled not only Matthew, who omitted it at 14:25, but also many commentators on Mark, especially those who employ the standard translation of παρέρχομαι: "go by, pass by."[67] Yet the verb can also mean "come to, come here, come."[68] I suggest that in the Semitic original the verb עבר was employed, which normally also means "to pass, cross,"[69] yet can also mean "to overtake."[70] This phrase probably also derives from Judaic comment on Egypt's or Pharaoh's wanting to "overtake" the

---

[65] Interestingly, instead of the "Do not fear" of Judg 6:23, Josephus has Gideon's visitor urge him to "take courage" (θαρσεῖν) in 5.214. This verb is also found in Mark 6:50 (θαρσεῖτε, and "do not fear"). See also *Ant.* 5.277 for an angel as a φάσματα.

[66] Cf. again the Hebrew New Testament of Delitzsch here (p. 74): מַרְאֶה-רוּחַ.

[67] Cf. BAGD 625,1. Several of these commentators are E. Klostermann, *Das Markusevangelium* (HNT 3; Tübingen: Mohr, 1950⁴) 65, who notes various opinions; M. Dibelius, *From Tradition to Gospel* (New York: Scribner's, no date [German original 1919]) 95; B. van Iersel, *Markus Kommentar* (Düsseldorf: Patmos, 1993) 143; and W. Lane, *The Gospel According to Mark* 236.

[68] BAGD 626, 3, citing Luke 12:37; 17:7; (and Acts 24:7). Cf. also John 6:19, which has: "and coming (γινόμενον) near the boat."

[69] Cf. BDB 716-717, 1.a; Jastrow 1038, 2).

[70] Jastrow 1038, 5): "to pass, overtake, precede."

Israelites in the middle of the Sea. Before commenting on that, however, the relevance of Job 4:15-16 should be noted here.

Eliphaz the Temanite, one of Job's three friends who come to comfort him, relates concerning one of his night visions:

15)   A spirit "glided past" my face;
      the hair of my flesh stood up.

16)   It stood still, but I could not discern its "appearance."
      A form was before my eyes;
      there was silence, then I heard a voice (RSV).

The "spirit" here is רוּחַ, meant as a "disembodied being,"[71] in other words an apparition / phantom / ghost. The verb חלף, here translated "glided past," means to pass on or away.[72] The Targum employs עבר for it.[73] The word translated "appearance" in v 16 is מַרְאֶה. I suggest that the occurrence of the latter term encouraged the Palestinian Jewish Christian author of Mark 6:45-51 to formulate Jesus' "coming" to the disciples in the boat as his עבר or "passing" them, just as the "spirit" glided past Eliphaz. This was then correctly translated by a Hellenistic Jewish Christian as παρέρχομαι in 6:48. Yet the origin of Jesus' "wanting" to pass by / overtake the disciples in the Sea derives from Judaic comment on Exodus 14.

Exod 14:10 says that when Pharaoh drew near, "Egypt moved after them (נֹסֵעַ אַחֲרֵיהֶם – the Israelites), and they were in great fear." Here the verb "moved" is singular. It was interpreted in some Judaic sources as the guardian angel or prince of Egypt, who "hovered" or "flew in the air," wanting to attack and destroy Israel. Therefore the Israelites were "in great fear."[74] *Pirq. R. El.* 42 repeats the motif of danger through the Egyptians. It states in regard to Exod 14:20, "The Egyptians 'desired' to follow after Israel..." (וְהָיוּ הַמִּצְרִים רָצִים לָבוֹא אַחֲרֵי יִשְׂרָאֵל).[75] The phrase is repeated in a similar context later.[76] I suggest that an earlier form of this

---

[71] BDB 925, 4.e.

[72] BDB 322; Jastrow 471, 2), to pass by, be gone.

[73] Cf. de Lagarde 88.

[74] Cf. *Exod. Rab.* Beshallaḥ 21/5 on Exod 14:15 (Soncino 3.264). See also Bo 15/15 on Exod 12:2 (Soncino 3.179, with Exod 14:23 related to v10), and *Deut. Rab.* Debarim 1/22 on Deut 2:31 (Soncino 7.24).

[75] Eshkol 160, Friedmann 329.

[76] Eshkol 161, with אַחֲרֵי; Friedlander 331. See also Philo, *Mos.* 2.248, where Pharaoh "came in hot pursuit, 'eager to' overtake (them)...." The term σπεύδω means both "to hasten" and "to be eager to..." (LSJ 1627). It seems to reflect רצה here, but could also be meant as רוּץ, running, hastening. The verb καταλαμβάνω

motif of "desiring" (רצה)[77] to come after or overtake was interpreted of *miṣraim*, considered to be singular, the guardian angel or prince of Egypt. It then formed the background of Jesus' "desiring" (θέλω)[78] to overtake or come to the disciples in the boat in the Sea of Galilee (Mark 6:48). He is considered an apparition (v 49), causing the disciples to be terrified and afraid (vv 49-50), just as the hovering in the air of the guardian angel of Egypt in Judaic tradition caused the Israelites to be in great fear (Exod 14:10).

11. *Crying Out.*

a) Mark 6:49 relates that when the disciples in their boat on the Sea of Galilee saw Jesus walking on the Sea, they thought he was an apparition / phantom / ghost and "cried out" (ἔκραξαν). Matthew in 14:26 adds "out of fear," but John does not have this motif of crying out in his version at 6:19. The verb κράζω means to cry out, scream, shriek.[79] It too was borrowed by the Palestinian Jewish Christian author of Mark 6:45-51 from early Judaic tradition on Exod 14:10.

b) As I noted above, the disciples' thinking Jesus, walking on the Sea towards them, was an apparition / phantom / ghost, is based in part on Judaic interpretation of Exod 14:10. It maintains that the guardian angel or prince of Egypt, hovering in the air, came towards the Israelites at the Sea. This resulted in their being in great fear and in their "crying out" to the Lord. Precisely this combination is also found in Mark 6:49-50.

The MT has at Exod 14:10 וַיִּצְעֲקוּ. The same verb, צָעַק, is employed at v 15, where the Lord asks Moses: "Why do you 'cry out' to Me?" It means to cry, cry out.[80] In his Hebrew New Testament, Delitzsch translates

---

(LSJ 897, 2.) is employed here of "overtaking" the Israelites; see LXX Exod 15:9. See also *Mos.* 1.168.

[77] Jastrow 1493, 2). It does not derive here from רוץ, "to run," although this verb is employed in a different form in *Mek.* Shirata 2 on Exod 15:1, "to run after" the Israelites (Lauterbach 2.21), and elsewhere. Here too God asks *the* horse, representing all of Egypt, why it "runs after" the Israelites. See also the comment in 2.19. Early word plays with רצה, to desire, are probable. The form "running to come," occurring twice in *Pirq. R. El.* 42, is however improbable.

[78] Did it also influence John's statement in 6:21, "They therefore 'wanted / desired' (θέλω) to take him into the boat"? The RSV incorrectly translates this as "Then they 'were glad' to take him into the boat." The NRSV, an improvement, has "they wanted."

[79] BAGD 447.

[80] BDB 858, 1.b. Cf. Jastrow 1294. It is also found in Exod 15:25, where Moses "cries out" to the Lord at Marah because there is nothing to drink.

ἔκραξαν in Mark 6:49 with וַיִּצְעֲקוּ.[81] When he retells the Israelites' crossing of the Reed Sea, *Pseudo-Philo* in 10:2 quotes Exod 14:10 with the Israelites' "crying out," and then in 4 adds the expression by way of emphasis to a quotation of Exod 3:13. It then quotes Exod 14:15, with "Why have you cried to Me?" in 5.[82] Josephus at this point interprets the "crying out" only of the female reaction: "wailing and lamentations of women and children, with death before their eyes" (*Ant.* 2.328).

In the school of R. Ishmael it was also taught that Israel at the Reed Sea resembled a dove which, in fleeing from a hawk, flew into the cleft of a rock but found a snake in it. With the snake inside and the hawk "hovering" outside, it began to "cry" (צווח) and to beat its wings in order to attract the attention of its owner, who should come and rescue it. The simile then quotes Exod 14:10.[83]

These examples demonstrate early haggadic retelling of the expression "crying out" in Exod 14:10, preceded by "being in great fear." The Palestinian Jewish Christian who related the disciples' "crying out" in Mark 6:49 was thus very probably neither the first person, nor the last, to employ the expression in a narrative based on Exod 14:10.[84]

12. *Being Terrified / in Great Fear.*

a) Mark 6:49 relates that when Jesus' disciples in the boat saw him walking on the Sea, they considered him to be an apparition / phantom / ghost, and they cried out. Verse 50 continues by stating: "For they all saw him and 'were terrified'" (ἐταράχθησαν).[85] The Matthean parallel in 14:26 also employs this verb and adds: "And they cried out 'in fear' (ἀπὸ τοῦ φόβου)." John 6:19 simply states: "They were afraid" (ἐφοβήθησαν).

The verb ταράσσω in the passive means to be troubled, frightened, terrified.[86] It too derives here from Judaic interpretation of Exod 14:10, just as "crying out" in Mark 6:49 does.

---

[81] P. 74. The United Bible Societies (p. 107) have the same verb: "they began to 'cry out.'"

[82] Cf. Harrington 1.116, with *exclamavit* in 10:4, and *OTP* 2.317.

[83] Cf. *Cant. Rab.* 2:14 § 2 (Donsqi 72-73; Soncino 9.129). The verb is found in Jastrow 1266: to cry out, shout.

[84] Since LXX Exod 14:10 employs the verb ἀναβοάω here (LSJ 99: "cry, shout aloud, esp. in sign of grief or astonishment"), the Hellenistic Jewish Christian translator of Mark 6:45-51 was not dependent on it here. His rendering of צעק with κράζω is, however, frequently found in the LXX (Hatch and Redpath 781-782).

[85] I shall comment on "Do not fear" in this verse in the next section.

[86] BAGD 805, 1) 2. Pass.

b) Exod 14:10 states that when the Israelites saw *miṣraim* moving (sing.) towards them, "they were in great fear" (וַיִּֽירְא֣וּ מְאֹד֒) and cried out to the Lord. The simple verb יָרֵא means to fear.[87] If the Semitic original of ἰδόντες and εἶδον (ὁράομαι) in Mark 6:49-50 was ראה, "to see," there may have been an intentional word play with the disciples' being exceedingly "afraid" (ירא) in v 50.

The author of Exod 14:10 thought the simple verb ירא inadequate to express the Israelites' great terror at the Reed Sea. Therefore he added מְאֹד, "exceedingly, greatly, very."[88] All the targums on this verse employ the verb דחל for ירא here. It also means to fear, be afraid of, but also to worship, revere.[89] They express מְאֹד with לחדא, singularly, very much.[90] I suggest that either the Hebrew or Aramaic form of "being exceedingly afraid" in Exod 14:10 stands behind the disciples' being "terrified" (ταράσσω, pass.) in the Sea of Galilee in Mark 6:50. The following Judaic interpretations of Exod 14:10 buttress this proposal.

Philo in *Mos.* 1.170 relates regarding the Israelites' seeing the Egyptians directly behind them at the Reed Sea: "At this strange, unexpected sight, they were 'panic-stricken.'"[91] They ask Moses: "Do you not see how great are our troubles, how impossible to escape?" (1.172) In 2.249 the Alexandrian states: "Thus, caught between the enemy and the sea, they 'despaired' of each of his own safety."[92] Philo then has Moses tell the Israelites in 2.251: "'Alarm' (δέος) you must needs feel. 'Terror' (φόβος) is near at hand: the danger is great." Here δέος, "fear, alarm," certainly reflects Exod 14:10's וַיִּֽירְא֣וּ מְאֹד, translated in Philo's LXX as ἐφοβήθησαν σφόδρα. It was thought of as more lasting than φόβος.[93]

Pseudo-Philo in 10:2 has the Israelites say in their very fearful situation: "Behold, now the time of our destruction has come." In 10:3 he relates of them: "Then in considering 'the fearful situation' of the

---

[87] BDB 431, Jastrow 593.

[88] BDB 547, Jastrow 721.

[89] Jastrow 292. Cf. also the Aramaic passages from Daniel cited in BDB 1087.

[90] Jastrow 425 on חד, II.

[91] Cf. LSJ 905 on καταπλαγής: panic-struck.

[92] Cf. LSJ 194 on ἀπογιγνώσκω, II. See also *Mos.* 2.247 and 250.

[93] Cf. the citation in LSJ 379 on this noun.

moment, the sons of Israel...."[94] The Latin *metus* here means "fear, apprehension, dread, anxiety."[95]

Finally, *Exod. Rab.* Beshallaḥ 21/5 on Exod 14:15 and Cant 2:14 states regarding the Israelites: "they raised their eyes heavenwards and saw the guardian angel of Egypt hovering in the air and 'became sore afraid,'" a quotation of Exod 14:10.[96] As noted several times above, the singular נֹסֵעַ, "moving," in the latter verse made this interpretation possible. The Israelites are "greatly afraid" when they see the prince of Egypt moving towards them at the Reed Sea. The disciples in the boat in the middle of the Sea of Galilee show the same reaction when they see Jesus walking towards them. For these reasons I suggest that Judaic tradition around וַיִּירְאוּ מְאֹד in Exod 14:10 provided the background for the disciples' "being terrified" (ταράσσομαι) in Mark 6:50. It is stronger than simply being afraid (ירא, φοβέομαι).

13. *Take Heart, Do Not Fear.*

a) When the disciples in a boat in the middle of the Sea of Galilee see Jesus walking towards them, they consider it an apparition / phantom / ghost and cry out in great terror. Jesus therefore speaks to them immediately and says: "Take heart, it is I; do not fear" (Mark 6:50).[97] The latter in Greek is: θαρσεῖτε, ἐγώ εἰμι· μὴ φοβεῖσθε. The first and last verbs here also derive from Judaic interpretation of Exod 14:13.

b) When the Israelites at the Reed Sea saw the guardian angel of Egypt moving towards them, hovering in the air, they were terrified and cried out (haggadah on Exod 14:10). Then Moses addressed them with the words: "Fear not, stand firm" (v 13). The first expression in Hebrew is אַל-תִּירָאוּ, for which the LXX has θαρσεῖτε. The verb θαρσέω primarily means to be of good courage.[98]

I suggest that the Palestinian Jewish Christian author of Mark 6:45-51 appropriated אַל-תִּירָא literally for the second half of Jesus' command in Mark 6:50. In his Hebrew New Testament, for example, Delitzsch

---

[94] *OTP* 2.317.

[95] *SC* 229, 1.114. See the *Chambers Murray latin-english Dictionary* 434. Like its Hebrew and Aramaic equivalents, *metus* can also mean "religious awe."

[96] Soncino 3.264. As analyzed above, Cant 2:14 is interpreted of the Israelites' dire straits. They are like a dove caught between a hissing serpent and a hawk, which hovers before it.

[97] Matthew reproduces this at 14:27; John in 6:20 only has "Do not fear."

[98] LSJ 784. They can also translate θάρσει as "fear not." See also BAGD 352, "have courage! don't be afraid!"

employs exactly the same words.[99] It was then appropriately translated later by a Hellenistic Jewish Christian as μὴ φοβεῖσθε.

The Palestinian Jewish Christian author of the narrative of Jesus' walking on the Sea knew of a double Judaic interpretation of "Do not fear" in Exod 14:13. He therefore has Jesus first say: "Take heart / courage," and only then "Do not fear."

Mek. Beshallaḥ 3 on Exod 14:13, for example, comments on "Do not fear" with the following: "Behold, Moses is 'encouraging' them (the Israelites)."[100] The verb זרז employed here for "encouraging" basically means to be strong.[1] Both Delitzsch and the United Bible Societies have the synonym חֲזָקוּ for θαρσεῖτε in Mark 6:50.[2] The verb חזק also means to be strong, to take courage.[3]

Because of this double interpretation of אל-תיראו in Exod 14:13 as "Do not fear" and "Be strong / Take courage," Josephus in *Ant.* 2.327 states that Moses "cheered" the Israelites at this point.[4] In *Mos.* 1.173 Philo also says in regard to the Israelites at the Reed Sea: Moses "silently interceded (prayed) with God to save them from their desperate afflictions, while the latter (his speech) 'encouraged and comforted' (ἐθάρσυνε[5] καὶ παρηγόρει) the loud-voiced malcontents. 'Do not lose heart (μὴ ἀναπίπτετε),' he said." In 2.252, after mentioning the Israelites' alarm, terror and danger in their situation at the Reed Sea, Moses tells them: "Yet be of good courage, faint not (θαρρεῖτε, μὴ ἀποκάμητε)." While employing the LXX as his biblical text, Philo betrays the same early Judaic double interpretation of "Do not fear" in Exod 14:13 as found in the Palestinian *Mekilta of Rabbi Ishmael.* Josephus' "cheering" may also betray knowledge of it.

I suggest therefore that this double interpretation of "Do not fear" in Judaic tradition on Exod 14:13 led the Palestinian Jewish Christian author of Mark 6:45-51 to have Jesus in v 50 first say: "Take heart / courage," and then "Do not fear."

---

[99] P. 74.

[100] Lauterbach 1.210, who has "rallying them."

[1] Jastrow 412. He translates the piel form in the corrected text of *b. Makk.* 23a as "encouraging."

[2] P. 74 and p. 107 respectively.

[3] Jastrow 444-445. Cf. the hithpael and the nithpael: to feel encouraged, take courage, as well as the parallel to *b. Makk.* 23a in *Sifre* as cited in n. 1.

[4] The verb παρορμάω employed here (LSJ 1343) means to urge on, stimulate, incite.

[5] This is the causal of θαρσέω (LSJ 785): encourage, embolden.

14. *It is I.*

a) When Jesus spoke to his disciples in the boat on the Sea of Galilee, he not only told them to take heart and not to fear. He also revealed who he was: "It is I / It's me" (ἐγώ εἰμι – Mark 6:50, as well as Matt 14:27 and John 6:20). This formula of self-revelation also derives from Judaic interpretation of the exodus event in Exodus 14.

b) Exod 14:4 says that when Pharaoh pursues the Israelites, the Lord will get glory over him and all his host. Then the Egyptians will know "that I am the LORD" (כִּי-אֲנִי יהוה). This is basically repeated in v 18: "And the Egyptians shall know 'that I am the LORD' (כִּי-אֲנִי יהוה) when I have gotten glory over Pharaoh, his chariots and his horsemen." *Targum Pseudo-Jonathan* and the *Fragment Targum* have in both verses: אֲרוּם אֲנָא הוּא יי, "that it is I, the LORD."[6] This interpretation must be very old, for the LXX already has for both verses: ὅτι ἐγώ εἰμι κύριος.[7] In his Hebrew New Testament, Delitzsch has כִּי-אֲנִי הוּא for Mark 6:50, the Hebrew equivalent of the Aramaic (except for "LORD") found in the targums. It seems quite probable, therefore, that the Palestinian Jewish Christian author of Mark 6:45-51 had in v 50: "Take heart, 'for it is I.' Do not fear." When a Hellenistic Jewish Christian translated this narrative into Greek, he omitted the כִּי or אֲרוּם, "for," which is not necessary in Greek. Recognizing the background to much of the narrative in Exodus 14, he may even have thought of the LXX at this point: ἐγώ εἰμι.

Another passage from the Hebrew Bible applied in Judaic tradition to the Lord's making a way in the sea is Isa 43:16, as noted above in section 9.2)c). It refers to the exodus event, as shown in v 17 of *Targum Jonathan*, which borrows the verb בלע, to swallow, from Exod 15:12.[8] Verse 2, "When you pass through the waters, I will be with you," is rendered in the Targum as: "At the first when you passed through the Reed Sea, My Memra was your support...."[9] Verse 5, "Fear not, for I am with you," recalls Jesus' words in Mark 6:50, "fear not." The Targum then interprets: "Fear not, for My Memra is your support."[10] After noting in v 10 that the Messiah is the Lord's servant, the Targum has Him say:

---

[6] Cf. Rieder 1.101, 102 and Maher 199-200 for the former, and Klein 1.75 and 2.41-42, MS "P," for the latter. *Neofiti 1* has this on Exod 14:4 (Díez Macho 2.87), but v 18 lacks הוּא (2.91). *Onqelos* has אֲרִי אֲנָא ה on both verses (Drazin 141 and 145).

[7] Stegner, "Jesus' Walking" 219 calls attention to the LXX here.

[8] Stenning 147.

[9] *Ibid*. 144-145.

[10] *Ibid*.

"understand 'that I am He; I am He' from the beginning...." This is the Aramaic ארי אנא הוא אנא הוא for the Hebrew כִּי אֲנִי הוּא.[11] In v 13 the Targum again has "I am He," אנא הוא, for the Hebrew אֲנִי הוּא.[12]

I suggest that this section of Isaiah 43, associated with the exodus via v 16, with the Lord's making a way through the sea, and interpreted messianically, in addition to Exod 14:4 and 18 influenced the Palestinian Jewish Christian author of Mark 6:50 to formulate in Hebrew or Aramaic: "Take heart, 'for it is I'; do not fear."

15. *The Wind Ceased.*

a) After Jesus in the middle of the Sea of Galilee revealed to his disciples who he was, and told them not to be afraid, he "entered the boat with them, and 'the wind ceased'" (Mark 6:51). The last phrase in Greek is: ἐκόπασεν ὁ ἄνεμος. It is repeated by Matthew in 14:32, but is lacking in John 6:21. The verb κοπάζω in the NT is only found here and in the story of the stilling of the storm in Mark 4:39. Yet it is not borrowed from that narrative, nor from its background in the book of Jonah. There the LXX does have κοπάζω in Jonah 1:11-12. Rather, the term derives from elsewhere.

The verb κοπάζω means to grow weary, abate, stop, rest, cease. Herodotus 7.191 even speaks of the wind as "ceasing," as in Mark 6:51.[13]

Gen 8:1-12 describes how after the flood, the waters gradually "subsided" or "abated" until the ground became dry and Noah and his extended family could depart from the ark. The verb κοπάζω is employed in the LXX in v 1 for שָׁכַךְ,[14] and in vv 8 and 11 for קַלַל.[15] In vv 3 and 5 the Hebrew verb חסר is another synonym.[16] The fourth and last synonym is found in v 3, שׁוּב, to return, abate.

---

[11] *Ibid.*

[12] *Ibid.* 146-147. Note also "I, even I, am the Lord" in v 11 (*ibid.* 144-145). For Isa 42:5 – 43:10 as the prophetic reading for the first Sabbath in Nisan in the Palestinian triennial lectionary system, thus associated with Passover, see the *Appendix* at the end of this chapter.

[13] LSJ 978, and BAGD 443.

[14] BDB 1013: decrease, abate. It does not have this meaning in rabbinic Hebrew (Jastrow 1573).

[15] BDB 886, 1: be slight, of water, "be abated." Nor does this verb have the same meaning in rabbinic Hebrew (Jastrow 1377).

[16] BDB 341: lack, need, be lacking, "decrease." I know of no occurrence in rabbinic Hebrew in the sense of waters or a wind as "abating" (Jastrow 489).

Ps 78:39 speaks of a wind which passes and does not "return," and Eccl 1:6 of a wind which does "return." While the first instance means to disappear and not to "cease," it nevertheless shows how a wind (רוּחַ, Greek πνεῦμα or ἄνεμος) could be thought of as causing "returning." This is indeed the case for the parting of the Reed Sea and the waters or Sea "returning" upon the Egyptians in Exodus 14-15.[17]

b) Before the Israelites passed through the Reed Sea, the Lord drove it back by a strong east wind all night, making the Sea dry land, and dividing the waters (Exod 14:21). In 15:8 the Song of Moses says that at the blast / wind (רוּחַ) of the Lord's nostrils the waters (of the Sea) were piled up. Yet v 10 also notes that the Lord blew with His wind, resulting in the Sea's covering them (the Egyptians, while the Israelites were already in safety on the east shore). The latter phenomenon is described in 14:26 and 28 as the waters' "returning" (שׁוּב) upon the Egyptians, and in v 27 of the Sea's "returning to its wonted flow" at the break of day (see also 15:19). Since κοπάζω is employed of a wind's ceasing, and is one Greek verb used to translate the synonyms of שׁוּב in Gen 8:1-12, I suggest that its employment in Mark 6:51 is based on Judaic interpretation of Exod 14:26-28. This is buttressed by the following passages.

Ezekiel the Tragedian in his *Exagōgē* 236-238 remarked concerning the Israelites after they passed through the Reed Sea: "For when they reached the farther shore a mighty wave 'gushed forth' hard by us (the Egyptians in the middle of the Sea)...." In 242 he notes that "The sea-path 'flooded,' all our host was lost."[18]

Philo of Alexandria describes the early dawn crossing of the Reed Sea by the Israelites. In *Mos.* 1.179 he then notes how the "returning tide" (παλιρροίη)[19] was "poured out"[20] by means of the north wind. This is the opposite direction from the south wind in LXX Exod 14:21, for which the Hebrew has the east wind. This flowing back or reflux then drowned the Egyptians to the last man, horse and chariot.

In *Mos.* 2.254 Philo describes the same moment by stating that the flowings (παλίρροια) of the Sea, "which had been stayed from their course and parted for a while 'return to their place'...." The latter is the

---

[17] For other waters' returning, cf. Ps 104:9 dealing with Creation, and Josh 4:18, concerned with the waters of the Jordan returning to their place after all the Israelites crossed the river. The latter is similar to the Reed Sea event.

[18] *OTP* 2.818.

[19] LSJ 1293: flowing back, reflux.

[20] LSJ 126 on ἀναχέω, passive.

Greek δίίστημι.[21] The waters then rush in, drowning the Egyptians, and "a mighty rushing wave...flings the corpses in heaps upon the opposite shore..." (255).

Pseudo-Philo in 10:6 also states in regard to Exod 14:27 that "the Lord commanded the sea, and it 'returned' to (the limits of) its flowings" (*et reversus est in fluxus suos*).[22]

Finally, Josephus in *Ant.* 2.343 notes that when the whole Egyptian military force was within the Reed Sea, "'back poured' (ἐπιχεῖται πάλιν) the sea, enveloping and with swelling wind-swept billows descending upon the Egyptians...." The verb ἐπιχέω here means to pour over,[23] and πάλιν, "again," clearly points to Josephus' attempt to render the שוב of Exod 14:26-28. He also notes that in the morning the tide brought the Egyptians' arms to the Hebrew camp (on the east shore), "and the force of the wind 'setting' in that direction," Moses collected them (2.349). The term for "setting" here is ἐκδίδωμι, which means to give up.[24] The wind is pictured as "relaxing" or "ceasing." Both Philo and Josephus are thus aware of early Judaic interpretation of the wind of Exod 15:10 as applied to the Sea's "returning" or ceasing in 14:26-28.[25]

The above early Judaic texts make it probable that the Palestinian Jewish Christian author of Mark 6:45-51, describing the incident in light of Judaic interpretation of Exodus 14-15, also interpreted the wind from 15:10 on the basis of the "returning" or "ceasing" from 14:26-28. He therefore noted the wind's "ceasing" in Mark 6:51. He may have employed רוּחַ with the verb שׁוּב, or שָׁתַק.[26] The Hellenistic Jewish Christian translator of Mark 6:45-51 then later rendered the latter by κοπάζω, for he

---

[21] LSJ 428: the sea made way, opened. Here it is meant as "return," as Colson translates.

[22] *SC* 229, 1.116. I modify Harrington's translation in *OTP* 2.317, in part employing the French rendering.

[23] LSJ 673.

[24] LSJ 494.

[25] *Midr. Pss.* 106/4 on Ps 106:7 (Buber 455, Braude 2.191) is related to this. Either R. Huna or R. Aḥa, both fourth generation Palestinian Amoraim (Strack and Stemberger, *Introduction* 103), taught: "It was not by a rebuke but by raising a wind (מנשׁפי, by My blowing) that God brought back the waters, as is said: 'Thou didst blow with Thy wind, the sea covered them' (Exod 15:10)."

[26] BDB 1060; it is employed in Jonah 1:11-12, where the Greek, as noted above, is κοπάζω. See also Jastrow 1640, and *y. Ber.* 9:1, 13b (Neusner 1.316). Another possibility is נוּחַ (Jastrow 885-886, with an example from *b. B. Meṣ.* 86a for a storm's "subsiding," as well as the sea's "subsiding" in *b. B. Baṭ.* 73a, Soncino 289).

was well aware of its LXX usage both in Gen 8:1-12 and in Jonah 1:11-12, and perhaps even of Greek usage for the wind's ceasing, as seen in Herodotus.

* * *

Here in Mark the disciples are described as rowing tortuously for most of the night into a head wind (from the east). When Jesus as the Messiah (see below, section II.) walks towards them and enters the boat, towards dawn, this reminded the original hearers, steeped in the Hebrew Bible and the Hebrew and Aramaic interpretations of it, of the Egyptians' making very difficult progress in their chariots in the Reed Sea because of the strong east wind blowing against them, and of the Sea's returning or ceasing in the early morning once the danger for the Israelites was past. For these Christians, Jesus was not only a second Moses, but even more. He was the final redeemer of Israel, the Messiah, who would lead them out of all their difficulties, however severe they might be. The motif of the wind's ceasing once Jesus enters the disciples' boat seeks to express this.

16. *Seeing the Lord, and Being Utterly Astounded.*

a) Mark 6:50 relates of the disciples in the boat on the Sea of Galilee: "Now when they 'saw' (ἰδόντες) him walking on the Sea...." Verse 51 emphasizes this motif: "For all 'saw' (εἶδον) him and were terrified." Then, after telling them who he was and not to be afraid, Jesus entered the boat, the wind ceased, "and they were 'utterly astounded'" (καὶ λίαν ἐν ἑαυτοῖς ἐξίσταντο). Some important Greek witnesses (ADWθ) add: "and marveled" (καὶ ἐθαύμαζον), as in Acts 2:7. Instead of the disciples' being utterly astounded, Matthew in 14:33 has them worship Jesus, saying: "Truly you are the Son of God." John 6:21 also omits the disciples' amazement. Instead, it notes that the boat immediately reached the land for which they departed.[27]

BAGD on ἐξίστημι 2.b. defines the verb so: "be amazed, be astonished, of the feeling of astonishment mingled with fear, caused by events which are miraculous, extraordinary, or difficult to understand...."[28] This fits the situation of Jesus' appearing as an apparition / phantom / ghost walking on the Sea, and the wind's ceasing when Jesus entered the boat, very well.

---

[27] This may be a haggadic development of Ps 107:29-30, where after the Lord causes the storm to be still, "He brought them to their desired haven." For the idea of a "miracle within a miracle," cf. *b. Soṭa* 47a (Soncino 245).

[28] P. 276; cf. LSJ 595, 3: to be astonished, amazed.

Both expressions, the disciples' "seeing" Jesus and their being "utterly astounded," also derive from Judaic interpretation of the Reed Sea event, especially Exod 14:31.

b)

1. The RSV of Exod 14:31 reads: "And Israel 'saw' (וַיַּרְא) the great work which the Lord did against the Egyptians, and the people 'feared' (וַיִּירְאוּ) the Lord...." There is a word play here between seeing, רָאה, and fearing, ירא. "The great work" is literally "the great hand," הַיָּד הַגְּדֹלָה. "Hand" is meant here as a "great achievement," a display of strength.[29] *Targum Neofiti 1* has here: "the strong (תקיפתא) hand," *Targum Onqelos* "the strength (גבורת) of the great hand," and both *Pseudo-Jonathan* and the *Fragment Targum* "the strength of the mighty hand."[30] They all mean, of course, the Israelites' "seeing" the miracle of the Lord's dividing the Reed Sea, saving them but drowning the pursuing Egyptians. This "seeing" was emphasized in Judaic traditions at an early point.

The Wisdom of Solomon, written in Egypt perhaps at the very beginning of the first century CE or, alternatively, during the reign of Gaius Caligula (37-41 CE),[31] states in 19:8 that the Israelites passed through the Reed Sea "after gazing on marvelous wonders" (θεωρήσαντες θαυμαστὰ τέρατα).

In *Ant.* 2.339 Josephus describes the Reed Sea as dividing, baring the soil for the Hebrews to flee through it. Moses then beholds "this clear manifestation of God and the sea withdrawn from its own bed to give them place...." Here Moses (and all the other Israelites) see the ἐπιφάνεια or epiphany of God, which is a miraculous deliverance (345).

In *Mek.* Shirata 3 on Exod 15:2 ("This is my God"), R. Eliezer (b. Hyrcanus), an older second generation Tanna,[32] states that even a (humble) maidservant "saw" at the Reed Sea what Isaiah and Ezekiel and all the prophets never "saw." God "revealed Himself" (נגלה) at the Sea, and as soon as the Israelites "saw" Him, they recognized Him and spoke Exod 15:2.[33] That is, they were privileged to see the Lord directly here.

---

[29] BDB 390 on יָד, 2; see also Jastrow 563, 2).

[30] Cf. respectively Díez Macho 1.95 and 449; Drazin 148-149; Rieder 1.103 and Maher 202; and Klein 1.77 and 2.244.

[31] Nickelsburg, *Jewish Literature* 184.

[32] Strack and Stemberger, *Introduction* 77.

[33] Lauterbach 2.24-25.

R. Judah b. Ilai, a third generation Tanna,[34] notes in *Cant. Rab.* 3:9 § 1: "At the Reed Sea they saw Him in the open (בְּפַרְהֶסְיָא),[35] as it says: 'And Israel saw the great work' – lit. 'hand' (Exod 14:31), and the children pointed to Him with the finger and said, 'This is my God, and I will glorify Him' (15:2)."[36] As above, the Israelites openly "see" God here, a tradition connected to Exod 14:31.

Finally, an anonymous commentator notes in *Midr. Pss.* 69/1 on Ps 69:1-2 that the verses are to be interpreted in light of Cant 7:7 – "How fair and pleasant were the Israelites when they stood at the Sea 'and beheld' (וראין) the Holy One, blessed be He! As Scripture says, 'And Israel saw the great work...' (Exod 14:31)." Shortly thereafter it states that the Israelites "beheld God upon (the waters of) the Sea," and they became water-lilies, as in Ps 69:1, "For the leader; upon Shoshannim ([water]-lilies)."[37] The English translator, W. Braude, had added the first words in parentheses, yet correctly, for the Israelites are thought of here as openly seeing the Lord above the Sea. *Pirq. R. El.* 42 directly states, for example, that "they saw the Holy One, blessed be He, walking before them" (over the Sea, or possibly in it), as Ps 68:24 and 77:19 are interpreted.[38]

Coupled with the passage cited above from Josephus, the latter rabbinic texts are amazingly direct in describing how the Israelites "beheld" the Lord at the Reed Sea in a very special way: openly.[39] These texts helped to prepare the way for the Palestinian Jewish Christian author of Mark 6:45-51, who emphasized that all the disciples "saw"

---

[34] Strack and Stemberger, *Introduction* 84-85.

[35] Jastrow 1217 on פרהסיא as from the Greek παρρησία. It means "outspokenness, frankness, freedom of speech" (LSJ 1344). See also BAGD 630 with μετά: "plainly," and παρρησίᾳ as "openly."

[36] Donsqi 93; Soncino 9.165, which I have slightly modified. Cf. Wisd 10:21b, as well as the many other sources cited in Ginzberg, *Legends* 3.34 and 6.13, notes 64-65.

[37] Buber 321, Braude 1.550.

[38] Eshkol 161, Friedlander 330. Stegner, "Jesus' Walking" 226-227, also calls attention to the above *Mekilta* passage, as well as to *Pirq. R. El.* 42 (he refers to Heil, *Jesus Walking* 51). He also notes Jer 32:21, which in the LXX (39:21) has "great visions" and in *Targum Jonathan* "the great vision" (Sperber 3.212 – חזונא רבא) for the Hebrew "great terror." R. Hayward in *The Targum of Jeremiah* 137, n. 14, notes that haggadic interpretations of Exod 15:2 may be meant. It is reflected in *Cant. Rab.* 3:9 § 1 cited above, with Exod 14:31 and 15:2; Wisd 10:21; and in *Targum Pseudo-Jonathan* (Rieder 1.104), as well as *Fragment Targum* (Klein 1.170 and 2.129) on Exod 15:2. *Neofiti 1*, "M," also has this (Díez Macho 2.97 and 450).

[39] This is especially significant in light of a passage like Exod 33:20.

Jesus, his own Lord, walking on the Sea of Galilee. This motif is in part based on Judaic interpretation of Exod 14:31a.

2. The disciples' being "utterly astounded" (ἐξίστημι) in Mark 6:51 after "seeing" the preceding events (Jesus' walking on the Sea, the wind's ceasing) is based on the phrase "and the people 'feared' the Lord" in Exod 14:31a. The Hebrew verb ירא here is translated by ἐξίστημι in LXX Ezek 2:6. In *Mos.* 1.180 Philo describes how the Israelites marvel when the Reed Sea returns due to the north wind, drowning the Egyptians. Then he states: "This great and marvelous work struck the Hebrews with amazement...." "This great...work" (τὸ μέγα τοῦτο...ἔργον) is based on "the great hand" of Exod 14:31, and "to strike with amazement" (καταπλαγής, from καταπλήσσω: strike with amazement, astound, terrify)[40] derives from "they feared" in the same verse. Philo does not reveal knowledge of the Hebrew text here, but of Judaic tradition on it which he learned in Alexandria from other older exegetes.[41] For him, God's work here is also "marvelous" (θαυμαστός),[42] the same root associated in some Greek MSS with "being astounded" in Mark 6:51.

The Alexandrian Jew Philo, writing in the first half of the first century CE, and dependent here on earlier tradition regarding Exod 14:31, shows how a Palestinian Jewish Christian wishing to describe the disciples' being "astounded" after seeing what they did, could also employ imagery from Palestinian Judaic interpretation of Exod 14:31 to do so.[43]

* * *

I suggest that the original narrative of Jesus' walking on the Sea ended at Mark 6:51. The account was joined, however, at an early, pre-Markan time to the feeding of the 5000 in vv 31-44. This is also the case in John 6:1-15 and 16-21.

---

[40] LSJ 905 and 906.

[41] Cf. for example *Ios.* 151 and 160.

[42] For the cognate verb, cf. *Mos.* 1.177 and Josephus, *Ant.* 2.347. See also Wisd 19:8 above.

[43] There was much more interchange between Alexandria and Jerusalem than was earlier thought. Cf. for example the fact that there was a synagogue of the Alexandrians in the Judean capital (Acts 6:9 and Str-B 2.663-664). Legal and haggadic traditions certainly went back and forth frequently.

While the motif of "hardening one's heart" in Mark 6:52 also occurs in Exod 14:4,8 and 17,[44] it was most probably the Evangelist Mark who first formulated this verse. He did the same in 8:17, where he has Jesus ask: "Why do you discuss the fact that you have no bread? Do you not perceive or understand (συνίημι, as in 6:52)? Are your hearts hardened?" In v 21 Jesus also asks: "Do you not yet understand (also συνίημι)?" For Mark, this lack of perception in 6:52 in regard to Jesus' true identity is part of the messianic secret. Even after Peter's telling Jesus he is the Christ in 8:29, thus long after the miraculous feeding of the 5000 and Jesus' walking on the Sea in chapter six, Mark has Jesus inform the disciples to tell no one about him (8:30). The same is true of the transfiguration in 9:2-8. After it, Jesus charges the disciples "to tell no one what they had seen until the Son of man should have risen from the dead" (v 9). Only the Resurrection itself in 16:1-8 removes the secret of who Jesus really is.

This is not true for Matthew, who ends his account of Jesus' walking on the Sea with the disciples' worshiping Jesus in the boat and saying: "Truly you are the Son of God" (14:33). The miracles of Jesus' walking on the Sea and the wind's ceasing when he (and Peter) entered the boat reveal for Matthew the true identity of Jesus already at this stage of the Gospel. In addition, Matthew inserts special Petrine material in vv 28-31, which also derives from Palestinian (or Syriac) Judaic tradition on Exodus 14-15. To this material I now turn.

17. *Peter the First Disciple, and Naḥshon of Judah, the First or Ruling Tribe.*

a) In Matt 14:28-31 Peter is the disciple in the boat on the Sea of Galilee who also walks on the water, yet for lack of sufficient faith sinks and needs to be rescued by Jesus. He is pictured here as representing the twelve disciples in the boat. He courageously enters the Sea first, (although the others do not follow).

Elsewhere Peter also plays the primary role among the disciples. He is the first disciple Jesus calls (Mark 1:16 par.; 3:16 par.); he is the first to proclaim Jesus the Christ (8:29 par.); he is named first in the inner circle of three (9:2 and 14:33 par.); the angel tells the women at the empty tomb to inform the disciples and Peter in Galilee (16:7 par.); Jesus appears to

---

[44] Cf. also Exod 4:21 in connection with miracles; 9:12; 10:20,27; and 11:10 with wonders. *Pseudo-Philo* 10:6 also states that after the Israelites passed through the Reed Sea, the Egyptians saw this and followed them. "And God hardened their perception, and they did not know that they were entering the sea" (*OTP* 2.317). The Latin is: *Et Deus obduravit sensum eorum, et non scierunt...* (*SC* 229, 1.116). This is somewhat reminiscent of the disciples' hardened heart, which caused them not to "perceive" the meaning of the (feeding of the 5000 with) loaves of bread.

him (there) first (1 Cor 15:5; cf. John 21); and according to Luke, he was the most important leader of the church in Jerusalem (Acts 1:13,15; 2:14, etc.; cf. Matt 16:18-19, also special Matthean material).

In Matt 14:28-31 Peter, the first of the disciples, is described in terms of Palestinian Judaic traditions on Naḥshon the son of Amminadab, the head of the tribe of Judah, which later ruled over all twelve tribes of Israel.

b) According to Num 1:7; 2:3; and 10:14 Naḥshon the son of Amminadab was the leader of the tribe of Judah. He was also the first of the twelve tribal leaders to present an offering to the tabernacle (Num 7:12).[45] Gen 49:10 states that the scepter shall not depart from this tribe, nor the ruler's staff. This information helps to understand the following Palestinian haggadic incident regarding Naḥshon at the Reed Sea. It is found in various sources.[46] They are narrated in the name of R. Ilai, R. Tarfon and R. Aqiva, second generation Tannaim,[47] and the third generation Tannaim R. Judah b. Ilai and R. Meir.[48]

According to this narrative, which also has numerous slight variants, showing its popularity, the Israelites were standing at the Reed Sea as in Exod 14:22. One said: "I do not want to go down to the Sea 'first' (תְּחִלָּה),"[49] and the others repeated this. While they stood there taking council / deliberating, Naḥshon the son of Amminadab jumped (forward) and descended "first" (תחלה) into the Sea and fell into its waves.[50]

---

[45] Naḥshon was privileged to make his offering on the "first day," and the other tribes on the following eleven days.

[46] Cf. *t. Ber.* 4:18 (Zuckermandel / Liebermann 12; Neusner 1.25-26); *Mek. Beshallaḥ* 6 on Exod 14:22 ("And the sons of Israel went into the middle of the Sea") in Lauterbach 1.232-237; *b. Soṭa* 36b (Soncino 182-183); *Exod. Rab. Beshallaḥ* 24/1 on Exod 15:22 (Mirqin 5.270; Soncino 3.294-295); *Num. Rab.* Naso 13/4 on Num 7:12 (Mirqin 10.55-56; Soncino 6.513); *Midr. Pss.* 68/14 on Ps 68:28 (Buber 320, Braude 1.547-548); 76/1 on Ps 76:2 (Buber 340, Braude 2.13); 76/2 on Ps 76:2 (Buber 341, Braude 2.13-14); 114/8 on Ps 114:2, "Judah became His sanctuary" (Buber 474, Braude 2.220-221); and *Pirq. R. El.* 42 (Eshkol 161, Friedlander 330-331).

[47] Cf. Strack and Stemberger, *Introduction* 80, for R. Ilai, a student of R. Eliezer b. Hyrcanus; 80 for R. Tarfon, the teacher of R. Judah b. Ilai; and 79-80 for R. Aqiva.

[48] *Ibid.*, 84-85 and 84, respectively.

[49] Jastrow 1661.

[50] Cf. for example *Mek. Beshallaḥ* 6 on Exod 14:22 (Lauterbach 1.234) in the name of R. Judah (b. Ilai). In *Num. Rab.* Naso 13/7 on Num 7:12, Naḥshon is called so because he was the first to go down into the surf / billow / gale (נַחְשׁוֹל – Jastrow

I suggest that Peter, the only one of the twelve disciples in the boat on the Sea of Galilee to enter the Sea, did so because he was otherwise the "first" of the disciples. The scene here is modeled on Naḥshon, from the "first" or ruling tribe of Judah, who "first" entered the Reed Sea.[51]

18. *Peter's Descending, and Naḥshon's Descending.*

a) Matt 14:29 states that when Jesus invited Peter to come to him upon the water, Peter "descended" (καταβαίνω) from the boat, walked on the water, and went towards Jesus. Later on, both he and Jesus "ascended" (ἀναβαίνω) into the boat in v 32. The expression "to descend" here is also borrowed from Naḥshon's behavior at the Sea.

b) As noted in 17.b) above, the Israelites, at the shore of the Reed Sea, told each other they did not want to "descend" (ירד) first into the Sea. While they were taking council / deliberating, however, Naḥshon jumped (forward), "descended" (ירד) first into the Sea and fell into its waves.[52]

I suggest that the author of the special material now found in Matt 14:28-31[53] also modeled Peter's "descending" into the Sea of Galilee on Naḥshon's "descending" to the Reed Sea and entering it.

19. *Peter's Descending in Faith, and Naḥshon's Descending in Faith.*

a) Peter asks Jesus to tell him to come to him upon the water. When Jesus does so, Peter descends from the boat, walks on the water and comes to Jesus (Matt 14:28-29).

While not mentioned explicitly, Peter's faith or trust in Jesus is implicitly emphasized here. Such faith while "descending into the Sea" is based on Judaic interpretation of Naḥshon's descending into the Sea.

b) In order to emphasize the importance of Naḥshon's descending into the Reed Sea first, as a representative of the tribe of Judah, the haggadah here quotes Hos 12:1 (Eng. 11:12). It applies the first part of the verse to those Israelites who refused to enter the Sea: "Ephraim has surrounded Me with lies, and the house of Israel with deceit." The second part is

---

897) of the Sea, a word play. See Mirqin 10.58, and Soncino 6.517. There is a parallel in *Pesiq. R.* 7/6 (Friedmann 28a, Braude 1.140).

[51] In his essay "The Concept of the So-called 'Divine Man' in Mark's Christology," O. Betz also calls attention to Naḥshon and Peter, yet only in a footnote (3) on p. 239. To my knowledge this was never developed elsewhere.

[52] Cf. n. 50.

[53] See below for several remarks on his identity.

applied[54] to Nahshon, the prince of Judah: "but Judah still rules with God, and 'is faithful' (נאמן) to the Holy One." Here Nahshon's faith / faithfulness is emphasized. This is interpreted in *Midr. Pss.* 76/2 on Ps 76:2 by the disciples of R. Tarfon as meaning that Judah (Nahshon here) "surrendered" (הִשְׁלִים) to God, hallowed His name, and "went down" into the Sea, thereby becoming worthy of the kingship, as Ps 114:2 is explained.[55]

The phrase from Hos 12:1, רָד עִם-אֵל, is also interpreted here as Judah's (Nahshon's) "descending (into the Sea because his trust was) with God."[56]

Nahshon's faith in God when descending into the Reed Sea provided the model upon which Peter's faith in his Lord Jesus was based when the "first" disciple descended into the Sea of Galilee.

20. *Peter's Fear and Little Faith, and the Israelites' Fear and Little Faith.*

a) While walking on the Sea of Galilee, Jesus told the disciples not to fear (Matt 14:27). Yet when Peter descended from the boat and walked upon the water towards Jesus, he "became afraid" (ἐφοβήθη) when he saw the (strong) wind,[57] and he began to sink. Then he cried out for the Lord to save him (v 30). Jesus caught Peter by the hand, yet reproached him with the words: "O man of little faith (ὀλιγόπιστε), why did you doubt?" (v 31).

While "being of little faith" is a favorite term of Matthew's,[58] it and the motif of "fear" derive from Judaic interpretation of the position of the Israelites at the Reed Sea, when Nahshon first entered it.

---

[54] As so often, only the first part of the verse is quoted in the sources. Familiarity with the rest of the text was simply assumed.

[55] Buber 341, Braude 2.14. See Jastrow 1585 on the hiphil 2) of שלם for surrender, and 1586, Af. 5) for surrender, hand over, entrust.

[56] Cf. the explanatory note (2) by A. Cohen in his rendering of *b. Soṭa* 37a (Soncino 183), as well as Braude's translation, "But Judah moreover went down with God," in *The Midrash on Psalms* 2.14.

[57] Normally one cannot "see" a wind, but only its effects such as waves. I suggest that the term רוּחַ here (wind; spirit, ghost) is still thought of partially in its second sense. Thus one can still "see" it, as in v 26.

[58] Cf. the noun in Matt 17:20, and the adjective in 6:30 (parallel in Luke 12:28); 8:26; and 16:8. They occur nowhere else in the NT.

b) In *Pirq. R. El.* 42 on the exodus, R. Aqiva[59] states that "the Israelites advanced to enter the Reed Sea (Exod 14:22), but they turned backwards, 'fearing' (יְרֵאִים) lest the waters would return upon them." Then the tribe of Judah (Naḥshon) sanctified God's great name and entered the Sea first, as Ps 114:2 is interpreted.[60]

Here the Israelites' "fear" at the Reed Sea follows directly after the strong east wind of the preceding verse, Exod 14:21. The same is true for Peter's reaction of fear in the Sea of Galilee when he sees the (strong) wind in Matt 14:30, although he is already in the Sea.

The synonymous expressions "of little faith" (קְטַן אמנה) and "lacking in faith" (מחוסר א') occur primarily in connection with the lack of faith shown by the Israelites when they tried to gather manna in the wilderness also on the seventh day in the neighboring chapter, Exodus 16.[61] Yet R. Huna, probably a fourth generation Palestinian Amora,[62] maintained in *b. Pesaḥ.* 118b: "The Israelites of that generation (*sc.* of the Egyptian exodus) were men 'of little faith' (קטני אמנה)...."[63] This is buttressed by the exposition of Ps 106:7, "But they were rebellious at the sea, even at the Reed Sea," by Rabbah b. Mari, a fourth generation Babylonian Amora, in regard to Exodus 14.[64] This doubling of "the Sea" was interpreted already at an early time to mean that the Israelites were rebellious not only at the Reed Sea, but also within it.[65]

I therefore suggest that the author of the special material now found in Matt 14:28-31 was aware of Judaic tradition on the Israelites' "fear" at

---

[59] I do not consider this a pseudonym here because of passages on the same topic from other second and third generation Tannaim.

[60] Eshkol 161; Friedlander 330-331, which I slightly modify (see also his notes).

[61] Cf. especially v 27, and *Mek.* Vayassa' 5 on this (Lauterbach 2.120), as well as other passages cited in Str-B 1.438-439. This topos certainly influenced Jesus' use of the term in Matt 6:30 // Luke 12:28, and Matthew's insertion of the expression in 16:8 in regard to the miraculous feeding of the 5000. (It is hardly accidental that John 6:22-59 on Jesus as the bread from heaven is in part based on Exodus 16 [cf. vv 4 and 15], as the preceding vv 16-21 with Jesus walking on the Sea are based on Exodus 14-15.)

[62] Strack and Stemberger, *Introduction* 103.

[63] Soncino 609. There is a parallel in *b. 'Arak.* 15a (Soncino 85).

[64] Strack and Stemberger, *Einleitung* 99. He was forgotten in the English translation on p. 105.

[65] Cf. for example R. Judah (b. Ilai) in *Sifre* Deut. Debarim on Deut 1:1 (Finkelstein 5, Hammer 25), and in *'Avot R. Nat.* A 34 (Schechter 98; Goldin 136) and B 38 (Saldarini 225). For the expression מחוסרי אמנה in regard to Exod 14:2, see *Mek. R. S.b. Yoḥ.* (Epstein and Melamed 48) and *Mek.* Beshallaḥ 2 (Lauterbach 1.190).

the Reed Sea in connection with Naḥshon's descent into it, and of the motif of being "of little faith" in connection with the Reed Sea. He then applied these terms to Peter, who because of the (strong) wind began to fear, resulting in Jesus' labeling him "of little faith" in the Sea of Galilee.

21. *Sinking.*

a) When Peter saw the (strong) wind (causing high waves on the Sea of Galilee), he became afraid, and having begun "to sink" (καταποντίζεσθαι), he cried out, saying: "Save me!" (Matt 14:30).

The verb καταποντίζω, in the passive "to sink,"[66] occurs in the NT only here and in 18:6. It is used in LXX Exod 15:4 in the active for God's sinking / drowning Pharaoh's select mounted viziers in the Red Sea. It translates the Hebrew טָבַע, "sink, sink down," here in the pual, meaning "be sunk."[67] In his Hebrew New Testament, Delitzsch also employs this verb at Matt 14:30.[68]

The basis for Peter's "sinking" in the Sea of Galilee, however, is found in Naḥshon's "sinking" in the Reed Sea.

b) In the Palestinian haggadah on Naḥshon's being the first to jump forward and descend into the Reed Sea, one tradition says "he fell into the waves of the sea."[69] Another states that "it (the sea) came down over him."[70] Ps 69:2-3 (Eng. 1-2) and 16 (Eng. 15) are then quoted at this point of Naḥshon. They read: 2) "the waters have come up to my neck (lit. 'soul'). 3) 'I sink' (טָבַעְתִּי) in deep mire, where there is no foothold; I have come into deep waters, and the flood sweeps over me." 16) "Do not let the flood sweep over me, or the deep swallow me up, or the Pit close its mouth over me" (NRSV).[71]

I therefore suggest that Naḥshon's "sinking" here in the Reed Sea after descending into it is the basis for Peter's "sinking" in the Sea of Galilee after descending into it.

---

[66] BAGD 417.

[67] BDB 371. Cf. also Jastrow 518.

[68] P. 27.

[69] Cf. *Mek.* Beshallaḥ 6 on Exod 14:22 (Lauterbach 1.234).

[70] *Midr. Pss.* 76/1 on Ps 76:2 (Buber 340, Braude 2.13). In 114/8 on Ps 114:2, it is all the Israelites who enter the Reed Sea until they reach "the ends of the Sea" (אפסי ים), i.e. its depths. See Buber 474, with a printing error, and Braude 2.220, with n. 17 on p. 510.

[71] Cf. n. 69.

22. *Save Me!*

a) When Peter began to sink in the Sea of Galilee, he cried out, saying: "Lord, save me!" (σῶσόν με – Matt 14:30). This expression also derives from the Naḥshon haggadah.

b) As stated above in 21.b), when Naḥshon descends into the Reed Sea, he falls into its waves, it comes down over him, or its waters come up to his neck causing him to "sink" (Ps 69:2-3). Above I intentionally omitted the first phrase from verse 2, quoted with it: "Save me, God!" (הוֹשִׁיעֵנִי אֱלֹהִים).

The author of the special material now found in Matt 14:28-31 borrowed this phrase[72] as applied to Naḥshon, beginning to sink in the Reed Sea, and reapplied it to Peter, beginning to sink in the Sea of Galilee. He simply changed "God" to "lord," later the Greek κύριε, in v 30. The latter was probably originally אֲדֹנִי,[73] or possibly מָרִי,[74] both meaning "my lord." When a Hellenistic Jewish Christian later translated "Save me!" into Greek, he employed σῶσόν με, just as in LXX Ps 68:2.

In light of Matt 14:33, where those in the boat "worship" Jesus, saying: "Truly you are the Son of God!" (or possibly "a son of God"), it must be asked whether the author meant more by אֲדֹנִי (κύριε) than merely "my lord." Theophanic language was usually first applied by Palestinian (and Hellenistic) Jewish Christians to Jesus in apocalyptic contexts.[75] Here, in the light of the background of the passage in the Reed Sea event, where in Judaic tradition God "manifested" Himself openly for all the Israelites to see Him, it appears that God language has consciously been applied to Jesus. "My lord" (אֲדֹנִי) became "my Lord" (אֲדֹנִי). That is a surprising development, especially for Palestinian or Syrian Jewish Christians. It would have been expected more readily in Gentile Christianity, and possibly already in Hellenistic Jewish Christianity.

---

[72] See also the Hebrew New Testament of Delitzsch on Matt 14:30 (p. 27): הוֹשִׁיעֵנִי. The narrator may also have thought of Jesus' name in Hebrew here: יֵשׁוּעַ.

[73] Delitzsch, *ibid.*, as well as the Hebrew New Testament of the United Bible Societies (p. 41).

[74] Jastrow 834 on מר, IV.

[75] See for example my 1971 Yale dissertation, *The Use of Day of the Lord and Theophany Traditions in 2 Thessalonians 1*, as well as the remarks by A. Yarbro Collins in "Rulers, Divine Men, and Walking on the Water (Mark 6:45-52)" 224.

23. *Stretching Out One's Hand and Taking / Rescuing Someone Sinking in the Sea.*

a) When Peter began to sink in the Sea of Galilee, he cried out for the Lord to save him. Then Jesus immediately "stretched out his hand and caught him" (ἐκτείνας τὴν χεῖρα ἐπελάβετο αὐτοῦ – Matt 14:31). This terminology of "stretching out one's hand," thereby rescuing a person sinking in the Sea, also derives from the Naḥshon haggadah.

b) After Naḥshon jumped forward first, descended to the Reed Sea and fell into its waves, Ps 69:2-3 are quoted of him, including his sinking / drowning (טבע). At that time Moses was standing and making extensive prayer to God, an interpretation of Moses' "crying" to Him in Exod 14:15. Therefore God said to him: "Moses, My beloved (Naḥshon) is sinking (משוקע)[76] in the water. The Sea is closing in upon him, and the enemy is pursuing. Yet you stand making extensive prayer before Me!" Moses then replied to Him: "Master of the Universe, what is 'in my hand' (בידי = in my power) to do?" God answered him: "Lift up your rod, and 'stretch out your hand' over the Sea and divide it, so that the people of Israel may go on dry ground through the Sea" (Exod 14:16).[77]

In the biblical text Moses now "stretches out his hand" over the Sea in v 21, and the motif is repeated in vv 26-27.[78] The fourfold mention of this expression in Exodus 14 shows its great importance for the narrative. In Judaic tradition on Exod 14:15-16, only by Moses' "stretching out his hand" is Naḥshon (and all of Israel) rescued from sinking / drowning in the Reed Sea.

The verb employed in Exod 14:16,21,26-27 for "stretching out" one's hand is נָטָה.[79] Since the latter is not used primarily in this sense in rabbinic Hebrew,[80] the Palestinian or Syrian Jewish Christian author of Matt 14:28-31 probably employed here a verb such as יָשַׁט, hiphil, "to stretch forth,"[81] or שָׁלַח, also "to stretch forth."[82] When a Hellenistic Jewish Christian, or perhaps Matthew himself, later translated this into

---

[76] Cf. BDB 1054 for שָׁקַע, sink, sink down, as well as Jastrow 1624.

[77] Cf. *Mek.* Beshallaḥ 6 on Exod 14:22 (Lauterbach 1.234-235).

[78] Cf. also God's stretching out His right hand in Exod 15:12.

[79] BDB 639.

[80] Jastrow 898.

[81] Jastrow 600. It is employed here in the Hebrew New Testament of the United Bible Societies (p. 41).

[82] Jastrow 1579-1580. In his Hebrew New Testament (p. 27), Delitzsch employs it at this point.

Greek, he recognized its background in Exod 14:16 and employed ἐκτείνω, as in the LXX of that verse (and 21,26-27).

The term ἐπιλαμβάνομαι employed in Matt 14:31 of Jesus' stretching out his hand and "catching"[83] Peter when he begins to sink in the Sea of Galilee, also derives from Judaic tradition on the Reed Sea. In *Exod. Rab.* Beshallaḥ 22/2 on Exod 14:26, "Stretch out your hand," R. Simeon b. Laqish, a second generation Palestinian Amora,[84] says that the Reed Sea enclosed the Israelites and Egyptians from all sides. When Moses asked God what he should then do (for the Israelites), He replied: "'You are not responsible as to what they should do, for I am going to perform a miracle (נֵס) for them.' At that moment God 'stretched forth His hand' (שָׁלַח...אֶת יָדוֹ) and 'brought them up' (הֶעֱלָן) out of the Sea, as it is said: 'He sent (יִשְׁלַח) from on high, He took me (יִקָּחֵנִי); He drew me out of many waters'" (Ps 18:17, Eng. 16). R. Abbahu, a third generation Palestinian Amora, then quotes Exod 15:6 in this regard: "Your right hand, O Lord."[85]

Here God's stretching out His hand and "bringing up" (hiphil of עלה) or "taking" (לקח) Israel out of the Reed Sea is labeled a miracle. Since לקח no longer seems to be used in rabbinic Hebrew for to take / catch, as in biblical Hebrew,[86] I suggest that the Hebrew or Aramaic original for Jesus' stretching out his hand and "catching" Peter in Matt 14:31 was חָזַק, hiphil, with בְּ.[87] This verb is employed here in the Hebrew New Testaments both of Delitzsch and the United Bible Societies.[88] When the narrative was later translated into Greek, the verb was rendered by ἐπιλαμβάνομαι, as very frequently in the LXX.[89]

It is possible that Jesus is described here as the Messiah, thought to be the second Moses. Just as the latter in Judaic tradition stretched out his hand, saving Naḥshon (Israel) from sinking in the Reed Sea, so Jesus stretched out his hand and saved Peter from sinking in the Sea of Galilee.

---

[83] BAGD 295. Cf. the simple form λαβεῖν for the disciples' wanting to "take" Jesus into the boat in John 6:21.

[84] Strack and Stemberger, *Introduction* 95. He was a brother-in-law of R. Yoḥanan, with whom he is in dialogue here.

[85] Mirqin 5.257; Soncino 3.276, which I slightly modify. Cf. the similar statements of R. Simeon b. Laqish and R. Yudan in *Midr. Pss.* 18/20 on Ps 18:17 (Buber 147, Braude 1.248). Ps 144:7 contains similar imagery.

[86] Jastrow 717, and BDB 542, 1. take, take in the hand.

[87] Jastrow 445, 4) to take a hold of , seize.

[88] Cf. pp. 27 and 41, respectively.

[89] Cf. Hatch-Redpath 523-524, (2).

In light of Ps 18:17 quoted above, however, it is more probable that a divine prerogative has been transferred here to Jesus, the narrator's Lord. Only God, or someone considered to be His Son, could rescue one from sinking in the Sea by "catching" him there. This is certainly one reason the disciples then "worship" Jesus and exclaim in Matt 14:33, "Truly you are the Son of God!" I thus now turn to the motif of "worshiping" Jesus.

24. *The Disciples' Worshiping Jesus.*

a) The eleven disciples viewed Jesus walking on the Sea and catching Peter when, out of lack of faith, he began to sink in it. After the two had joined them in the boat, the wind ceased. These events then caused (all twelve of) the disciples to "worship" or "revere" (προσκυνέω)[90] Jesus, saying: "Truly you are the Son of God!" (Matt 14:33). Matthew's "Vorlage," Mark 6:51, simply has: "And he went up to them into the boat, the wind ceased, and 'they were utterly astounded.'" John 6:21 also has nothing about worshiping Jesus here.

b) As I pointed out in section 16. above, the verb "they were astounded" in Mark 6:51 is ultimately based on an interpretation of "and the people 'feared' (ירא) the Lord" in Exod 14:31a. This only came about after the Israelites had also "seen" (ראה) the Egyptians dead upon the seashore (v 30), and after they had "seen" the great work which the Lord did against the Egyptians. The result was the people's "fearing" the Lord, believing in both Him and His servant Moses (v 31). Then they sang the Song at the Sea (Exod 15:1-18), a form of worshiping the Lord for His having redeemed them (14:30;15:13) from drowning there.

Also as noted above, according to *Mek.* Shirata 3 on Exod 15:2, the Israelites saw God openly at the Reed Sea, something not one of the prophets had experienced before. As soon as they saw Him after He had revealed Himself, "they recognized Him, and they all opened their mouths and said: 'This is my God, and I will glorify Him.'"[91] This glorification of the Lord by *all* the Israelites after their redemption at the Reed Sea provided part of the thought background for all the disciples' worshiping Jesus after he saved them from the (strong) wind and Peter from sinking in the Sea.

The verb יָרֵא in Exod 14:31 not only means "to fear" in the sense of being afraid of something. It can also mean "to fear, reverence, honor"

---

[90] BAGD 716: "(fall down and) worship, do obeisance to, prostrate oneself before, do reverence to, welcome respectfully."

[91] Lauterbach 2.24-25.

someone, including God.[92] The same is true for the Aramaic equivalent found in the targums, דְּחַל, דחיל.[93] I therefore suggest that the Semitic behind προσκυνέω in Matt 14:33 was originally also ירא, now understood not as the disciples' "fearing" Jesus, but as showing reverence to him, standing in awe of him, "worshiping" him. When the incident was retold often enough in a Palestinian or Syrian Jewish Christian community, the hithpael of the synonymous verb שָׁחָה was employed as a variant. It means to bow down, prostrate oneself, for example before God.[94] Both Delitzsch and the United Bible Societies correctly employ it in Matt 14:33,[95] for προσκυνέω in the LXX almost always translates the hithpael of שָׁחָה.[96]

The result of the people's "fearing" or "revering" the Lord in Exod 14:31 was that they believed both in Him and in His servant Moses. When the disciples in Matt 14:33 feared / revered / worshiped Jesus as the Son of God after what he had done, he is represented not only as taking on a divine prerogative. He is also pictured as a second Moses, in whom one should also believe. As noted before, Moses was considered to be the first redeemer of Israel primarily because of his activity at the exodus. The Messiah was to be his future successor, the final or great redeemer of Israel. Jesus' activity of saving the twelve disciples fighting a strong head wind on the Sea of Galilee, and of saving Peter sinking in the Sea, are based on Judaic interpretation of the redemption of the Israelites from a strong east wind at the Reed Sea, and of Nahshon's sinking in the Sea when he entered it first and fell into the waves up to his neck. Here Jesus' redemptive messianic activity is shown to have already begun, even before his death on the Cross and resurrection from the dead on Easter Sunday. In addition, Jesus' miraculous walking on the Sea also represents him as the Messiah (see section II. below), and the wind's ceasing due to his presence in the boat presents him as having the power of God, who alone can control the wind, as at the Reed Sea (Exod 14:21; 15:8 and 10). For Matthew, such deeds show that Jesus is not only the Messiah, but also the Son of God. This is the first time in the Gospel that humans call him this, Peter's confession coming only later in 16:16.

---

[92] BDB 431.3.

[93] Jastrow 292: to fear, be afraid of, shun; to worship, revere. Cf. דחילו as fear, worship, and דחלא as fearer, worshiper.

[94] BDB 1005, 2; Jastrow 1547.

[95] Cf. p. 27 and p. 42 respectively.

[96] See Hatch-Redpath 1217-1218.

* * *

The above first sixteen comparisons between narratives of Jesus' disciples fighting a strong head wind in order to cross the Sea of Galilee, and Judaic interpretation of the narrative of the Israelites' crossing the Reed Sea with a strong east wind, all based on Exodus 14 (and in part 15), may of course be questioned individually. Some of the arguments are admittedly stronger than others. Yet *cumulatively* they provide convincing evidence that the first Palestinian Jewish Christian narrator of Mark 6:45-51 primarily based his account on the early Judaic traditions on Exodus 14-15 described above in section b) of each comparison.

Matthew's special material in 14:28-31 and 33, analyzed in sections 17-24, was also based on the same complex of Judaic traditions, especially in regard to Naḥshon as the representative of the twelve tribes who was the first to leap into the water at the Reed Sea and to sink up to his neck leading to his request: "Save me!" Along with major commentators, I consider Matthew to be bilingual and probably to have written his Gospel in an area such as Antioch in Syria which was also so.[97] There Palestinian / Syrian Jewish Christians further developed the oral Semitic original of what is now found in Mark 6:45-51, adding to it special Petrine material in light of the Naḥshon haggadah.[98] The latter material, now found in Matt 14:28-31 and 33, was probably already translated into Greek in Matthew's bilingual Christian community.[99] If

---

[97] Cf. R. Gundry, *Matthew*. A Commentary on His Handbook for a Mixed Church under Persecution (Grand Rapids, Michigan: Eerdmans, 1994[2]) 608 for Syria. For Matthew's occasional independent use of the Hebrew OT text, see F. Beare, *The Gospel According to Matthew* (Oxford: Blackwell, 1981) 10, and 8-10 for Syria or Phoenicia. D. Harrington notes Matthew's "special interest in the Hebrew Scriptures" and thinks of Syria, yet also Palestine itself. See his *The Gospel of Matthew* (Sacra Pagina 1; Collegeville, Minnesota: Glazier, 1991) 8-10. U. Luz in *Das Evangelium nach Matthäus (Mt 1-7)* (EKK 1/1; Zurich, Benziger; Neukirchen-Vluyn: Neukirchener, 1992[3]) 75 says the provenance of Matthew was "certainly a larger Syrian city." A. Schlatter in *Der Evangelist Matthäus* (Stuttgart: Calwer, 1948[3]) 8 maintains "The bilingualism of its (the Gospel's) author is constantly visible."

[98] W. Grundmann in *Das Evangelium nach Matthäus* (THNT 1; Berlin: Evangelische Verlagsanstalt, 1975[4]) 366 also thinks of an oral Peter tradition, formulated in writing by Matthew, and inserted here. For the latter, see already G. Kilpatrick, *The Origins of the Gospel According to St. Matthew* (Oxford: Clarendon, 1946) 41.

[99] Cf. E. Schweizer, art. υἱός κτλ. in *TDNT* 8.380 for Matt 14:33 as derived from tradition and not from Matthew himself. E. Klostermann in *Das Matthäusevangelium* (HNT 4; Tübingen: Mohr, 1927[2]) 130 states that vv 28-31 are certainly not the creation of Matthew, but a piece of tradition which especially dealt with Peter, like Acts 1-2.

not, he could have done this himself and added it to the narrative he already found in Greek in Mark 6:45-52. The result would have been the same.

*   *   *

One final aspect of the narrative in Mark 6:45-51 has not yet been analyzed. It is Jesus' "walking" on the Sea, which in Matt 14:29 is supplemented by Peter's walking on the water. The first derives from a different corpus of Judaic tradition, that concerning the Spirit of God as "hovering" over the water. To this I now turn.

II. The Messiah as Hovering Over the Water in Gen 1:2.

Before analyzing the messianic interpretation of the "Spirit" of God as "hovering" over the water at Creation in Gen 1:2, it is first helpful to note the similar role of other figures in Judaic thought.

Already in the Hebrew Bible it is wisdom by which the Lord founded the earth (Prov 3:19). The Lord created it "before the beginning of the earth" (8:23); it was then beside Him like a "master workman" (v 30). In *b. Ḥag.* 12a, for example, the first generation Babylonian / Palestinian Amora Rab[1] states that wisdom was the first of ten things by which the world was created. This is based on Prov 3:19.[2] It is thus understandable that *Frag. Targ.* Gen 1:1 has "'With wisdom' the Lord created and perfected the heavens and the earth."[3] The same is true for *Targum Neofiti 1* here.[4]

Another means of creation in Judaic thought was the "word" of the Lord. Ps 33:6 states: "By the word (דָּבָר) of the Lord the heavens were made...." The second generation Palestinian Amora R. Yoḥanan,[5] for example, notes in *Gen. Rab.* Bereshit 12/10 on Gen 2:4 that God did not create the world through labor or exhausting toil, but "By the word of

---

[1] Strack and Stemberger, *Introduction* 93, better known as Abba Arikha.

[2] Soncino 65.

[3] Klein 1.43 and 126, and 2.3 and 90.

[4] Díez Macho 1.3 and 497.

[5] Strack and Stemberger, *Introduction* 94-95.

the Lord" (Ps 33:6).[6] Ben Zoma, a second generation Tanna,[7] employed the verse similarly.[8]

Yet the Messiah was also somehow thought to be active already at the Creation. Ps 72:17 states: "May his name endure forever, his fame continue as long as the sun!" This verse is frequently applied in Judaic sources to the messianic king.[9] Already in the LXX (71:17), however, it is interpreted: "before the sun (πρὸ τοῦ ἡλίου) his name endures." That is, before the creation of light in Gen 1:3 and lights in the firmament (vv 14-18), the Messiah's name existed. Psalm 110 is also frequently interpreted messianically in Judaic sources.[10] The LXX (109:3) already has the Lord say: "I have begotten you from the womb 'before the morning' (πρὸ Ἑωσφόρου)." These two passages from the LXX, certainly pre-Christian, show the great age of the Messiah's name, his "existence," at the very beginning of Creation. Thus, the basic content of a targumic passage such as *Targ. Ps.-Jon.* Mic 5:1 (Eng. 2) regarding the messianic ruler who comes from Bethlehem is not necessarily late. It speaks of him as "him whose name was mentioned from of old, from ancient times."[11] This interprets

---

[6] Theodor and Albeck 108; Soncino 1.95. Cf. John 1:1-3.

[7] Strack and Stemberger, *Introduction* 82.

[8] Cf. *Gen. Rab.* Bereshith 4/6 on Gen 1:7 (Theodor and Albeck 30; Soncino 1.31). The second half of Ps 33:6 reads: "and all their host (were made) by the breath (*ruah*) of His mouth." This verse is cited in *b. Roš Haš.* 32a (Soncino 156) as the last of the "ten utterances" by which the world was created, the others being found in Genesis 1. In the Tannaitic parallel *Gen. Rab.* Bereshith 17/1 on Gen 2:8 (Theodor and Albeck 151, with other similar traditions cited in the note on line 4; Soncino 1.132), Gen 1:2, "And the *ruah* of God hovered," is listed as the second of the ten utterances. It is explicitly defended by the Tanna R. Jacob B. Kirshai / Qorshai, one of the teachers of Rabbi (Str-B 5/6.168 and 4.845). Here the role of the hovering *ruah* of God is emphasized at Creation, which may then have made it easier to interpret the same *ruah* of the royal Messiah, definitely thought to be present at Creation. See below.

[9] Cf. *b. Pesah.* 54a (Soncino 265) in a baraitha, which says the name of the Messiah is one of the seven things which were created before the world came into being. Parallels are found in *b. Ned.* 39b (Soncino 125) and *Midr. Pss.* 72/6 on Ps 72:17 (Braude 1.563). For the Messiah's name as one of six things created before the world came into being, see *Gen. Rab.* Bereshit 1/4 on Gen 1:1 (Soncino 1.6); *Pesiq. Rab Kah.* 22/5a (Braude and Kapstein 349); *Eliyyahu Rabbah* (31) 29 in Braude and Kapstein 388-389; and *Midr. Pss.* 93/3 on Ps 93:2 (Braude 2.125). In *b. Sanh.* 98b (Soncino 667) and *Lam. Rab.* 1:16 § 51 (Soncino 7.138) the Messiah's name is Yinnon, from Ps 72:17.

[10] Cf. the many sources cited in Str-B 4.452-465.

[11] Sperber 3.446. Cathcart and Gordon 122 also call attention in n. 3 to *Targ. Jon.* Zech 4:7 (Sperber 3.482), and other passages.

the phrase מִקֶּדֶם in the Hebrew, which is associated with the first words of the Bible. Gen 1:1 has בְּרֵאשִׁית, which in *Targum Onqelos*, for example, is בקדמין.[12]

The above Palestinian Judaic passages[13] regarding the Messiah as already present at or even before Creation show how God's Spirit in Gen 1:2 could also be thought of in a similar way. The spirit in Isa 57:16, "from Me proceeds the Spirit (רוּחַ), and I have made the breath of life," was interpreted of the messianic king for example in *Gen. Rab.* Bereshith 24/4 on Gen 5:1.[14] Isa 61:1 also has: "The Spirit of the Lord God is upon me, because the Lord has anointed me...." This is interpreted of the Holy Spirit in connection with the redemption in *Lam. Rab.* 3:49-50 § 9,[15] but definitely of the Messiah Jesus in Luke 4:18 and 21. Isa 11:1 also speaks of a shoot which will come forth from Jesse, a branch from his roots. Verse two continues: "And the Spirit of the Lord shall rest upon him, the spirit of wisdom and understanding...." This passage was interpreted messianically in many Judaic sources.[16] One of them deals with Gen 1:2.

Pesiq. R. 33/6 says that at the beginning of the creation of the world the messianic king was born / came into existence (נולד), for he arose in (God's) plan even before the world was created. Thus it says: "And there came forth a shoot from the stump of Jesse" (Isa 11:1). It does not say

---

[12] Sperber 1.1. The LXX already has ἀπ᾽ ἀρχῆς in Mic 5:1, "from the beginning," similar to LXX Gen 1:1's ἐν ἀρχῇ. See also *Targ. Neofiti 1* Gen 1:1 for מלקדמין (Díez Macho 1.3 and 497).

[13] This means that the Hellenistic passages in the NT letters which speak of Jesus the Messiah's existence or role at Creation are not of basic relevance here. Cf. for example 1 Cor 8:6; 2 Cor 8:9; Eph 1:4; Col 1:15-20; Heb 1:2; 1 Pet 1:20; and 2 Pet 3:5.

[14] Theodor and Albeck 233; Soncino 1.201, with n. 3. The LXX of Isa 57:16 already states: "For the Spirit will proceed from Me," which is probably meant messianically. Parallels with the "royal Messiah" are found in *Lev. Rab.* Thazria 15/1 on Lev 13:2 (Soncino 4.188-189) and *Qoh. Rab.* 1:6 § 1 (Soncino 8.19). He is called the Son of David in *b. Yebam.* 62a (Soncino 415) and 63b (Soncino 426), *'Avoda Zara* 5a (Soncino 20), *Nid.* 13b (Soncino 89), and *Kallah Rabbati* 2:4, 52a (Soncino 430).

[15] Soncino 7.209-210. See also 4Q Messianic Apocalypse (4Q 521) with the Messiah in Martínez 394, yet his role is not clear in regard to Isa 61:1. For the text, cf. p. 113 here.

[16] Cf. *b. Sanh.* 93b (Soncino 626); *Gen. Rab.* Vayechi, New Version, 97 on Gen 49:8 (Soncino 2.902); *Num. Rab.* Naso 13/11 on Num 7:13 (Soncino 6.523); and *Ruth Rab.* 7/2 on Ruth 3:15 (Soncino 8.83). Isa 11:1 is interpreted messianically in *b. Sanh.* 43a (Soncino 282 – on one of the disciples of Jesus!); *y. Ber.* 2:3 (Neusner / Zahavy 1.89) and *Lam. Rab.* 1:16 § 51 (Soncino 7.137) of the Messiah as born in Bethlehem; *Midr. Pss.* 72/3 (Braude 2.560); and *Targum Jonathan* (Stenning 40-41).

here: "And there shall come forth" (וְיָצָא), but "And there came forth" (וַיֵּצֵא). The Parma MS then adds: "implying that the shoot from the stump of Jesse had already come forth."[17]

The midrash then interprets Gen 1:1-2 in light of the oppression of Israel by the four kingdoms, the last being wicked Edom (Rome), and the redeemer, the messianic king. It proceeds by asking from where one can prove that the messianic king existed from the beginning of (God's) creation of the world. "And the spirit (רוּחַ) of God hovered (מְרַחֶפֶת)" – this is the messianic king. Thus it says: "And the Spirit (רוּחַ) of the Lord shall rest upon him" (Isa 11:2).[18]

R. Simeon b. Laqish, a second generation Palestinian Amora,[19] also comments in *Gen. Rab.* Bereshith 2/4 on "the spirit of God" in Gen 1:2, which "hovers," as the spirit of the Messiah. He also cites Isa 11:2.[20]

The "hovering" of the Messiah is rare, but it may be very early. Line 1 of fragment 2, column 2, of 4Q Messianic Apocalypse (4Q 521) has "His (the Lord's) Messiah." In line 6 it then states: "And 'His Spirit will hover' (רוחו תרחף) over the poor...."[21] This is the only known occurrence of the verb at Qumran.[22] J. Collins notes that lines 1-8 here reflect Psalm 146.[23]

---

[17] Friedmann 152b; Braude 641, with the reading from the Parma MS in his note 30.

[18] Friedmann 152b, Braude 642-643.

[19] Strack and Stemberger, *Introduction* 95.

[20] Theodor and Albeck 16-17; Soncino 1.17. It is also found in Yalquṭ Shem'oni 1.4 (Kook 1.14). In *Lev. Rab.* Thazria 14/1 on Lev 12:2 (Mirqin 7.154; Soncino 4.178), R. Simeon (Resh) Laqish also interprets Gen 1:2 as the spirit of the messianic king. In *Gen. Rab.* Bereshit 8/1 on Gen 1:26, "Let us make man in our image, after our likeness" (Theodor and Albeck 56; Soncino 1.55), R. Simeon b. Laqish interprets Gen 1:2 of the soul of Adam, with Isa 11:2. This I think is clearly anti-Christian and / or anti-messianic because of the plural "Let us...." See already R. Ishmael in *Midr. Terumah* 2 on Gen 1:2, quoted in *Encyclopedia of Biblical Interpretation* 1.19-20. I. Lévi, "L'esprit de Dieu et l'esprit de Messie" in the *David Simonsen Festschrift* (Copenhagen: Hertz, 1923) 104, considers the two opinions of R. Simeon b. Laqish to be simply two interpretations of the same words, a frequent occurrence in rabbinic writings. While some chapters of *Pesiqta Rabbati* are often considered late (34-37; see Braude 1.22-23), the parallels in *Genesis Rabbah* and *Leviticus Rabbah* in regard to Gen 1:2 show that at least this section of the midrashic work is contemporary with them.

[21] Cf. the Hebrew in E. Puech, "Une apocalypse messianique (4Q 521)" in *RevQ* 15/60 (1992) 485. I slightly modify the English of J. Collins, *The Scepter and the Star. The Messiahs of the Dead Sea Scrolls and Other Ancient Literature* (New York: Doubleday, 1995) 117. See also Martínez 394, who less accurately has: "and upon the poor he will place his spirit...."

Verse 6 states that the Lord "made heaven and earth, the sea, and all that is in them," so the Spirit of the Messiah could derive here from Gen 1:2.

In addition, 11Q Melchizedek, column 2, line 18, interprets the messenger of Isa 52:7 as "[the ano]inted of the spirit about whom Dan[iel] spoke...."[24] While this is ostensibly the eschatological agent Melchizedek here, it should be noted that *Lev. Rab.* Tzab 9/9 has "the Rabbis" on the messenger of Isa 52:7 say: "Great is peace, for when the messianic king comes, he will only commence with peace."[25]

The term MŠYḤ HRWḤ is thus attested at Qumran, although not necessarily of the Davidic Messiah. In addition, the Lord's Spirit, His Messiah, can also be described as "hovering" over others.

The "hovering" of the messianic king in Gen 1:2, as noted above, is the verb רָחַף.[26] It occurs in the Hebrew Bible only here and in Deut 32:11, where it describes an eagle "hovering" or "fluttering" over the young in its nest. In *t. Ḥag.* 2:6 it is related that R. Joshua met Ben Zoma, a second generation Tanna,[27] in a piazza and asked him where he came from. Ben Zoma replied that he was considering the works of Creation (Genesis 1) and ascertained that there was "not even a handbreath (of distance) between the upper waters and the nether waters." He then buttresses his argument by citing Gen 1:2 and Deut 33:11-12. In regard to the latter he says: "Just as the eagle hovers / flutters above its nest, touching but not touching, so there is no more space between the upper waters and the nether waters than a handbreadth."[28]

---

[22] Cf. Charlesworth, *Graphic Concordance to the Dead Sea Scrolls* 488, who in 1991 was not yet aware of the verb in 4Q 521. In an oral communication, Professor Charlesworth calls my attention also to Odes Sol 24:1 (*OTP* 2. 757), where at Jesus' baptism "The dove 'fluttered' over the head of our Lord Messiah, because he was her head." See also 28:1 (2.759).

[23] *The Scepter and the Star* 117.

[24] Martínez 140. This reading (MŠYḤ HRW [Ḥ]) is based on a reconsideration of the text by E. Puech, "Notes sur le Manuscrit XIQ Melkîsédek" in *RevQ* 48/12 (1987) 489 and 499. He dates it from ca. 75-50 BCE (pp. 507-508). Dan 9:25-26 may be meant.

[25] Mirqin 7.100; Soncino 4.120, which I modify. Cf. the messianic king as prince of peace in Isa 9:5.

[26] BDB 934. For the combination of the Lord's "passing by" (פסח) and "hovering" (עוּף) like a bird, see Isa 31:5, BDB 733,1.b., and *Mek. R. Ish.* Pisḥa 7 on Exod 12:13 (Lauterbach 1.56, with a parallel on p. 87).

[27] See n. 7.

[28] Zuckermandel and Liebermann 234; Neusner 2.313. Parallels are found in *b. Ḥag.* 15a (Soncino 92), and *y. Ḥag.* 2:1, 77a-b (Neusner 20.44).

This example shows that when the messianic king is described as "hovering" over the waters of Gen 1:2, he is directly above them, with hardly any distance in between. He would appear to be walking on the water. I would therefore suggest that the Palestinian Jewish Christian author of Mark 6:45-51 was acquainted with this messianic interpretation of Gen 1:2 in an earlier form. With it in mind, he described Jesus as the Messiah, who now "walked" upon the Sea of Galilee. Since the verb רחף was not used in rabbinic Hebrew[29] (and only once at Qumran), he employed הָלַךְ, "to walk." Later a Hellenistic Jewish Christian correctly translated this into Greek as περιπατέω.

The Palestinian Jewish Christian author of Mark 6:45-51 was also encouraged to appropriate the imagery of "hovering" in Gen 1:2 because the waters there were connected in Judaic tradition to the waters of the Reed Sea in Exodus 14. *Mek.* Beshallaḥ 5 on Exod 14:21, "and the waters were divided," for example interprets the plural here to mean that "all the waters in the world" were then divided, even the upper and the nether waters (Gen 1:6-8). When the water of the Reed Sea later returned to its place (Exod 14:28), "all the waters of the world likewise returned."[30] In addition, according to *Exod. Rab.* Beshallaḥ 21/6 on Exod 14:15, R. Eleazar ha-Qappar, a fourth generation Tanna,[31] has God instruct Moses on the real meaning of Gen 1:9, "Let the waters under the heavens be gathered together." "It was I who made a condition at the very beginning that I would one day (in the future) divide it; for it says, 'And the Sea returned to its strength (*le-ethano*) when the morning appeared' (Exod 14:27), that is, in accordance with the condition which I made with it at its creation."[32]

These texts show how the Palestinian Jewish Christian author of Mark 6:45-51 could easily have employed the motif of the messianic king's "hovering" over the water from earlier Judaic interpretation of Gen 1:2. This water, the water of Creation, was associated directly with that of the Reed Sea, which first divided and then returned.

---

[29] The only text Jastrow can cite in 1468 is *b. Ḥag.* 15a, which interprets the verb in Gen 1:2. Levy does not even list it.

[30] Lauterbach 1.231-232; cf. n. 10 on p. 231.

[31] Strack and Stemberger, *Introduction* 88-89.

[32] Mirqin 5.250-251; Soncino 3.267. See also *Mek.* Beshallaḥ 4 on Exod 14:15, with Gen 1:9 (Lauterbach 1.216). See also Wisd 19:6, which states concerning the Reed Sea event: "the whole creation in its nature was fashioned anew...." The next verse deals with "dry land emerging where water has stood before."

* * *

If the above proposal is basically correct, it shows that the author of what is now found in Mark 6:45-51 based his narrative almost exclusively on Palestinian Judaic traditions regarding two texts in the Hebrew Bible. Both were extremely well-known and important, the story of Creation in Genesis 1, and the crossing of the Reed Sea in Exodus 14-15, central to Israel's history of redemption. This is why they were interpreted so early and so much, and this is also why he reinterpreted them in light of his belief in Jesus as the Messiah.

III. The Extent of the Original Narrative.

To begin with the conclusion of the episode, it is very probable that the Evangelist Mark himself composed 6:52. As remarked above in section II. 16, the original narrative logically closed with the disciples' being "utterly astounded" in v 51. It is based on Judaic interpretation of Exod 14:31, which also concludes that narrative before the recital of the "Song at the Sea" in chapter 15. My reasons for Mark's formulating 6:52 were given above on p. 98.

While v 45 could also go back to Mark, I suggest that it already connected the feeding of the 5000 in 6:31-44 with the account of Jesus' walking on the Sea in vv 46-51 in Greek, before Mark appropriated it and included it in his Gospel. The similar and apparently independent connection of the two stories in John 6:1-15 and 16-21 buttresses this suggestion.

It would also be strange for an independent narrative such as Jesus' walking on the Sea to begin with Mark 6: 46a, "When he had taken leave of them...." The referent of "them" would originally have to have been spelled out, or the narrative began after it. Yet then "the boat" in v 47 would appear suddenly, also without a referent. For the narrative, it is imperative that the disciples later be alone in the boat in the middle of the Sea when Jesus comes to them. Thus a narrative means had to be found to keep Jesus on the land. Since his going to a mountain to pray is based on Moses' similar behavior at the Reed Sea, this was very probably in the original episode. Yet the motif of "crossing" or "passing through" the Sea in v 45 also was derived from the crossing or passing through of the Reed Sea in Exodus 14-15. Thus it too very probably belonged to the original anecdote. The latter may have begun: "Once Jesus urged his disciples to enter their boat on the Sea and to precede him to the other side, to Bethsaida. After he had taken leave of them...."

Here "immediately" in Mark 6:45 is omitted, as is "while he dismissed the crowd." The first now clearly connects the narratives of the feeding of the 5000 and Jesus' walking on the Sea, and the second refers back to it. There is no reason to believe, however, that they were not already in the Greek version which Mark appropriated. They were needed to connect the two narratives.

Otherwise, as A. Yarbro Collins states, "there is no compelling evidence of editorial activity in vv 46-51."[33] After inserting v 52 for his own theological reasons (the messianic secret), Mark continued by composing v 53. He may have changed Bethsaida on the NE side of the Sea in v 45 to Gennesaret on the WNW side of the Sea in v 53 in order to have the people who had witnessed the feeding of the 5000 "immediately recognize him." In contrast to the disciples (v 52), they react very positively to the (first) miracle and rapidly fetch their sick in order for Jesus, who had just performed the feeding miracle (or two miracles), to heal them. Their response is appropriate. The disciples' reaction shows their inability to believe at this stage of the Gospel. It was Matthew in 14:33 who first changed the disciples' utter astonishment and lack of a positive response into an acclamation of faith on their part. They worship Jesus and say: "Truly you are the Son of God!"

IV.   A Concrete Cause for the Origin and Date of the Original Narrative.

The Roman emperor Gaius Caligula, who reigned from 37-41 CE,[34] thought of himself as divine, lord of both land and sea. He crossed an entire Italian bay, riding a horse or in a chariot, or walking, and insisted on having a colossal statue of himself as god installed in the Jerusalem Temple. A Palestinian Jewish Christian reacted to this severe blasphemy by composing a narrative which demonstrated that only Jesus as the Messiah could walk on the Sea. The following elucidates this thesis.

Louis Ginzberg once wrote: "The deification of the Roman Caesars was well known to the Jews, and occupied their imagination to a great extent."[35] This was, of course, based on the First Commandment, which prohibits any other human or non-human god in addition to the LORD (Exod 20:3; Deut 5:7), who brought the Israelites out of bondage in Egypt. For this reason first century Palestinian Jews vehemently opposed any human's calling himself or herself a god and demanding adoration, especially from them.

The author of Mark 6:45 (as described above in III.) to v51 based his account to a great extent on Judaic interpretation of Exodus 14-15. There

---

[33] "Rulers, Divine Men, and Walking on the Water (Mark 6:45-52)" 208.

[34] Schürer, *The history* 1.388.

[35] *The Legends* 6.423, n. 99.

Pharaoh is also described as declaring himself to be god, the lord of the entire world. In *Mek.* Beshallaḥ 2 on Exod 14:5, for example, Pharaoh is portrayed as ruling from one end of the world to the other.[36] R. Ḥiyya b. Abba, a fifth generation Tanna,[37] said that on the occasion of Pharaoh's birthday he received ambassadors, "when all kings came to pay him honor, bringing with them gifts of crowns with which they crowned him *cosmocrator* (קוֹזְמוֹקְרָטוֹר)...."[38] This title, "lord of the world," was employed for the Roman emperors, so it is probably meant satirically here. This is definitely the case in *Exod. Rab.* Va'era 9/8 on Exod 7:15a, which says Pharaoh "used to boast that he was a god and did not require to ease himself."[39] According to *Mek.* Shirata 8 on Exod 15:11, the wicked Egyptian king even called himself a god. This is based on his boasting: "The river (Nile) is mine" (Ezek 29:9), and "I have made myself" (or "I have made it myself" – v 3).[40]

Pharaoh's great arrogance recalled for the Palestinian Jewish Christian narrator that of his own contemporary, the Roman emperor Gaius Caligula. According to both Jewish and non-Jewish sources, Gaius gradually became mad, finally demanding that he even be worshiped as god. His madness was coupled with his insolence[41] and his thirst for blood.[42] Josephus notes that "It was his object to be and to be thought stronger than religion or the law...."[43] Suetonius remarks that Gaius set up a temple to his own godhead in Rome. "In this temple was a life-sized statue of the emperor in gold, which was dressed each day in clothing

---

[36] Lauterbach 1.196.

[37] Strack and Stemberger, *Introduction* 90.

[38] *Exod. Rab.* Shemoth 5/14 on Exod 5:1 (Mirqin 5.97; Soncino 3.93). A parallel is found in *Tanḥ.* Va'era 5 (Eshkol 1.241). See other references to the noun in Jastrow 1325, who points out that it is the same as κοσμοκράτωρ.

[39] Mirqin 5.127; Soncino 3.126. A parallel is found in *Tanḥ.* B Va'era 16 (Buber 2.31; Bietenhard 1.326).

[40] Lauterbach 2.61. Cf. the note in the RSV on Ezek 29:3, "Heb *I have made myself.*" See also *Exod. Rab.* Shemoth 5/14 on Exod 5:2 (Mirqin 5.98; Soncino 3.95), and Va'era 8/1-2 (Mirqin 5.118-119; Soncino 3.115-117). A parallel is found in *Tanḥ.* B Va'era 8 on Exod 7:1 (Buber 23; Bietenhard 1.318-319).

[41] Josephus, *Ant.* 19.1. On his insolence (ὕβρις), cf. 22,78,82,129; 18.280; and *Bell.* 2.184. Philo in *Leg. Gai.* 78 and 93 notes that Gaius first compared himself to the demigods, then to the full gods.

[42] Dio Cassius in *Roman History* 10.2 for example speaks of Gaius' delight in the deaths of others, and of "his insatiable desire for the sight of blood." Cf. also the Jewish *Sib. Or.* 12.60 (*OTP* 1.446): "He will kill the heads of the senate."

[43] *Ant.* 19.202.

such as he wore himself."[44] In the temple of Jupiter Capitolinus in Rome, most honored of the temples, Gaius even dared to speak to Jupiter as his brother. In fact, he considered himself to be Jupiter / Zeus.[45]

At the beginning of his reign in 37 CE, Gaius was regarded as "savior and benefactor" (ὁ σωτὴρ καὶ εὐεργέτης).[46] As successor of Tiberius, he became the sovereign of earth and sea,[47] just as Pharaoh was thought to be *cosmocrator* in the Judaic sources cited above. Josephus notes that Gaius "imagined himself a god because of the greatness of his empire...."[48] Suetonius remarks that he cared "for nothing so much as to do what men said was impossible. So he built moles out into the deep and stormy sea...."[49] He had even intended to have a canal dug through the Corinthian Isthmus in Greece.[50] This was certainly an attempt to outdo the Persian King Xerxes, who in fact did build a canal through the isthmus of Mount Athos so that his ships could pass through it.[51]

Of direct relevance to Mark 6:45-51 is the incident of Gaius' building a bridge over the bay between Baiae and Puteoli just west of modern Naples.[52] Suetonius notes that many people thought he did so to rival

---

[44] *Lives of the Caesars*, "Gaius Caligula" 22.3 in the LCL translation of J. Rolfe. Suetonius published the *Lives of the Caesars* in 120 CE (LCL Suetonius, I.xii).

[45] Josephus, *Ant.* 19.4. Cf. Suetonius, "Gaius Caligula" 22.4. For his calling himself Jupiter Latiaris, see Dio Cassius, *Roman History* 59.28.5 (cf. also 8). See also the incident at the birth of his daughter in Josephus, *Ant.* 19.11, as well as his order to have a copy of his own head replace that on the statue of Jupiter (Zeus) of Olympia, to be brought from Greece to Rome (Suetonius, "Gaius Caligula" 22.2). In 52 Suetonius notes that Gaius would exhibit himself with a thunderbolt in his hand, one of the insignia of Jupiter. On this, see also Dio Cassius, *Roman History* 26.5,7-8.

[46] Philo, *Leg. Gai.* 22. The first term may have encouraged the appropriation of "Save me" from Ps 69:2 in Matt 14:30, part of the Naḥshon haggadah.

[47] *Leg. Gai.* 8 and 44. Cf. 247, where Gaius is "the ruler and master of them all...."

[48] *Ant.* 18.256.

[49] "Gaius Caligula" 37.2.

[50] *Ibid.* 21.

[51] Cf. Herodotus 7.22-24. The Greek historian considered this an example of Xerxes' "arrogance" (24), for he could easily have drawn his ships across the land. See also Isocrates' *Panegyricus* 89, which mentions Xerxes' "arrogance." An Athenian, Isocrates was born in 436 and died in 338 BCE. See the LCL edition by G. Norlin, I.xi. Dion Chysostomos has Socrates mention the incident in the *Orationes* 3.31. See the text in de Budé, *Dionis Chrysostomi Orationes* 1.49.

[52] Puteoli is the modern Pozzuoli. It was "the main port for trade with the east and also an important site for eastern communities" (Schürer, *The history* 3.110). It was called Dicaearchia by the Greeks (Josephus, *Vita* 16) and already had a

Xerxes.[53] Herodotus, the fifth century BCE Greek historian,[54] describes the Persian king as crossing over (διαβαίνω) the Hellespont above Troy in order to wage war on the Greeks by having 360 ships placed together on one side and 314 on the other. After being joined into a bridge, brushwood was put on top of them and earth heaped onto this, which was then stamped down. At one point the sacred chariot of Zeus, drawn by eight white horses, was followed by Xerxes. According to Herodotus, it took seven days and nights for Xerxes' entire Persian army to "cross over," the land army numbering 1,700,000 men. The historian relates that a tale has a man there call Xerxes Zeus because of this fantastic feat.[55]

Here a Persian king is thought at least by some to be equal to Zeus for his ability to "cross over" the sea at the Hellespont.

Gaius was certainly aware of this account[56] because his project of building a bridge upon the sea between Baiae and Puteoli in Italy followed it very closely, except that in his madness he made sure the distance was greater.[57] Josephus in *Ant.* 19.6 says Gaius "considered it his privilege as 'lord of the sea' (δεσπότῃ ὄντι τῆς θαλάσσης) to require the same service from the sea as he received from the land." Suetonius relates that Gaius rode back and forth for two days on the pontoon bridge, composed of merchant ships anchored in a double line with a mound of earth heaped onto them to resemble the Appian Way. On the first day he rode horseback, with a crown of oak leaves and a cloak made

---

Jewish colony at the time of Herod the Great's death in 4 BCE (*Bell.* 2.104 and *Ant.* 17.328). Some of them had probably become Christians by the time Paul landed there on the way to Rome (Acts 28:13-14). Baiae was a favorite residence of the Roman emperors, including Gaius Caligula (*Ant.* 18.248-249). On the latter, see also Philo, *Leg. Gai.* 185.

[53] "Gaius Caligula" 19.3. Dio Cassius, *Roman History* 17.11, states: "as for Darius and Xerxes, he made all manner of fun of them, claiming that he had bridged a far greater expanse of sea than they had done." The work was composed ca. 200-220 CE. See the LCL edition, I.xi.

[54] Cf. the LCL translation by A. Godley in 1.vii.

[55] Cf. 7.35-60, with Xerxes as Zeus in 56. The term "crossing over" is found in 35 and 54-56.

[56] Cf. Isocrates, *Panegyricus* 89: "a plan whose fame is on the lips of all mankind – a plan by which, having bridged the Hellespont and channeled Athos, he (Xerxes) sailed his ships across the mainland, and marched his troops across the main." English by G. Norlin in the LCL edition.

[57] Suetonius in "Gaius Caligula" 19.1 says it was about 3600 paces, or over 3 1/2 Roman miles (see n. "d"). Josephus in *Ant.* 19.6 has 30 furlongs, and Dio Cassius in *Roman History* 59.17.1 speaks of 26 furlongs.

of gold cloth, on the second in a chariot.[58] Josephus notes that Gaius "drove (ἤλαυνεν) in his chariot. That way of traveling, he said, befitted his being a god."[59]

Here the same Greek verb for Gaius' "driving" (ἐλαύνω) his chariot is employed as for the disciples' "rowing" their boat against a (strong) head wind in Mark 6:48. Gaius thought his driving his chariot over the sea was appropriate to his divinity, just as Xerxes was compared to Zeus for performing a similar feat. The Palestinian Jewish Christian narrator of Jesus' walking on the Sea consciously created an account in which his own Lord, Jesus the Christ, was shown to be superior to a maniacal Roman emperor, thought by many to be the lord of the sea. Gaius needed hundreds of ships to perform his feat, as did Xerxes. He thus merely seemed to be walking or riding on the water. However, Jesus the Messiah, the Spirit of God who hovers over the waters, himself walked upon the water of the Sea of Galilee from the shore to the middle of the Sea. Instead of cruelly drowning others such as those Gaius bid come to him, Jesus rescued the disciples from their precarious situation. When he entered the boat, the wind ceased. He, Jesus, is the true lord of the elements.

I suggest that this event served as the main inspiration for the Palestinian Jewish Christian author of Mark 6:45-51.[60] Josephus and Seneca seem to locate the account at the end of Gaius' emperorship, i.e. sometime in 40 CE.[61] Even if it was a year or two earlier, news of such a fantastic feat spread immediately throughout the entire Roman Empire, including Palestine. It is thus probable that the counter-episode in Mark 6:45-51 was first narrated already at the beginning of the forties.

---

[58] "Gaius Caligula" 19.1-2. In 32.1 he notes that at the dedication of the bridge, he had a number of people join him from the shore, and then cruelly had them all thrown overboard, (presumably to drown). On this, see also Dio Cassius, *Roman History* 17.1-11. Dio notes that the crescent-shaped bay was illuminated all night from fire on the nearby hills, for it was Gaius' "wish to make the night day, as he had made the sea land" (9).

[59] *Ant.* 19.6. Paradoxically, Suetonius in "Gaius Caligula" 54.2 notes that Gaius could not even swim.

[60] The independent narrative of Jesus' stilling the storm in Mark 4:35-41 may have been similarly inspired as an intentional Jewish Christian contrast to the account of Julius Caesar's inability to cross the sea in a storm in 48 BCE. Cf. Plutarch, *Lives*, "Caesar" 38, and Dio Cassius, *Roman History* 46. Some scholars believe Fourth Maccabees was written as a reaction to Gaius Caligula's attempt to set up a statue of himself in the Jerusalem Temple. See Nickelsburg, *Jewish Literature* 226, with n. 40, as well as already R. Townshend in *APOT* 2.653-654.

[61] Cf. *Ant.* 19.6, and L. Feldman's n. "g" on this. The reference is to Seneca's "Ad Pavlinvm, De Brevitate Vitae" 18.5-6 (Basore 2.346-349).

A second factor in the reign of the insane Gaius Caligula encouraged the Palestinian Jewish Christian to create his account. First Maccabees was written sometime between 104-63 BCE in Hebrew.[62] It describes how Antiochus IV Epiphanes in 169 BCE "arrogantly" (ἐν ὑπερηφανίᾳ) entered the Jerusalem sanctuary and stole Temple vessels and treasures (1:21-24).[63] Two years later, in 167 BCE, his representative in Jerusalem, backed by a large military force, defiled the sanctuary (v 37), which "became desolate" (ἠρημώθη) as a desert (v 39). In the same year Antiochus' forces "created a 'desolating sacrilege' (βδέλυγμα ἐρημώσεως) upon the (Temple) altar of burnt offering" (v 54). This was an altar to Olympian Zeus and possibly a statue of the godhead. Second Maccabees, written in Greek sometime between 103-76 BCE,[64] relates in 6:2 that Antiochus sent his representative to "pollute (μολῦναι) the Temple in Jerusalem and call it the temple of Olympian Zeus."

Significantly, just before this the author of Second Maccabees describes Antiochus' personal plundering of the Temple. Then he adds that Antiochus thought "in his arrogance that he could sail on the land 'and walk on the sea' (καὶ τὸ πέλαγος πορευτόν) because his mind was elated" (5:21). Here, like Gaius Caligula, the ruler of the entire Seleucid Empire is described in his insolence as considering himself a god,[65] who can even "walk on the sea." The Palestinian Jewish Christian author of Mark 6:45-51 may thus also have had Antiochus in mind when he created his counter-account of Jesus' walking on the Sea.

This is made even more probable by the "desolating sacrilege" Antiochus had erected in the Jerusalem Temple. Dan 11:31 and 12:11 (cf. also 9:27) mention it specifically, and they are referred to in Mark 13:14, which reads: "But when you see the 'desolating sacrilege' (τὸ βδέλυγμα τῆς ἐρημώσεως), him standing (ἑστηκότα) where he ought not to be (let the reader understand), then let those who are in Judea flee to the hills...." Matthew in 24:15 specifically refers to "the desolating sacrilege spoken of by the prophet Daniel," and Luke in 21:20 interprets the verse

---

[62] Nickelsburg, *Jewish Literature* 117.

[63] His arrogance in v 21 is emphasized in v 24: "he spoke with great arrogance."

[64] Nickelsburg, *Jewish Literature* 121 and the chart on p. 320 for Alexander Jannaeus.

[65] In their n. "a" on Philo's *Leg. Gai.* 346, F. Colson and W. Rouse call attention to the fact that "coins of Antiochus Epiphanes bear the inscription Ἀντιόχου θεοῦ ἐπιφανοῦς." See also Isocrates, *Panegyricus* 89, on Xerxes' crossing the Hellespont. He "rose to such a pitch of 'arrogance' (ὑπερηφανία)...," and intended to leave a memorial "which would not be of a human nature."

of the Roman siege of Jerusalem in 70 CE: "But when you see Jerusalem surrounded by enemies, then know that its desolation has come near."

Matthew in 24:15 intentionally has the neuter "standing" (ἑστός) follow the neuter "desolating sacrilege." In his "Vorlage," however, Mark 13:14 has ἑστηκότα, masculine, thus a different entity than the neuter "desolating sacrilege." For Mark this masculine participle, purposely veiled in apocalyptic style, very probably referred to the Roman general Titus' "standing" in the holy place of the Jerusalem Temple when his army captured Jerusalem, as Josephus specifically states in *Bell.* 6.260.[66] Many scholars view the Gospel of Mark as having been finished at about this time.[67]

Yet Mark 13:14 was probably already part of a thought unit before Mark incorporated it into his Gospel. Along with other exegetes, I believe it originally referred to the Roman emperor Gaius Caligula's attempt to erect his own statue in the Jerusalem Temple in 40 CE.[68] Philo relates for example that in his zeal for self-deification, Gaius had the Jewish synagogues in other cities after Alexandria filled "with images and statues of himself in bodily form." He then proceeded to change the Jerusalem Temple into one of his own, "to bear the name of Gaius, 'The New Zeus Made Manifest'" (Διὸς Ἐπιφανοῦς Νέου – *Leg. Gai.* 346). A Jewish messenger had earlier informed Philo and other Alexandrian representatives in Puteoli that "Our Temple is lost. Gaius has ordered a colossal statue (ἀνδριάντα κολοσσιαῖον) to be set up within the inner sanctuary dedicated to himself under the name of Zeus" (188). It was to be coated with gold (203) and to be erected in the Holy of Holies, to which only the high priest had access once a year (306).[69]

---

[66] Mark could not openly name Titus, the son of Vespasian, who had been declared Roman Emperor while in Palestine in 69 CE. Cf. Josephus, *Bell.* 4.619. Thus the parenthesis, "let the reader understand."

[67] Cf. J. Marcus, "The Jewish War and the Sitz im Leben of Mark" in *JBL* 111 (1992) 460; D. Lührmann, *Das Markus-Evangelium* (HNT 3; Tübingen: Mohr, 1987) 6; and J. Gnilka, *Das Evangelium nach Markus (Mk 1–8,26)* (EKKNT II/1; Zurich, Benziger; Neukirchen-Vluyn: Neukirchener, 1989³) 34.

[68] Cf. W. Schmithals, *Das Evangelium nach Markus. Kapitel 9,2–16* (ÖTKNT 2/2; Gütersloh: Mohn; Würzburg: Echter, 1979) 564-565, and other authors cited by Grundmann, *Das Evangelium nach Markus* 356. See now also N. Taylor, "Palestinian Christianity and the Caligula Crisis. Part I: Social and Historical Reconstruction" in *JSNT* 61 (1996) 101-124, and "Part II. The Markan Eschatological Discourse" in 62 (1996) 13-41. Taylor has no reference to Jesus' walking on the Sea.

[69] Cf. Josephus, *Ant.* 18.281. Tacitus in *The Histories* 5.9 notes that Gaius ordered *effigiem eius in templum locare*. C. Moore in Tacitus, *The Histories* I.viii states that he was born "not far from 55-56 A.D.," and died in 117 or somewhat later (x).

The masculine noun ἀνδρίας means "image of a man, statue."[70] I suggest that the neuter "desolating sacrilege" in Mark 13:14, an expression intended to describe the general state of desolation, is followed by the masculine in order to clarify its meaning. "The one standing where he ought not to" is the (in Greek male) statue of Gaius Caligula to be set up within the innermost sanctuary of the Jerusalem Temple. Non-Jews, however, were prohibited from entering even the area before it upon penalty of death.[71]

Today it is hard to imagine what effect Gaius' plan had upon all Jews of the time, but especially those in Palestine. They knew that Gaius had a special hatred of them because they alone, of all the nations subjugated by the Romans, refused to acknowledge him as a god.[72] Philo, who with others journeyed from Alexandria to Rome to persuade Gaius to abandon his endeavor, thought it would be "a calamity worse than death" (*Leg. Gai.* 233). He notes that "it is to be feared that the overthrow of the Temple will be accompanied by an order for the annihilation of our common (Jewish) name and nation..." (194).[73] Josephus relates for example how tens of thousands of Jews first went to protest against Gaius' intended action to the Roman legate of Syria, Petronius, in Ptolemais. They told him he should first slay them all. The same scene repeated itself at their encounter with Petronius at Tiberias, where for

---

[70] LSJ 128.

[71] Cf. Philo, *Leg. Gai.* 212, as well as other texts cited in Str-B 2.761-762 on Acts 21:28.

[72] Cf. Josephus, *Ant.* 18.261, as well as Philo, *Leg. Gai.* 115-117; 133 for Gaius' "indescribable hatred of the Jews"; 198 for only the Jews as resisting his plan; 201 for "the extreme hostility which Gaius felt toward the whole Jewish race"; 256, where Gaius says the Jews are "the nation which is my worst enemy"; as well as 265, 332 and 353.

[73] This fear was justified. Josephus in *Ant.* 19.15 says that "our own nation was brought to the very verge of ruin and would have been destroyed but for his sudden death...." In *Bell.* 2.197 the Jewish historian notes that if Gaius insisted on his plan, "he must first sacrifice the entire Jewish nation." In 185 he relates that if the Jews refused Gaius' wishes, the Syrian legate Petronius with his legions and Syrian auxiliaries was ordered to kill the leaders of the plot and reduce the rest of the whole nation to utter slavery (thus to be sold as slaves to other countries in the Empire). Cf. also Tacitus, *The Histories* 5.9, who relates regarding Gaius' order that the Jews erect his image in the Temple: "they rather took up arms, which uprising the death of Gaius ended." From the Roman viewpoint, such sedition had to be ended militarily. Josephus in *Ant.* 18.270 says the Jews thought the danger of actual war with the Romans was great at this point. See also the note in Dio Cassius, *Roman History* 25.5, that Gaius once "almost destroyed the whole (Roman) senate because it had not voted him divine honors."

forty days they made their supplications, baring their throats to show their willingness to be slain.[74] Through Petronius' delaying tactics and the death of Gaius on January 24, 41 CE, the terrible danger was finally averted.[75]

This major threat of the annihilation or enslavement of at least all of Palestinian Judaism provided the background to the original version of Mark 13:14, before Mark later appropriated it into his Gospel. Yet it also provided the major impetus for the Palestinian Jewish Christian author of Mark 6:45-51 to compose his narrative. Jesus, who walked on the Sea of Galilee, performed a feat which was far greater than that of Gaius, the Roman "lord of land and sea," who rode a horse and a chariot over a man-made sea bridge, or raced across it. Jesus the Messiah, the Spirit of God who "hovers" over the waters, is the true lord / Lord of the natural elements, for his Father is God Almighty, the maker of heaven and earth. He does not have to insist, like Gaius, on his divinity, for his Father is the only true God, working through him. The author of Mark 6:45-51 was still reticent in applying the title "Son of God" to Jesus here. Later, in a mixed Jewish / non-Jewish environment, Matthew could more easily have the disciples in the boat proclaim: "Truly you are the Son of God!" (14:33). This is described as their "worshiping" (προσκυνέω) or "prostrating themselves" before him. It intentionally stands in contrast, for example, to the predecessor of Petronius as Roman legate to Syria, Vitellius. Summoned back to Rome to be killed by Gaius because of his ineptness in handling the Jews' resistance to the setting up of the emperor's statue in the Jerusalem Temple, he could only save his life by calling Gaius by the names of numerous gods and by "worshiping" (προσκυνέω) him.[76]

---

[74] Cf. *Ant.* 18.263-279; *Bell.* 2.195-196; Philo, *Leg. Gai.* 209,215,223,225-230, and Agrippa's petition to Gaius, for example in 292.

[75] Cf. Josephus, *Ant.* 18.305 and note "b" on the latter. See also Suetonius, "Gaius Caligula" 58.1. In 59 he states that Gaius was only twenty-nine years old at the time of his death. Note also Acts 12:22-23, where Herod Agrippa I's death is attributed to his not giving God the glory. In Caesarea the people had shouted to him: "The voice of a god, and not of man!" Although the name Caligula is garbled, the annulment of his decree in regard to the Jerusalem sanctuary through his being killed is noted in *t. Soṭa* 13:6 (Zuckermandel / Liebermann 319; Neusner 3.202). Parallels are found in *y. Soṭa* 9:13, 24b (Neusner 27.259-260);*b. Soṭa* 33a (Soncino 163); and *Cant. Rab.* 8:9 § 3 (Soncino 9.316).

[76] Cf. Dio Cassius, *Roman History* 27.5, and Josephus, *Ant.* 18.261, for Petronius as the successor of Vitellius. Philo in *Leg. Gai.* 116 notes that some nations "even introduced into Italy the barbarian practice of 'prostrating themselves' (προσκύνησις)..." in regard to acknowledging Gaius as a god. Philo also remarks that a multitude of Jews rushed to Phoenicia to Petronius and fell to the ground

The above proposal argues strongly for a dating of the original version of Mark 6:45-51 as already at the beginning of the forties, shortly after the death of Gaius in 41 CE. After it had been translated into Greek by a Hellenistic Jewish Christian, it was appropriated by Mark into his Gospel about a quarter century later. In the meantime it had also developed into the variant narrative now found in John 6:16-21, and in light of the Naḥshon haggadah it had elsewhere also acquired the special Petrine material now incorporated in Matt 14:28-31.

V. The Original Language and the Provenance of the Narrative.

K. Clemen was acquainted with seven different writers who believed Mark 6:45-51 derived from a Buddha narrative,[77] presumably passed on to the West in Greek. R. Reitzenstein maintained that a pagan miracle account was copied and superseded here.[78] K. Kertelge sees its background in the Hellenistic concept of a "divine man."[79] Omitting any discussion of Judaic sources, W. Berg points to Hellenistic Jewish Christianity as the source of the tradition because of its apparent synthesis of OT and Hellenistic thought.[80] J. Gnilka agrees with him in this respect,[81] and W. Schmithals speaks of the narrator as living in a "Jewish-Hellenistic environment."[82] Finally, W. Stegner calls attention to a number of expressions in Exodus 14, but thinks that "Mark was working with a pre-Markan Greek account first formulated by Jewish Christians." In regard to the Exodus narrative he remarks: "the audience

---

before him (προσπίπτω – 228), which was to be interpreted as prostrating themselves before Gaius (230). See also Josephus, *Ant.* 18.271 for the Jews' "falling on their faces" at a second encounter in Tiberias. For them, this gesture was that of acknowledging a king or emperor, but not of worshiping or doing obeisance to Gaius as a god. See LSJ 1518 on προσκυνέω for the two different interpretations of the verb. For prostrating oneself before Gaius Caesar as a god, see also Suetonius, *Lives of the Caesars,* "Vitellius" 2.5.

[77] Cf. his *Religionsgeschichtliche Erklärung des Neuen Testaments* (Giessen: Töpelmann, 1924²) 238.

[78] *Hellenistische Wundererzählungen* (Stuttgart: Teubner, 1906) 125.

[79] *Die Wunder Jesu im Markusevangelium* (SANT 23; Munich: Kösel, 1970) 148-149.

[80] *Die Rezeption* 326.

[81] *Das Evangelium nach Markus (MK 1–8,26)* 267.

[82] *Das Evangelium nach Markus, Kapitel 1–9,1* (ÖTKNT 2/1; Gütersloh: Mohn; Würzburg: Echter, 1979) 333.

who heard the story about Jesus would recall the familiar story from the Septuagint."[83]

All of the authors mentioned above thus presuppose that Mark 6:45-51 was first related or composed in Greek. I also believe that when the Evangelist Mark appropriated the narrative, it was already in Greek. The account of Xerxes' crossing the Hellespont was also in Greek, as was that of Gaius Caligula's crossing the bay at Puteoli,[84] and his resolve to erect a colossal gold statue of himself as god in the Holy of Holies of the Jerusalem Temple. Antiochus IV Epiphanes' boast that he could walk on the sea was certainly also in Greek originally, as it is now in 2 Macc 5:21.

Yet in section I above I pointed out a large number of motifs and expressions in Mark 6:45-51 which are still found in Judaic sources on Exodus 14-15. Almost all of them are or originally were in Hebrew, with only a few, such as the targums, in Aramaic. In a number of instances I noted that the author did not employ a LXX term from Exodus 14-15, which would have been expected if his mother tongue was Greek. In addition, the background of Jesus' walking on the Sea derives in part from Judaic interpretation of the royal Messiah as the Spirit who "hovers" over the water in Gen 1:2. This tradition is found only in Hebrew sources. The same is true for the Naḥshon haggadah which formed the background of the special Petrine material in Matt 14:28-31.

For the above reasons I suggest that the narrative of Mark 6:45-51 was originally composed in Hebrew. This would also account for word plays such as "seeing" (רָאָה), "fearing" (יָרֵא), and "apparition / phantom / ghost" (מַרְאֶה). "Crossing" (עָבַר), "shore" (עֵבֶר) and "evening" (עֶרֶב) are other possible word plays. They are a part of the author's narrative artistry. Yet Aramaic, the language of the larger population, is certainly also possible. My main point is that the account was originally composed in one of these two Semitic languages. As a very colorful, moving episode, it was translated by a Hellenistic Jewish Christian into Greek at a relatively early date, perhaps already in the forties. It was in this Greek form, coupled to the feeding of the 5000, that it then became available to the Evangelist Mark.

Palestine was thus the place of the narrative's origin. While it is impossible to be more specific, it is tempting to imagine the author as a Galilean Jewish Christian who was very well acquainted with his own Sea of Galilee and the dangerous winds which come down from the NE there, even today. This knowledge aided him in thinking of the LORD's

---

[83] "Jesus' Walking on the Water" 215.

[84] Although this was probably originally composed in Latin, it would have been translated immediately into Greek for the eastern Mediterranean area.

major salvific action at the Sea of Reeds in Exodus 14-15, especially as described in the great amount of Judaic interpretation on it, with which he was personally acquainted.

VI. The Historicity and Purpose of the Narrative.

Very few commentators, even those of an Evangelical bent, deal directly with the question of historicity in regard to the story of Jesus' walking on the Sea.[85] V. Taylor maintained, however, that "the basic assumption of actual events remembered and interpreted is fully justified." He could only justify this assertion by having Jesus "wading through the surf near the hidden shore...."[86] P. Lapide also appears to favor the historicity of the narrative under the presupposition that it was an "optical illusion of the disciples." In the semi-darkness of the late twilight his walking on or along the shore, above the level of the lake (Heb. על הים), appeared to them to be upon the water, in part because their minds were agitated by the storm.[87]

Yet all attempts to preserve the historicity of the narrative are doomed to failure because they do not recognize that this is a haggadic account. In section II. 9.b) above I cited the incident in *y. Sanh.* 7:13, 25d where a heretic spoke an incantation near Tiberias on the Sea of Galilee in the presence of Rabbis Eliezer, Joshua and Aqiva. At this point the Sea divided itself, which the heretic related to Moses' dividing the Reed Sea. No contemporary Jew considered this dividing of the Sea of Galilee to be historical. Since it swallowed up the heretic when he entered it, like Moses, it was a narrative device designed to express the religious truth that heretics cannot be victorious. Indeed, God will provide a way to eliminate them.

Another example is the following statement in *y. 'Aboda Zara* 3:1, 42c: "When R. Ḥanina of Bet Hauran died, the Sea of Tiberias split open."[88] Here too a religious, not an historical truth is expressed. God's creation was so sad at the death of a famous rabbi that it joined in the

---

[85] Typical is W. Stegner's observation that "the possible historical event, the point of departure for the story... is difficult to determine." See his "Jesus' Walking on the Water" 216, referring to A.-M. Denis. Stegner intentionally avoids "the historical question."

[86] *The Gospel According to St Mark* 326 and 327, respectively.

[87] *Er wandelte nicht auf dem Meer* 21.

[88] Neusner 33.112. Str-B 5/6.137 only notes that he was a Palestinian.

bereavement. This is the same religious truth expressed by the *prodigia* at Jesus' Crucifixion.[89]

M. Herr has written that "the *aggadah* does contain truth which is greater than that of historical and philological reality, and more important than that of the natural sciences."[90] It would thus simply not be fair to ask the question: "Is the narrative now found in Mark 6:45-51 true or not?" Historically it is not. Yet, like many other haggadic narratives created within Palestinian Judaism at that time, *it is true in a religious sense*. To these religious truths I now turn.

M. Hooker has written regarding Jesus' walking on the Sea that "Mark appears to consider its significance plain, but the modern reader often feels as perplexed as the disciples."[91] C. Mann also states in this regard: "All in all, it must be said that if the narrative is not a doublet of 4:35-41, its purpose is wholly obscure."[92] These statements are close to resignation, which is not necessary if one considers the religious truths the narrative seeks to express.

1) As the (twelve tribes of the) Israelites at the Reed Sea were hemmed in on all sides and had to go ahead, to pass through or cross the deep waters, so Jesus' twelve disciples and the Christians who are the author's contemporaries have to move through situations in which "rowing" is also very torturous or difficult. This does not necessarily mean physical

---

[89] Cf. the analysis in my *Samuel, Saul and Jesus. Three Early Palestinian Jewish Christian Gospel Haggadoth* (USFSHJ 105; Atlanta: Scholars Press, 1994) 115-157. See also other sources cited in Str-B 1.1040-1042.

[90] Cf. his art. "Aggadah" in *EJ* (1971) 2.355. For other Jewish Christian examples of haggadic narratives which express religious truths, see "The Child Jesus in the Temple (Luke 2:41-51a), and Judaic Traditions on the Child Samuel in the Temple (1 Samuel 1-3)" in *Samuel, Saul and Jesus* 1-64; "The Release of Barabbas (Mark 15:6-15 par.; John 18:39-40), and Judaic Traditions on the Book of Esther" in *Barabbas and Esther* 1-27; *Water into Wine, and the Beheading of John the Baptist. Early Jewish-Christian Interpretation of Esther 1 in John 2:1-11 and Mark 6:17-29* (BJS 150; Atlanta: Scholars Press, 1988); and the chapter "Die Weihnachtsgeschichte im Lichte jüdischer Traditionen vom Mose-Kind und Hirten-Messias (Lukas 2,1-20)" in *Weihnachtsgeschichte, Barmherziger Samariter, Verlorener Sohn. Studien zu ihrem jüdischen Hintergrund* (ANTZ 2; Berlin: Institut Kirche und Judentum, 1988) 11-58.

[91] *The Gospel According to St Mark* 169.

[92] *Mark* 306.

persecution,[93] although this was also sporadically the case.[94] Rather, it could mean the tremendous *fear* of persecution, indeed the annihilation or selling into slavery of all Jews in Palestine. This tendency had already begun for example in Alexandria, where statues of the mad Gaius Caligula were erected in all the synagogues, as well as in other nearby cities. No difference would have been made here between Jews and Jewish Christians. Also, there may have been some resistance in Palestine from fellow Jews because Jewish Christians now believed that the Messiah had already come and would return very soon. Yet "messianic" conditions had definitely not yet arrived. Not only was Jesus ignobly put to death on a cross like a criminal. Rome still ruled with an iron hand; Israel was still subjugated; and the wolf did not dwell with the lamb yet (Isa 11:6). So how could Jesus of Nazareth be the Messiah? In addition, in spite of several glowing summary passages in Acts (2:47; 4:4; 5:14; 6:1,7), the disciples and other early evangelists were often frustrated by resistance to their work.[95] Yet as God "saved" and "redeemed" the Israelites at the Reed Sea through Moses, the first redeemer of Israel (Exod 14:30 and 15:13), so He will also aid the hearers of the narrative in Mark 6:45-51 through Jesus, the Messiah, the last or great redeemer of Israel. Jesus will not leave them alone in a difficult situation, but will come to them and help them, especially when the wind blows strongly against them. In such situations they should not *fear*, but take heart, for Jesus is with them. In the related special Petrine material in Matt 14:28-31, this motif is spelled out even more. The disciples (the author's fellow Christians) should not be of little faith. Jesus will help / save them when they begin to sink.

2) In contrast to elsewhere, the LORD appeared openly at the Reed Sea in Judaic tradition so that all the Israelites clearly saw and recognized Him, a privilege not even granted to the prophets. Josephus for example emphasizes "the clear manifestation of God" at this point. When Jesus, the Christians' Lord, appears to them on the Sea of Galilee, he shows them that he is the Son of God (spelled out in Matt 14:33), and he performs his Father's will by repeating His act of aid / salvation at the Reed Sea. The narrative of Mark 6:45-51 is thus not a veiled Resurrection appearance such as those found in Luke 24:36-43 and John 21, as often

---

[93] Against Lane, *The Gospel According to Mark* 239: "it provided the martyrs with the assurance of Jesus' saving nearness to all who believe and obey him."

[94] Cf. Gal 1:22 for Paul as a persecutor; 1 Thess 2:14; Acts 7:58; 8:1 and 11:19; 12:1-2; and Josephus, *Ant.* 20.200.

[95] Cf. Luke 5:5, "We toiled all night and took nothing!" See W. Schmithals, *Das Evangelium nach Markus, Kapitel 1–9,1* (334).

maintained. Rather, Jesus' manifestation at the Sea of Galilee recalls his Father's manifestation at the Reed Sea.[96]

3) Jesus' walking on the Sea is also intended to demonstrate that he is the royal Messiah, the Spirit of God who already "hovered" over the waters at Creation in Gen 1:2, a passage very well-known to every Palestinian Jew and Jewish Christian.

4) Mortals such as Xerxes, Antiochus IV Epiphanes and Gaius Caligula were thought by others to be, or themselves arrogantly claimed and even acted as if they were, lord of the sea, and that they could ride or walk over it because they were ostensibly divine. Yet they only pretended to do so, running or riding for example over ships fastened together. Jesus is presented in Mark 6:45-51 as actually walking on the Sea. It is he, and not a mad and bloodthirsty emperor, who in fact is "divine," i.e. the Son of God and as such also lord of the elements.[97] Thus the head wind also ceases when Jesus reveals himself and enters the boat. What the Father is described as doing in the Hebrew Bible, His going through the sea (Ps 77:20; 68:25; Isa 43:16-17), His Son now also does. God language is thus applied to Jesus here at a relatively early time, very probably already at the beginning of the forties, and in a non-apocalyptic context. Jesus, who walks on the Sea, is the true σωτήρ of the world, the *cosmocrator*, the lord of land and sea, and not the Roman emperor, who demanded that he be worshiped as a god, or even as *the* god, Jupiter / Zeus.

*   *   *

We should be very grateful today for the above four religious truths expressed in the narrative of Jesus' walking on the Sea. The Palestinian Jewish Christian who first composed the account employed many elements from early Judaic tradition on Exodus 14-15 and Gen 1:2 to form a narrative which has offered encouragement to countless disciples of Jesus throughout the centuries. In addition, it has given artists the opportunity to present a fascinating dramatic scene.[98]

---

[96] The narrative thus does not emphasize that Jesus' walking over the waters shows he is the lord or conqueror of death. Against E. Lohmeyer, *Das Evangelium des Markus* (Meyer 1,2; Göttingen: Vandehoeck & Ruprecht, 1963[16]) 135, and M. Dibelius, *From Tradition to Gospel* 227 on the mythical waters of death.

[97] Note also the contrast made by the Evangelist John between the people's wanting to make Jesus a political "king" in 6:15, and his ruling the elements of nature in 16-21.

[98] It is represented for example in the mosaic altar picture rescued in 1944 from my first parish, the Genezarethgemeinde, in Berlin-Neukölln, and in the stained

Appendix: The Lectionary Readings in Nisan.

The oldest Jewish lectionary system in Palestine was triennial.[99] While it is notoriously difficult to date liturgical materials, what has remained from the earliest available sources may indicate, at least in part, why certain texts important in the above study were associated by the author of Mark 6:45-51 and the author of the special Petrine material in Matt 14:28-31.

The first month in the Jewish calendar is Nisan, in which Passover occurs (Exod 12:2). In the first year of the triennial cycle, Gen 1:1 – 2:3 was read on the first Sabbath of Nisan.[100] That is, Gen 1:2 was included, which in Judaic tradition has the Spirit of God "hovering" over the waters interpreted as the royal Messiah. As pointed out above, this is the major background for Jesus' "walking" on the Sea of Galilee in Mark 6:48-49.

Secondly, Isa 42:5 – 43:10 is the haftarah or prophetic reading for the same first Sabbath in Nisan.[101] Verse 5 begins with God's creating the heavens and earth, as in Genesis 1. Isa 43:1 repeats the creation motif and has God say in v 2: "When you pass through the waters, I will be with you," which recalls the dividing of the Reed Sea at the exodus. As noted above, the Targum interprets this section of Isaiah as referring to the exodus from Egypt, and it has the Lord's servant in v 10 as the Messiah. In addition, one "that I am He" passage occurs in the same verse, of relevance to Mark 6:50. Another occurs in v 13, and vv 16-17 specifically deal with the Reed Sea event, with v 16 having the LORD make a way through the Sea, cited in several Judaic sources in connection with Exodus 14-15. While Isa 43:13 and 16-17 apparently did not belong to the haftarah as such, the hearers knew their Scriptures so well as to probably also associate them with the preceding.

---

glass window behind the altar of the Lutherhaus in my present congregation, the Luthergemeinde in Berlin-Reinickendorf.

[99] Cf. the articles "Triennial Cycle" by J. Jacobs in *JE* (1905) 12.254-257, "Sidra" by J. Jacobs and I. Dobsevage in *JE* (1905) 11.328-329, "Haftarah" also by J. Jacobs and I. Dobsevage in *JE* (1905) 6.135-137, and the art. "Triennial Cycle" by "Ed." in *EJ* (1971) 15.1386-1389.

[100] Cf. the art. "Sidra" in *JE* (1905) 11.328, and the table in *EJ* (1971) 15.1387.

[101] Cf. the art. "Haftarah" in *JE* (1905) 6.136. It is also for the annual cycle, but when the triennial was reduced to an annual cycle, the first of the three readings was usually retained. See also the table in *EJ* (1971) 15.1387.

Thirdly, Num 6:22 – 7:47 was also read on the first Sabbath of Nisan in the third year of the lectionary cycle.[102] It not only includes the Aaronic benediction (6:24-26), but also the tribal leaders' offerings for the tabernacle and the altar. Num 7:12 for example has Nahshon of the tribe of Judah as making his offering on the *first* of twelve days, one for each tribe. As noted above, the Nahshon haggadah provides the major background for the special Petrine material in Matt 14:28-31.

Are the above three observations simply accidental? In spite of the serious problem of dating the sources in which these data occur, I consider this very improbable. If at least these three readings from the Pentateuch and the prophets were already employed in Palestine in the first half of the first century CE,[103] it is understandable that the Palestinian Jewish Christian author of Mark 6:45-51, who based his narrative on Judaic interpretation of the Passover texts Exodus 14-15, may also have been influenced by Genesis 1. The same is true for the author of Matt 14:28-31 in regard to Num 7:12-17 on Nahshon.

John relates his version of Jesus' walking on the Sea in 6:16-21 as occurring on the same evening as the feeding of the 5000. In v 4 the Evangelist notes that "the Passover, the feast of the Jews, was at hand." If this notice of time may also be assumed for the Markan account, it would not only explain the (strong) head wind of 6:48, typical especially of this time of the year on the Sea of Galilee, but also the Palestinian Jewish Christian's use of Passover imagery from Exodus 14-15, and of Genesis 1, in the narrative.[104] Unfortunately, more cannot be said.

---

[102] Cf. the table in *EJ* (1971) 15.1388, and the editors' remark in 1389: "Numbers (6:22ff.), always read at the beginning of Nisan (in the third year), corresponds to the biblical date of Moses' inauguration of the tabernacle." See also *JE* (1905) 11.329, Nr. 110, for Num 6:22–7:47.

[103] Cf. Luke 4:17 for the book of Isaiah given to Jesus to read (as a haftarah) on the Sabbath in the synagogue at Nazareth. While I do not consider this scene historical, it nevertheless speaks in favor of the first-century use of prophetic readings in the Palestinian synagogues.

[104] Here I oppose the lectionary readings proposed by A. Guilding in her *The Fourth Gospel and Worship* 67, who deals with Gen 2:4ff., Isa 51:6-16, and 63:11ff. in regard to Exodus 15. She thinks they substantiate the "theme of death and resurrection" she finds in the Johannine account (p. 66). I do not perceive this theme here.

"Christ Before Pilate." Reproduced in O. Benesch, *The Drawings of Rembrandt* (London: The Phaidon Press, 1957) 6.408; Cat. No. A 115, figure 1670.

Chapter Three

The Release of Barabbas Revisited

(Mark 15:6-15; Matt 27:15-26; Luke 23:18-25; John 18:39-40)

I. Introduction

One of the most puzzling Gospel narratives is that of the Roman procurator Pontius Pilate's releasing the imprisoned revolutionary Barabbas and then delivering Jesus to be crucified (Mark 15:6-15 par.).[1] P. Winter calls it the "Most enigmatical of all parts of the Gospel Story of Jesus' trial,"[2] and R. Brown states at the end of his own exhaustive analysis of this pericope that "historical criticism cannot overcome the lack of comparative material, and the Barabbas case is particularly frustrating on that score."[3] The following study attempts to provide such

---

[1] For extensive bibliography, see R. Brown, *The Death of the Messiah*. From Gethsemane to the Grave (New York: Doubleday, 1994) 1.672-673, who examines the narrative on pp. 787-820; F. Neirynck et al., ed., *The Gospel of Mark: A Cumulative Bibliography 1950-1990* (Louvain: Peeters, 1992) 616; and R. Gundry, *Mark* 929-939. I previously dealt with the pericope in "The Release of Barabbas (Mark 15:6-15 par.; John 18:39-40) and Judaic Traditions on the Book of Esther" in my *Barabbas and Esther* 1-27. It must now be revised in the light of the results of this study.

[2] Cf. his *On the Trial of Jesus* (Berlin: de Gruyter, 1974[2]) 131. On p. 142 he states that "The Barabbas episode remains an enigma." J. Derrett in *The Making of Mark*, Vol. II (Shipston-on-Stour, Warwickshire: Drinkwater, 1985) 262 maintains: "Unfortunately, this is the most awkward section in the gospel."

[3] *The Death of the Messiah* 1.820.

comparative material, all datable to within the very end of the first century BCE and the first half of the first century CE. Before I present it, it will be helpful to first note numerous peculiarities in the Barabbas narrative.

Mark 15:7 states that Barabbas was imprisoned with the "rebels" or "revolutionaries" (στασιαστής – only here in the NT)[4] who had committed murder during "the insurrection" (στάσις – only here and in Luke 23:19 and 24 in the Gospels).[5] It should be noted that at least here in Mark it is not expressly stated that Barabbas himself committed murder(s).[6] Only Luke 23:19 and 25, as well as Acts 3:14, maintain this. John 18:40 calls Barabbas a λῃστής, which can mean both "robber / bandit" and "revolutionary / insurrectionist," most probably the latter here.[7] This also best explains the connection to the two λῃσταί crucified with Jesus (Mark 15:27 par.). They were not executed for merely robbing or stealing something, but ostensibly for participating in the insurrection of v 7.

It is presupposed that "the" insurrection in Mark 15:7 is known to the original Palestinian Jewish Christian hearers of this segment of the Passion Narrative, and perhaps later to the first readers of Mark's Gospel. Luke 23:19 states in this regard that "a certain insurrection" had taken place "in the city," i.e., in Jerusalem. Yet no such political revolt is recorded for the time usually associated with Jesus' crucifixion, ca. 30 CE. For this reason R. Brown, for example, thinks only of "a local riot" here.[8] Yet "the" insurrection points to something much larger, a major rebellion. The problem cannot be solved by simply assuming it was on a small scale and therefore not noted by historians such as Josephus. The problem remains.

---

[4] BAGD 764; LSJ 1633: "one who stirs up sedition." A textual variant has "fellow revolutionaries."

[5] BAGD 764,2.: "uprising, riot, revolt, rebellion." Matthew omits this term, but speaks of a "riot" (θόρυβος – BAGD 363: turmoil, excitement, uproar) as beginning in 27:24.

[6] The RSV is misleading in translating: "And among the rebels in prison, who had committed murder in the insurrection, there was a man called Barabbas." The NRSV has corrected this to: "Now a man called Barabbas was in prison with the rebels who had committed murder during the insurrection."

[7] BAGD 473.

[8] *The Death of the Messiah* 1.796; cf. "a riot" in 819. He is followed by D. Juel in *Mark* (Augsburg Commentary on the New Testament; Minneapolis: Augsburg Fortress, 1990) 215: "a small rebellion, a guerrilla action."

In addition, Matthew states in 27:16 that "they (the Roman authorities in Jerusalem) then had an ἐπίσημος prisoner[9] called Barabbas." Both the RSV and the NRSV render this adjective by "notorious" on the basis of the entire context. Yet ἐπίσημος, occurring only here in the Gospels, can also mean "prominent, outstanding."[10] It is thus possible that the model or "Vorlage" of Barabbas was a prominent Jerusalem Jew who had participated in an insurrection there, but himself had not committed murder. The historical source I describe below deals with precisely such a person.

Mark 15:6 also states that he (Pilate) used to "release" for them (the crowd or people) one prisoner whom they requested. The verb ἀπολύω means here to "set free, release, pardon" a prisoner.[11] The importance of this motif in the present narrative is emphasized by its repetition in vv 9, 11 and 15.[12]

Connected to this is the crowd's or people's "asking for" or "demanding" the release of Barabbas. This is expressed in Mark 15:6 by παραιτέομαι,[13] and in v 8 by the simple form αἰτέομαι.[14] Matt 27:20 also has the latter verb, as do Luke 23:23 and 25. Luke 23:24 speaks of the chief priests', rulers', and people's (v 13) "demand" (αἴτημα, found only here in the Gospels).[15] This motif is also conveyed by the crowd's "wanting" (θέλω) Barabbas and not Jesus in Matt 27:15 and 17, and by the noun "wish / will" (θέλημα) in Luke 23:25. In the Markan narrative, the crowd demands the release of Barabbas and the death of Jesus in 15:8, 11 and 13-14. In 23:22, Luke expressly states that Pilate attempts three separate times to release Jesus in spite of the crowd's demands.

If there were thus an historical model upon which the Barabbas narrative was based, the motifs of "releasing" and "asking for /

---

[9] The noun δέσμιος only occurs here, in v 15, and in Mark 15:6 in the Gospels. Mark 15:7 has the perf. pass. participle δεδεμένος, "imprisoned," from δέω. Luke 23:19 and 25 state that Barabbas had been thrown into "prison" (φυλακή).

[10] BAGD 298. Such is the meaning, for example, in the only other NT occurrence, Rom 16:7.

[11] BAGD 96,1.

[12] Cf. also four times in Matthew (27:15,17,21 and 26), five in John (18:39 twice; 19:10 and 12 twice, its only occurrences in John), and five in Luke (23:16, [17], 18, 20, 22, 25; see also Acts 3:13).

[13] BAGD 616,1.: ask for, request. This is the only occurrence of the verb in this sense in the Gospels.

[14] BAGD 25: ask, ask for, demand.

[15] BAGD 26: request, demand.

demanding" should be found in it. As I point out below, this is indeed the case.

The same is true for the "custom" of a Roman procurator's releasing a prisoner to the people of Jerusalem once a year at the festival of Passover. The NRSV of Mark 15:6 states of Pilate: "Now at the festival 'he used to release' a prisoner for them, anyone for whom they asked." The imperfect of ἀπολύω is employed here: ἀπέλυεν. It implies a repetition of the action.[16] The same applies to ἐποίει in v 8, where the NRSV has: "according to his custom." Matt 27:15 notes that at the festival the governor "was accustomed" to release a prisoner for the crowd, anyone whom they wanted. The verb εἴωθα here is the pluperfect of ἔθω, "to be accustomed, to be wont."[17] It is related to the noun ἔθος, "custom, habit."[18] John 18:39 has Pilate expressly tell "the Jews": "But you have 'a custom' (συνήθεια)[19] that I release someone for you at the Passover."[20] While Passover is not specifically named in the Synoptic Barabbas accounts, it is definitely the "festival" (ἑορτή) mentioned in Mark 15:6 par. This is shown by 14:1-2, 12 and 16. The nocturnal hearing of Jesus at the high priest's residence (14:53-72), the consultation with the whole council (15:1), the "trial" before Pilate (15:1-5), and the crucifixion itself all took place according to Mark during the first day of Passover, the 15th of Nisan, which extended from sundown to sundown. The Barabbas episode also took place on the same day.

Yet neither in Jewish nor Greek and Roman accounts is there one single source alluding to the custom of a Paschal pardon or amnesty by a Roman procurator in Jerusalem.[21] This leads one to ask whether "the insurrection" mentioned in Mark 15:7, which according to Luke 23:19 had taken place "in the city" (of Jerusalem), may not be based on an *earlier* historical event which also occurred in connection with Passover. Palestinian Jewish Christians may then have reshaped it into the present Barabbas narrative.

---

[16] In rabbinic Hebrew this is expressed by היה followed by a participle. Cf. the United Bible Societies' Hebrew New Testament (p. 117): הָיָה מְשַׁחְרֵר. The Aramaic could be נהג, נהיג (Jastrow 881); see also the noun מנהגא (Jastrow 797).

[17] BAGD 234. Cf. also LSJ 480. The expression ὡς εἴωθε, for example, means "as is the custom." See also Luke 4:16 and Acts 17:2 – "according to the custom of...."

[18] LSJ 480.

[19] BAGD 789,2.b: custom, habit, usage. It occurs in this sense in the NT only here and in 1 Cor 11:16.

[20] Cf. also the textually uncertain Luke 23:17, which states that Pilate was "obliged" (ἀνάγκην δὲ εἶχεν) to release someone for them at the festival.

[21] I review the evidence in *Barabbas and Esther* 2-3.

Several other relevant observations should also be made at this point. In Mark's account the crowd first remains calm and then, having been "stirred up" (ἀνασείω),[22] "cries out" or "screams" (κράζω)[23] in 15:13 (ostensibly "again"): "Crucify him!" When Pilate asks them what evil Jesus has done, the crowd gives no answer, but "cries out / screams" even louder (v 14): "Crucify him!" In 27:23 Matthew changes the aorist to the imperfect, indicating repetition. In 23:18, Luke employs ἀνακράζω, stating that the crowd shouted out "all together."[24] In v 21 Luke uses the imperfect of ἐπιφωνέω, to cry out (loudly).[25] In v 23 he notes that "they kept urgently demanding 'with loud shouts' (φωναῖς μεγάλαις) that (Jesus) should be crucified." In John 18:40 and 19:6, 12 and 15 the verb κραυγάζω is employed, "to cry out / scream" excitedly.[26] The crowd's loudly crying out / screaming / shouting is thus a major motif in the Barabbas narrative.

This crying out finally leads to Pilate's giving up on trying to release innocent Jesus. He accedes to their wishes and releases Barabbas, who is thought to be still in prison and not present with Jesus before Pilate. That is, he gives the order to have him released. After having Jesus scourged, Pilate then hands him over to be crucified (Mark 15:15).

Pilate is pictured here as wishing "to satisfy the crowd" (τῷ ὄχλῳ τὸ ἱκανὸν ποιῆσαι - v 15) through the above actions. This phrase has been thought to be a Latinism, even to indicate a Roman origin for Mark's Gospel: *satisfacere alicui* = to satisfy someone.[27] Yet the expression can also mean "to do someone a favor."[28] Both translations, however, are very improbable for the procurator, who never would have allowed himself to be subject to the whims of a crowd, especially an uncontrollable one which bordered on a riot. Pilate was well-known as having no respect for Jewish religious and national feelings. On the

---

[22] BAGD 60. The verb occurs in the NT only here and in Luke 23:5, where the chief priests and the multitudes maintain that it is Jesus himself who (seditiously, against Caesar – v 2) stirs up the people.

[23] BAGD 447.

[24] παμπληθεί: BAGD 607, only here in the NT.

[25] BAGD 304. It is found only here in the Gospels, and elsewhere only twice in Acts. It appears to be a verb preferred by Luke.

[26] BAGD 449.

[27] Cf. BAGD 374 on ἱκανὸν ποιεῖν τινι, as well as LSJ 825,II.2, and BDF § 5,3 (p. 6).

[28] *Ibid.*

contrary, his reputation was for extreme cruelty, including the execution of many innocent Jewish citizens.[29]

It is thus historically very difficult to believe in the willingness of Pilate to plead numerous times with the Jerusalem crowd for the release of Jesus. Instead, he had the prophet from Nazareth executed on the charge of claiming to be "The King of the Jews" (15:26) and thus an insurrectionist and enemy of the only real king, Caesar in Rome, Pilate's superior.[30] Nor would this military man have ever acceded to the release of a "notorious" insurrectionist, Barabbas, who would then have caused him even more major problems. It must be asked whether the very improbable picture of Pilate presented here in the Barabbas episode may rather be due to a "Vorlage," in which someone like him was willing to appease the crowd in Jerusalem by releasing prisoner/s to them at Passover. As I shall show below, this was the case.

In Mark 15:9 and 12 Pilate labels Jesus "The King of the Jews." While Pilate had already asked him whether he was this in v 2, and the inscription of the charge against Jesus read so on the Cross (v 26), it must also be asked whether the two-fold emphasis on the title in the relatively short Barabbas episode may be an intentional contrast to someone who was, or was considered, the "King of the Jews." I shall also point this out below.

Finally, as part of his special material, Matthew in 27:19 notes that during the Barabbas narrative Pilate sat on the βῆμα or "judicial bench / tribunal"[31] in Jerusalem. This noun only occurs here and in the comparable scene of John 19:13 in the Gospels. As I indicate in the following, it too plays a role in the historical "Vorlage" of the Barabbas incident.

* * *

All of the rare or unusual vocabulary, the numerous historical and psychological improbabilities,[32] and the conspicuous inconcinnities

---

[29] Cf. Luke 13:1; Josephus, *Bell.* 2.176-177 and *Ant.* 18.62; and Philo, *Leg. Gai.* 301-302, who speaks of "the executions without trial constantly repeated, the ceaseless and supremely grievous cruelty" (English by F. Colson in the LCL); as well as other sources cited in Schürer, *The history* 1.383-387.

[30] The Evangelist John emphasizes this motif in 19:12 and 15, which leads to Pilate's handing Jesus over to be crucified.

[31] BAGD 140.

[32] Cf. also the message of Pilate's wife to him in Matt 27:19, based on a dream. I proposed a possible background to this in *Barabbas and Esther* 22. See also now the dream of Glaphyra, the wife of Archelaus, in Josephus, *Bell.* 2.114-116 and *Ant.* 17.349-353. Archelaus, sitting on a *bēma* in the Jerusalem Temple before a

mentioned above indicate that the Barabbas narrative is basically a Christian composition. The following sections describe the major historical background of the episode. As I will point out at the end of this study, the incidents analyzed here were then later creatively reworked in a typically Palestinian Jewish Christian haggadic manner to produce the present forms of the Barabbas accounts in the Gospels.[33]

Section II. describes Herod the Great, "King of the Jews," who himself was once "released" or acquitted even though the Sanhedrin in Jerusalem wanted to condemn him for killing fellow Jews without a trial; his lack of respect for Jewish customs; and his great fear of insurrections, including the major one which occurred in Jerusalem shortly before his death in 4 BCE.

Section III. analyzes the latter insurrection as dealt with by his son and successor Archelaus directly after Herod's death. The scene of Archelaus on a *bēma* in the Jerusalem Temple, acceding to the demands of the crowd in regard to the recent insurrection, including the release of prisoners now at Passover, provides the major background to the Barabbas narrative in the Gospels.

Section IV. describes the popularity of the Roman governor of Syria, Vitellius, who in 36 CE performed an act of "releasing" at Passover in Jerusalem, which aided a Palestinian Jewish Christian in connecting motifs from the insurrection episode of 4 BCE to ca. 30 CE. Section V. then deals with the original language and date of the Barabbas narrative, and Section VI. concludes with the purpose(s) of the original account and Mark's redaction of it.

II. An Insurrection in Jerusalem in 4 BCE

Before analyzing the major insurrection in Jerusalem against Herod's rule at the very end of his life in 4 BCE ("D"), it will be helpful to briefly sketch A) his own "release" from the Jewish high court there, B) his lack of respect for Jewish religious beliefs and customs, and C) his great fear of insurrections and how he handled them.

In the following I employ two major sources, both by Josephus. The Jewish historian, a native of Jerusalem born in 37/38 CE, first wrote his account of the Jewish-Roman war of 66-70 CE *(Bellum)* in his native

---

shouting crowd, like Pilate, plays a major role in the historical "Vorlage" of the Barabbas narrative. See below.

[33] I by no means wish to underestimate the independent literary artistry of the individual Gospel writers, especially that of Matthew and Luke, who had Mark before them, as well as access to special traditions.

tongue, Aramaic.[34] This version is unfortunately lost. The Greek version, which appeared sometime between 75-79 CE and was in part compiled with the aid of King Agrippa II, Herod's great-grandson, and some of his relatives, was a complete rewriting of the Aramaic.[35] The much more expansive *Jewish Antiquities* were completed by Josephus in 93-94 CE (*Ant.* 20.267).

A) *Herod's "Release" and "Releasing / Remitting."*

In *Bell.* 1.204-215 and *Ant.* 14.158-184, Josephus describes how the youthful Herod killed the bandit chief Ezekias and many of the bandits with him on the border to Syria. The chief Jews of Jerusalem maintained that this violated the Law, "which forbids us to slay a man, even an evildoer, unless he has first been condemned by the Synhedrion to suffer this fate."[36] The mothers of the murdered bandits begged Hyrcanus daily in the Jerusalem Temple to have the Sanhedrin try Herod there. Hyrcanus thereupon summoned him, yet Sextus, the Roman governor of Syria, wrote Hyrcanus to "release" or acquit (ἀπολῦσαι) him of the charges.[37] At Herod's trial, one of the members of the council, Samaias, rebuked the other members for their cowardice in not condemning Herod, who had dared to appear there with troops in order to kill them if they condemned him. Samaias maintained that out of respect for Hyrcanus they wished to "release" (ἀπολῦσαι) Herod.[38] Hyrcanus noted that the Sanhedrin intended to put Herod to death, so he advised the latter to escape, and he went off to Damascus. Angry because of his treatment before the Sanhedrin, Herod later returned with an army to attack Jerusalem. Yet his father and brother requested him to recall his "release / acquittal" (ἄφεσις).[39] Later, however, when he became king,

---

[34] Cf. *Bell.* 1.3. See also *Vita* 5 for his birth date, and 7 for Jerusalem.

[35] Cf. H. Thackeray's remarks in LCL II.ix-xii. On King Agrippa II, see *Vita* 362-366, promising little known, personal information to Josephus. Agrippa II was the son of Agrippa I, who in turn was the son of Aristobulus, the son of Herod the Great. On Agrippa II, see Schürer, *The history* 1.471-483; on Herod the Great, 1.287-329. For the latter, see especially A. Schalit, *König Herodes. Der Mann und sein Werk* (SJ IV; Berlin: de Gruyter, 1969).

[36] *Ant.* 14.167; cf. *Bell.* 1.209. The translation is that of R. Marcus. The statement is also relevant to Jesus' "trial" before the Sanhedrin.

[37] *Ant.* 14.170; cf. *Bell.* 1.211. The latter reference also employs ἀποψηφίζομαι (LSJ 228) for voting death away from one, refusing to condemn one; acquitting.

[38] *Ant.* 14.174. In 179 Hyrcanus' cowardice is mentioned.

[39] *Ant.* 14.182; *Bell.* 1.214.

out of revenge Herod killed everyone in the Sanhedrin except Samaias (*Ant.* 14.175).[40]

Here Herod the Great is not condemned to death by the Jerusalem Sanhedrin for murdering persons without a trial. Due to Roman pressure, Hyrcanus instead "releases" him. The same verb, ἀπολύω, is employed here as in the Barabbas narrative.

The noun ἄφεσις, applied here to Herod's "release,"[41] can also be employed for the release or "remission" of taxes. Since this is relevant to Sections III. and IV. below, it should be noted already at this point that Herod levied extremely heavy taxes upon the inhabitants of his kingdom. This was partly due to his extensive building activity, as well as to his support for other (non-Jewish) projects abroad, which impoverished his own people.[42]

However, at times Herod "remitted" taxes. To appease his citizens, who thought he disdained their religion and customs, ca. 20 BCE he remitted (ἀφίημι) a third of their taxes (*Ant.* 15. 365). Perhaps in 14 BCE, Herod also proclaimed to the assembled inhabitants of Jerusalem that he would remit (ἀφίημι) a fourth of the taxes from the past year (*Ant.* 16.64).[43]

The Greek verbs ἀπολύω and ἀφίημι, with the noun ἄφεσις, can thus mean not only the "release" or acquittal of a person on trial, but also the release or remission of taxes. The same is true for the Semitic verb שבק and the noun שיבוקא.[44] Both meanings are important in regard to the sources to be analyzed in Sections III. and IV. below.

---

[40] On this, cf. the similar incident with Baba b. Buta in *b. B. Bat.* 3b-4a (Soncino 10-11); *Num. Rab.* Naso 14/8 on Num 7:64 (Soncino 6.603); and Josephus, *Ant.* 15.259-266.

[41] LSJ 288: letting go, release. With φόνος it means "quittance" from murder. The verb ἀφίημι (LSJ 290, II.b) can mean to "acquit" of a charge, to acquit someone of murder.

[42] Cf. *Ant.* 17.304-308, which mentions the annual tribute on everyone, as well as bribery; 17.204; and *Bell.* 2.4. See also Schürer, *The history* 1.416, and Schalit, *König Herodes* 262-298, for the sources of Herod's income. On the building projects at home and abroad, as well as Herod's support for foreign cities and the Olympic games, see *Bell.* 1.401-428.

[43] On the date, cf. n. "b" in VIII. 215 of the LCL edition.

[44] Cf. Jastrow 1516-1517 and 1557, together with the examples I cite in *Barabbas and Esther* 19-21. There I also call attention to the nouns דּוֹרִיָה and דְּרוֹר (Jastrow 290 and 322) as remission of tribute or fine, pardon; amnesty. To my knowledge the verb שחרר, to set free (Jastrow 1552; the cognate noun is שִׁחְרוּר, 1560), is not also employed of taxes. It is primarily used of the emancipation of slaves.

B)	*Herod's Lack of Respect for Jewish Religious Beliefs and Customs.*

Josephus notes in *Ant.* 15. 267 that Herod departed in major ways from "the native customs" (τῶν πατρίων ἐθνῶν), which led to piety (εὐσέβεια) among the people. Instead, by introducing foreign practices, "he gradually corrupted the ancient way of life." He "established athletic contests every fifth year in honour of Caesar, and he built a theatre in Jerusalem, and after that a very large amphitheatre," which were against Jewish customs (268). Athletes from many different countries, chariot races, wild beasts such as lions which fought against each other or condemned men, were all extremely costly. For the Jews, however, "it meant an open break with the customs (τῶν...ἐθῶν) held in honour by them" (274). Such behavior was "impious" (ἀσεβές – 275). While Herod, in order to pacify the people, removed the ornaments on the trophies which had been set up in the area of the contests, about ten of his opponents continued in their belief that the activities named above were against their tradition (ἔθος), that these violated their national customs (τὰ πάτρια – 281). When the men then tried to kill Herod in the theatre with their daggers, an informant caused them to be apprehended, and they were executed after being severely tortured (281-290).

The above is a concrete example of the Jews' strong conviction that Herod had disrespect for their religious beliefs and customs. Another instance of this was his later erecting a large golden eagle over the great gate of the Jerusalem Temple. It led to the major insurrection of relevance to the Barabbas narrative, and I shall describe it in D) below.

C)	*Herod's Fear of Insurrection and His Preventive Measures.*

The attempt on his life described above led Herod to fear open rebellion (ἀπόστασις – *Ant.* 15. 291), so that he built various fortresses within his realm in addition to maintaining a system of informers (295). He allowed no public meetings, no one was allowed to walk together with others, all were carefully observed. If someone was caught, the punishment was severe, and many were taken to the fortress of Hyrcania SE of Jerusalem and murdered there. Herod himself was reported to put on civilian clothes and mingle among the crowds in order to perceive their mood towards him. Those who disagreed with the above measures were persecuted. Finally, Herod even demanded from all citizens an oath of loyalty that they would agree to his rule.[45]

---

[45] *Ant.* 15.366-370. Only several leading scholars and the Essenes were exempted from taking the oath.

This thumbnail sketch provides the background to the major insurrection of relevance to the Barabbas narrative.

D) *The Jerusalem Insurrection of 4 BCE Shortly Before Passover.*

In *Bell.* 1.648-655 and *Ant.* 17.149-167, Josephus describes how Herod, who died at about the age of seventy,[46] had to come to terms with a major insurrection at the very end of his life in 4 BCE.

In Jerusalem there were at this time two scholars, the most learned of the Jews, "unrivaled interpreters of the ancestral laws," or "profound experts in the laws of their country," and highly esteemed by the whole nation because of their lectures on the laws, which were attended daily (in the Temple) by a large number of young men.[47] Their names were Judas the son of Sariphaeus or Sepphoraeus, and Matthias the son of Margalothus or Margalus.[48] When they learned that Herod's sickness was terminal, they "aroused" or "stirred up" (ἐξαίρω)[49] these youth to "pull down all the works built by the king in violation of the laws of their fathers."[50] It was against the Law to set up in the Temple images or busts or a work with the name of any living being.[51] Yet with much expense Herod had nevertheless erected a golden eagle as a votive offering over the great gate of the Temple. The same scholars and their adherents had reproached Herod about this matter before.[52]

When a rumor spread that Herod had died, the two scholars' "stirring up" (ἐξαίρω) their disciples caused the latter to take action. At noon they ascended (to the roof of the Temple), pulled down the eagle, and cut it up with axes. The head officer approached with a force of Temple police, however, and arrested at least forty of the youth, as well as Judas and Matthias. Brought to Herod, they defended their action before him.[53]

---

[46] *Bell.* 1.647 and *Ant.* 17.148. Since the two accounts appear to derive in part from separate sources, I cite from the relevant sections of each. The reader should always compare both.

[47] *Ant.* 17.149 and *Bell.* 1.648-649.

[48] On the Greek variants to their names, cf. Schalit, *König Herodes* 638, who also proposes Semitic equivalents.

[49] LSJ 582,3.

[50] *Ant.* 17.150; cf. *Bell.* 1.649.

[51] This was based on the First Commandment. See Exod 20:3-6.

[52] *Ant.* 17.150-151; *Bell.* 1.649-650.

[53] *Ant.* 17.155-160; *Bell.* 1.651-653.

At this point the shorter account in *Bellum* differs from that in *Antiquities*. *Bell.* 1.654-655 says that Herod then had himself brought to a public assembly (presumably in Jerusalem), where he castigated the men's false zeal for the Law. Since he suspected they actually intended something else (insurrection), he demanded their punishment. The assembled people, in fear of their own lives, asked Herod only to punish the actual perpetrators and those who instigated the matter. Consenting, Herod had those who let themselves down from the roof and the (two) scholars burned alive. He then handed over the others who had been arrested to his adjutants ἀνελεῖν. The verb ἀναιρέω can mean both to take up and carry off, bear away (here to prison), and to make away with, destroy, kill.[54] While the latter meaning is probable here in Greek, the Aramaic original may well have meant "to bear away" (to prison to be sentenced later). As I shall point out in Section III. below, the releasing of prisoners by Archelaus after Herod's death in part very probably refers back to these men.

The *Antiquities* version in 17.160-167, in contrast, relates that Herod had those arrested bound and sent to Jericho. He then summoned the Jewish magistrates (from Jerusalem) and had them all gather in the amphitheatre. From a couch he defended his votive offering and castigated the sacrilegious deed of those who pulled it down. He then deposed the high priest Matthias from office for partial responsibility for the deed. "As for the other Matthias, who had 'stirred up the sedition' (ἐγηγέρκει τὴν στάσιν), he burnt him alive along with some of his companions." Josephus in conclusion notes that there was an eclipse of the moon that night, (which was March 13, 4 BCE).[55]

It should be noted here that in contrast to the *Bellum* account, only the scholar Matthias "and some of his companions" (καὶ ἄνδρας ἐκ τῶν ἑταίρων αὐτοῦ) are mentioned as being burned alive. If the other famous scholar, Judas, had been in his source, Josephus would certainly have mentioned him. The account thus appears to assume (in spite of 17. 157 and 214) that Judas and others who were not burned alive were imprisoned. This is important for the possible identity of "Barabbas" in Section V. below.

Finally, it is striking here that one Matthias, the high priest, is deposed from office for his involvement in the insurrection. "The other Matthias," the instigator of the insurrection, is killed. Some MSS of Matt 27:16 and 17 read "Jesus Barabbas," who in v 17 would then be contrasted to "Jesus Christ." Here too, one man is let off and the other is

---

[54] LSJ 106.

[55] Translation by R. Marcus. On the date of the eclipse, cf. n. "b" in VIII. 449.

killed. The source of the variant Matthean account may have borrowed this motif from the incident related above.

* * *

The preceding description of the insurrection (στάσις) against Herod the Great in the early spring of 4 BCE in Jerusalem is very important for the populace's reaction to his death, which occurred only shortly thereafter. His son and successor, Archelaus, had to deal with the consequences of this insurrection at the festival of Passover. To this I now turn.

III. Archelaus' Handling of the Insurrection, with a Release of Prisoners

In *Bell.* 2.1-13 and *Ant.* 17.200-218 Josephus describes how, after the death of his father Herod, Archelaus dealt with the insurrection described above. While analyzing the incident, I shall point out the many striking similarities to the Barabbas narrative.

1. A *bēma*.

After mourning for seven days and feasting the crowds in Jerusalem, Archelaus went up to the Temple (τὸ ἱερόν). Well received by the populace, he ascended an elevated platform (βῆμα) which had been made and sat down on a throne of gold,[56] from which he addressed the mass of the people.[57] This recalls the Jerusalem crowd scene and the specific mention of the *bēma* of Pilate in the Barabbas narrative at Matt 27:19 and John 19:13, the only occurrences of the term in the Gospels.[58] The Matthean passage with *bēma* attests the further development of the Markan account, while the Johannine occurrence most probably points to an independent development of the tradition.

---

[56] This is also referred to in *Bell.* 2.27 and *Ant.* 17.232.

[57] *Bell.* 2.2 and *Ant.* 17.201. While *Bellum* has τὸ πλῆθος, *Antiquities* reads τοὺς ὁμίλους. On the latter, cf. LSJ 1222: any assembled throng of people; esp. the mass of the people, the crowd; mob.

[58] For the *bēma* or tribunal of Pilate in Jerusalem in connection with a tumult (ταραχή: LSJ 1758) at which the multitude shouted out, cf. Josephus, *Bell.* 2.175 and 176. The parallel in *Ant.* 18.60-62 speaks of many thousands who cried out at this insurrection (στάσις) by rioters (θορυβέω). In *Ant.* 18.57, Pilate's *bēma* in the stadium of Caesarea is mentioned. Josephus also notes in 14.228 that the consul Lucius Lentulus "released" (ἀπολύω) before his tribunal those Jews in Ephesus from military service who were Roman citizens. See also 230, and 240, where they are described as being "accustomed" (εἰώθασιν) to observing Jewish rites there. Pilate's "releasing" Barabbas from his tribunal should be compared.

2. The Crowd.

First the crowd (ὄχλος)[59] praised Archelaus. The same term is employed for the "crowd" before Pilate in Mark 15:8, 11 and 15, as well as in Matt 27:15 and 24.

3. Requests / Demands.

Then the crowd made "requests" (αἰτήσεις) for favors from Archelaus (*Ant.* 17.204; cf. also 209). In *Bell.* 2.4, Josephus describes these as "large demands" (μεγάλοις αἰτήμασιν). *Ant.* 17.232 refers back to them as Archelaus' having assented to "the requests (αἰτήσεων) of those making a petition (αἰτουμένοις) in public."[60] The three requests are then listed in *Ant.* 17.204-205 and *Bell.* 2.4.

The requesting / demanding and the requests / demands made here recall the Jerusalem crowd's παραιτέομαι in Mark 15:6; the αἰτέομαι in 15:8, Matt 27:20, and Luke 23:23 and 25, as well as the αἴτημα in Luke 23:24; and θέλω in Matt 27:15 and 17, with θέλημα in Luke 23:25. It is striking that, as there are three requests or demands in the Archelaus scene, so Pilate responds three times to the crowd's demands (expressly stated in Luke 23:22). While no number appears in the Markan narrative, the triad is also found in 15:8, 11 and 13-14.

4. Crying Out.

In the Archelaus narrative the crowd at this point "cried out" in its demands. *Bell.* 2.4 employs the verb βοάω, while *Ant.* 17.204 has the noun βοή.[61] The crowd later continues its crying out in *Bell.* 2.7 (ἀναβοάω), and in *Ant.* 17.206 (βοή) and 210 (βοάω).

This crying out or shouting of the crowd before Archelaus recalls the crowd's κράζω before Pilate in Mark 15:13 and 14 and Matt 27:23. Luke 23:18 has ἀνακράζω, in v 21 ἐπιφωνέω, and in v 23 φωναῖς μεγάλαις. John 18:40, as well as 19:6, 12 and 15, employ the verb κραυγάζω. All these terms have the same meaning of crying out, shouting.

5. Releasing Prisoners.

In the Archelaus scene the crowd made three requests / demands. 1) Some of them cried out that Archelaus should lighten their annual

---

[59] *Ant.* 17.204. BAGD 600 has crowd, throng, (multitude) of people. *Bell.* 2.4 again reads τὸ πλῆθος.

[60] *Bell.* 2.28 paraphrases this.

[61] The verb βοάω means to cry aloud, shout (LSJ 319), the noun the same (320).

taxes (εἰσφοραί), i.e. they wanted a reduction in the excessive annual tax Herod levied. 2) Some demanded the "release" (ἀπόλυσις) of the prisoners (pl. of δεσμότης) who had been incarcerated by Herod, (for these were many and of long duration). 3) Some demanded the removal (pl. of ἄρσις) of the duties which "had been levied upon public purchases and sales and which had been ruthlessly exacted" (*Ant.* 17.204-205). *Bell.* 2.4 places the second request last: "some (demanded that he) 'release' (ἀπολύειν) the prisoners." Here no mention is made of "older" prisoners, and the reader assumes that those taken by Herod at the recent insurrection and not executed are meant.

In *Ant.* 17.205 Josephus states that Archelaus by no means opposed (ἀντιλέγω – these requests). In *Bell.* 2.4 this is more explicit. Archelaus readily "assented" (ἐπινεύω)[62] to all (three of the demands). Then he made a sacrifice in the Temple and participated in a banquet with his friends.

The texts here do not explicitly mention an order of Archelaus to "release" the prisoners taken by his father Herod at the recent insurrection. Yet in *Bell.* 2.28 he was later reproached before Caesar in Rome for having "released" (λύσας) those imprisoned by his father for the most important reasons, (certainly including the recent open rebellion).[63] The context thus suggests that those participants who were not burned to death or executed after the incident of the golden eagle were imprisoned, as I interpreted *Bell.* 1.655 and *Ant.* 17.167 above. Archelaus, sitting on a *bēma* in the Jerusalem Temple, with the crowd shouting out and making demands before him, is thus most probably pictured here as also "releasing" those left in prison from the recent insurrection.

I suggest that this is the background for Pilate, who, sitting on a *bēma* in Jerusalem, with the crowd shouting out and making demands of him, "released" Barabbas to them. He was one of the prisoners from "the" insurrection. In both the Archelaus and Pilate scenes, the verb ἀπολύω

---

[62] LSJ 648: nod to, nod assent; approve; grant.

[63] *Ant.* 17.232 refers to Archelaus' assenting to the requests of those who publicly petitioned him (in the Jerusalem Temple). In 233 the speaker reproaches him for another, separate act, the release (ἄφεσις) of prisoners from the hippodrome (in Jericho). The latter were notable Jews from all over the nation (174-175), whom Herod wanted to have killed at his death so that the whole country would mourn. They, however, were later dismissed by others (193). In *The Death of the Messiah* 1.818, R. Brown notes *Bell.* 2.28, yet he does not connect it to Passover and its customs. A. Schlatter on Matt 27:15 had already called attention to *Bell.* 2.4 in his *Der Evangelist Matthäus* (Stuttgart: Calwer, 1929) 771.

(together with the noun ἀπόλυσις) plays a decisive role, emphasized by its repetition, for example in Mark 15:6, 9, 11 and 15.

At the end of this Section, number 9., I will also propose that the name "Barabbas" may derive from a major imprisoned participant in the insurrection against Herod.

The above proposal in regard to the release of someone imprisoned for insurrection is made even more probable by the following related motif in the same Archelaus scene.

6.   *Flattering / Conciliating.*

Josephus relates in *Bell.* 2.4 that when the Jerusalem crowd made its three requests, Archelaus readily assented to all of them, "θεραπεύων the multitude." The verb θεραπεύω here means to "pay court to, flatter, wheedle, conciliate."[64] Archelaus was both attempting to "ingratiate" himself with the crowd, and to "placate / appease / conciliate" it. He wanted to gain its favor in regard to his future reign as king over them, but also in order to show his understanding for their grievances, which were many and justified.[65]

This motif is the background for Mark 15:15, "So Pilate, wishing 'to satisfy the crowd' (τῷ ὄχλῳ τὸ ἱκανὸν ποιῆσαι), released Barabbas for them." As indicated in the Introduction, the Greek can mean to satisfy, but also to do someone a favor. The same is true for θεραπεύω. It is thus very improbable that the Markan phrase is a Latinism, *satisfacere*. It is also historically very improbable that Pilate, known for his extreme cruelty and disrespect for Jewish customs, as the Roman procurator would have assented to the release of an insurrectionist. His ingratiating, conciliatory behavior in regard to releasing a prisoner is rather due to the background of the scene in the Archelaus episode.

7.   *The Festival of Passover and Ancestral Custom.*

The latter sentence in 6. is also true for the festival of Passover. First Archelaus attempted to conciliate the Jerusalem crowd, after which he banqueted with his friends. Then the revolutionaries, who out of fear of Herod had not been able to mourn those convicted of pulling down and cutting up the golden eagle from the Temple gate, on the same evening

---

[64] LSJ 793, II.2. *Ant.* 17.204 employs the adverb θεραπευτικῶς before the requests. While preceded by "mildly," due to its root it can also mean in an ingratiating, conciliatory way.

[65] Cf. the end of *Bell.* 2.3, and especially *Ant.* 17.201 and 203. See also Archelaus' assent to the removal of the high priest in 17.207. It is treated differently in *Bell.* 2.7-8.

began to scream (βοή and ἀναβοάω) and wail for the victims who had died on behalf of their ancestral laws and the Temple. Archelaus thus feared a political uproar (κίνημα). He counseled them that the appearance of insurrection (στασιάζω) should not be made. The danger of an insurrection (στάσις) was growing fast, however, because a mass of people was now entering Jerusalem.[66]

a) *The Festival of Passover.*

The pilgrimage "festival" (ἑορτή) of Passover, also called Unleavened Bread, had now arrived (*Ant.* 17.213 and *Bell.* 2.10). The same "festival" is also mentioned in *Ant.* 17.218, 230 and 237, and *Bell.* 2.13 and 30.

This is the background of the "festival" (ἑορτή) in Mark 15:6 and Matt 27:15, equated with Passover in John 18:39 (cf. also Mark 14:2 and 1; Matt 26:5 and 2; Luke 22:1; and John 13:1, 29).

b) *Ancestral Custom.*

For his non-Jewish readers, Josephus at this point in *Bell.* 2.10 simply notes that the festival of Unleavened Bread, called by the Jews Passover, "is an occasion for the contribution of a multitude of sacrifices, and a vast crowd streamed in from the country for the ceremony." In *Ant.* 17.213-214, however, he describes it more extensively:

> At this time there came round the festival during which it is "the ancestral custom" of the Jews to serve unleavened bread. The festival is called Passover, being a commemoration of their departure from Egypt. They celebrate it with gladness, and "it is their custom" to slaughter a greater number of sacrifices at this (festival) than at any other, and an innumerable multitude of people come down from the country and even from abroad to worship God.[67]

The Greek for "the ancestral custom" here is πάτριον. This had become a technical term. In LSJ 1348 πάτριόν ἐστιν (sc. αὐτοῖς) is defined as "it is 'an hereditary custom' [among them]." τὰ πάτρια are "hereditary customs."

The second phrase in the above quotation, "it is their custom" (ἐστὶν αὐτοῖς νόμιμον), is very similar. νόμιμος means "conformable to custom, usage, or law"; "customary, prescriptive." The verb νομίζω with the

---

[66] Cf. *Ant.* 17.206-212 and *Bell.* 2.5-9.

[67] English by R. Marcus in the LCL edition, which I have only altered at one point. Josephus as a native of Jerusalem would not have written "come down," but "come up" to the city. Perhaps a Greek assistant chose the term. Cf. also n. "c" on 17.214. See also *Ant.* 2.313 for the feast *Pascha*, celebrated κατὰ τὸ ἔθος.

infinitive is defined as "'to be accustomed' to do," and νομίζεται with the infinitive as "'it is customary' for them to....."[68]

I propose that the strong emphasis here on what is "customary" at Passover formed the background for a Palestinian Jewish Christian who described the Barabbas scene in terms of the Archelaus insurrection episode.

In the Introduction I pointed out the various terms employed in the four Gospels for the "custom" of releasing a prisoner at the festival (of Passover), from the imperfect verbs in Mark 15:6 (ἀπολύω) and 8 (ποιέω), to the pluperfect of ἔθω in Matt 27:15, to the noun συνήθεια in John 18:39.

It should also be noted that the Passover "custom" in Josephus is described directly after the crowd demanded from Archelaus the release of prisoners from the recent insurrection. It was thus easy for another person aware of this account in a Semitic source to associate the two and make out of them a Passover "custom" on the part of a ruler in Jerusalem. As J. Bauer has shown, the invention of such a custom within a narrative is also known from elsewhere.[69]

*   *   *

One factor which made the Passover festival of 4 BCE stick in the minds of Palestinian Jews for so long was the terrible bloodshed which took place at this time. The followers of Judas and Matthias now stood together in the Temple, gathering more adherents for their insurrection (στάσις). In his effort to prevent it from spreading to the multitude of the pilgrims, Archelaus dispatched a tribune with a cohort of soldiers, especially to arrest the leaders of the *stasis*. Angered by the appearance of the military, the people threw stones at them, killing most of the cohort. This in turn caused Archelaus to send his entire army, together with the cavalry, against them, killing about 3000 people. Josephus relates that the massacre occurred at the very moment the people were sacrificing around the sanctuary (ναός). It was thus probably on the late afternoon of the fourteenth of Nisan[70] when thousands of people slaughtered their Passover lambs in the Temple in order to eat them together at home in the evening, when the fifteenth of Nisan or first day of the festival actually began. The worshipers, both foreigners and Palestinian Jews, were themselves slaughtered "just like sacrificial victims." An opponent

---

[68] Cf. LSJ 1179 for both the noun and the verb (I.4).

[69] Cf. the examples he cites from Apuleius, Aristophanes and Vergil in "'Literarische' Namen und 'literarische' Bräuche (zu Joh 2,10 und 18,39)" in *BZ* n.s. 26 (1982) 258-264, especially his reference to F. Fröhlke on p. 262.

[70] Cf. Exod 12:6, "between the two evenings."

of Archelaus later in Rome described these victims as "poor people who had come for a festival and, while offering their sacrifices, had themselves been brutally immolated." This filled the Temple with more corpses than a foreign army would have produced.[71]

The utter brutality of Archelaus, and the extremely high number of innocent victims (ca. 3000), caused this incidence of insurrection at Passover in Jerusalem to remain imprinted in the minds of Palestinian Jews for a very long time, including that of the Jewish Christian author of the Barabbas narrative. It may also be reflected in two other Gospel accounts.[72]

Before making a proposal in regard to the origin of the name "Barabbas" itself, I would like to make one more point of comparison between the Archelaus and the Pilate / Barabbas episodes.

8. *The King of the Jews.*

In Rome Herod's friend Antony caused Octavian and the Senate to make Herod "the King of the Jews" in 40 BCE: βασιλεὺς Ἰουδαίων.[73] For thirty-six years he bore this title until his death in 4 BCE. That is, when Judas and Matthias and their followers had to answer for their causing the golden eagle over the large gate of the Jerusalem Temple to be removed just before Herod died, they stood before the King of the Jews.

In his final testament Herod named his son Archelaus his successor. This decision, however, had to be confirmed by Caesar in Rome. When Herod died, the army at Jericho already then wanted to place the diadem on Archelaus' head, which he rejected. Nevertheless, after Herod's funeral he addressed the multitude in the Temple from a "golden

---

[71] *Bell.* 2.30; cf. also *Ant.* 17.237. On the whole incident, see *Bell.* 2.10-13 and *Ant.* 17.214-218. On the similarity of Archelaus' and Pilate's actions in this regard, see Luke 13:1.

[72] Archelaus' slaughter of some 3000 people could provide the background to Matthew's remark in 2:22. Joseph, having heard that Archelaus now ruled in Judea instead of his father Herod, "was afraid" to go there and thus proceeded on to Nazareth. Archelaus' massacre may also stand behind Luke 19:27 ("slay [these enemies] before me"), part of Jesus' parable of the pounds (vv 12-27). It deals with a nobleman who went off to a far country to receive a kingdom, as Archelaus proceeded to Rome to have his kingship confirmed by Caesar. A counter faction opposed it there (cf. v 14) because he was so severe / cruel (vv 21-22). On a pre-Lucan form of this parable, see J. Jeremias, *The Parables of Jesus* (New York: Scribner's, 1963) 59. He considers the massacre to have taken place after Archelaus' return to Judea, yet it occurred before he left for Rome.

[73] See *Bell.* 1.282, and *Ant.* 14.385, with reference to Strabo, Appian and Tacitus in n. "h." See also *Bell.* 1.665 and *Ant.* 17.191.

throne" on a *bēma* erected there.[74] He told them that he reckoned with his being declared King, (i.e. King of the Jews, with the same title and kingdom as his father). Later in Rome his adversaries maintained that at this point Archelaus had already acted as King, performing the deeds mentioned above as well as similar ones.[75]

That is, when the followers of Judas and Matthias in Jerusalem demanded the "release" of those who had been imprisoned by his father Herod after the insurrection and Archelaus acceded to this, they regarded him already at that moment as their king, the King of the Jews, even if the formal recognition of this title by Caesar had not yet been granted.[76]

Archelaus as "the King of the Jews" *in spe* thus may have provided a foil to Jesus as "the King of the Jews" in the Barabbas narrative at Mark 15:9 and 12 (cf. also vv 2 and 26). The crowd shouted for the release of Barabbas, someone taken prisoner with the insurrectionists who had committed murder in "the" insurrection (v 7). The first hearers of this episode before it entered the Gospels, Palestinian Jewish Christians, may have been aware of its background in the Archelaus insurrection episode. If so, they would have appreciated the portrayal of Pilate partially in terms of Archelaus, the King of the Jews *in spe*. The Roman procurator, representing the only true king / Caesar in Rome, Tiberias, attempts to release Jesus, whom he twice calls "the King of the Jews" within the short span of ten verses.

9. *The Name Barabbas.*

Finally, I would like to make a proposal in regard to the origin of the enigmatic name "Barabbas" (Βαραββᾶs). Because so many of the expressions and motifs in the Pilate / Barabbas narrative derive from the episode of the insurrection under Judas and Matthias, it is reasonable to ask whether the name Barabbas could also come from there.

As noted above, Josephus calls both Judas and Matthias σοφισταί.[77] He is not influenced by the LXX in this respect, for there *sophistai* are foreign wise men except for Dan 4:18, where Daniel is labeled "head of the *sophistai*." Nor does Josephus mean the Greek Sophists, unless

---

[74] *Bell.* 2.1-3; *Ant.* 17.201-203.

[75] *Bell.* 2.26-28; *Ant.* 17.231-236.

[76] Cf. *Ant.* 17.204 and Josephus' already speaking of him as king in 206.

[77] *Bell.* 1.648, 650, 655-656 and 2.10; *Ant.* 17.152, 155. The only other occurrences of the term in Josephus are for Judas the Galilean (*Bell.* 2.118) and his son Menahem (2.433, 445), and "reprobate sophists" in *Ap.* 2.236.

sophistēs is reduced to a "sage" here.[78] Rather, he is trying to express for non-Jewish readers what Judas and Matthias stood for. In *Ant.* 17.149 Josephus calls them ἐξηγηταὶ τῶν πατρίων νόμων, "interpreters of the ancestral laws" (cf. also 214 and 216). He says they were the most learned or erudite of the Jews and educated the youth, which made them very popular with the people (of Jerusalem). In *Bell.* 1.648 the Jewish historian notes that in the city they were very highly reputed (μάλιστα δοκοῦντες) for their exacting investigations of the laws of the country. Because of this, they were deemed worthy of great honor by the whole nation. When they interpreted the laws, an army of young men attended (649).

In other words, Judas and Matthias were the most famous "rabbis" of the time.[79] The term רִבִּי, later a title, is literally "my *teacher*, my master."[80] A rabbi was considered more than a חָכָם, a wise man or scholar, itself also later a title.[81] Unfortunately, it is notoriously difficult to date the times when these designations were first employed.[82] The same is true for רִבָּן, which also means chief, *teacher*.[83] Both Judas and Matthias, the most prominent teachers of the Law in Jerusalem in 4 BCE, could each have already been designated as a *rabban*, meant primarily as teacher. Another usage of the term is as a proper title for a scholar. In this case, for example, the first would have been called Rabban Judas, bar (son of) Sepphoraeus.

A third use of *rabban* is as a special honorary title given to scholars as of the time of Gamaliel I, the Elder, the grandson of Hillel, active ca. 25-50 CE and according to Acts 5:34 "a teacher of the law, held in honor by all the people."[84] Since Judas and Matthias were the most learned of the Jews in Jerusalem in regard to "teaching" the laws to the youth, they were deemed worthy of great honor by the whole nation (see above). This recalls the similar description of Rabban Gamaliel in Acts 5:34. However, the special honorary title "Rabban" may not have already been applied to teachers before Gamaliel I, the Elder.

---

[78] LSJ 1622.

[79] Schürer employs this term in *The history* 1.294, 325 and 330.

[80] Jastrow 1442.

[81] *Ibid.*, 463.

[82] Cf. also "Rabbouni" in Mark 10:51 and John 20:16 (defined as "teacher").

[83] Jastrow 1444.

[84] Cf. Acts 22:3 and the many Tannaitic instances of him as "Rabban" cited in Str-B 2.636-639. Billerbeck correctly calls attention to the fact that Gamaliel was not also designated Nasi. That title was retroactively applied to him.

It is therefore best to presuppose the Aramaic plural of *rabban*, רַבָּנִי or רַבָּנָן,[85] behind *sophistai* as employed by Josephus for Judas and Matthias. They are the highly reputed "teachers" of the Law who incited their disciples to carry out the insurrection of 4 BCE in Jerusalem, with its terrible death toll of some 3000 victims.

As I noted above, one source which Josephus employs emphasizes that Herod the Great had Matthias, who had incited (sing.) the insurrection, burned alive as well as some of his companions (*Ant.* 17.167). In 206 some of the Jews who desired sedition later began to mourn in Jerusalem for Matthias and those killed with him by Herod. Here Matthias is emphasized as the ringleader, and Judas is not mentioned by name, which one would expect (as in 214). According to this source, then, it is possible that later Palestinian hearers or readers of this pre-Josephus tradition believed that "Rabban" Judas was first sent to prison by Herod. Archelaus then acceded to the crowd's shouting out in Jerusalem and released to them the prisoners taken in the insurrection, even including Judas.[86] This could explain why Matt 27:16 has Barabbas as a "prominent" prisoner.[87]

Judas is thought of here as *Rabban*, a prominent "teacher." Since Palestinian Jewish Christians knew he was not active at the time of Jesus, the author of the Christian narrative of Pilate's releasing a prisoner at Passover may himself simply have added here Bar (son) to Rabban. "Bar" before another name often became a proper name among later rabbis, such as the fifth generation Tanna Bar Qappara and his nephew Bar Pedayah.[88] The Aramaic in the course of many years of oral

---

[85] Jastrow 1444. It should be recalled that the first version of Josephus' *Bellum* was in Aramaic. The plural רבנין is employed of "teachers" for example in association with disciples in *Cant. Rab.* 1:10 § 2 (Donsqi 51, Soncino 9.74), and רבנן of "teachers" in connection with wisdom in *Gen. Rab.* Ḥayye Sarah 61/1 on Gen 25:1 (Theodor and Albeck 657, Soncino 2.540, Neusner 2.331). Examples from Jastrow.

[86] Cf. *Bell.* 2.28 for the assertion that Archelaus released those imprisoned by his father for the most severe reasons (Thackeray: "the gravest crimes"), certainly including the recent insurrection.

[87] Cf. also some textual witnesses in John 18:40, which have Barabbas as an ἀρχιληστής, a "chief" insurrectionist (Brown, *The Death of the Messiah* 1.797, n. 19).

[88] Cf. Strack and Stemberger, *Introduction* 90-91 and 92. For other names beginning with Bar, see Str-B 5/6.126-127, and the index volume of the Soncino edition of the Babylonian Talmud (18.637). No rabbi is known who was simply called Bar Abba. There was, however, someone by the name of Naḥman bar Abba, for which one textual tradition has Naḥman Bar Rabba (רבא or רבה). See *b. Šabb.* 25b (Soncino 111; Goldschmidt 373) and *'Aboda Zara* 39a (Soncino 190; Goldschmidt 929). In Schürer, *The history* 1.385, n. 138, an inscription with בר רבן

transmission may then have been elided to one word, Barrabban.[89] When translated into Greek, the typical ending "s" was later substituted for "n."[90] A (fictitious) son or Bar of the prominent teacher Judas, referred to as teacher / Rabban, thus may have evolved from Bar Rabban to Barrabban, and then to Barabbas when translated by a Hellenistic Jewish Christian into Greek. This means that it would not derive from בר אבא, as so often proposed.

Historically, however, it is improbable that Herod would not also have had the insurrectionist Judas executed, as explicitly stated in Josephus' other source.[91] A Palestinian Jewish Christian may have known of a tradition that a son of either Judas or Matthias was not executed along with about forty other youthful followers of the two scholars at the time of the insurrection, but was rather imprisoned by Herod on the grounds of complicity and later released by Archelaus. Since the personal name of the son was either unknown or unimportant to him, he designated him as Bar Rabban, a son of either the Rabban Judas or the Rabban Matthias. This may then have evolved into Barabbas, in the same way as described above.

The latter proposals are, to be sure, an historical reconstruction. They are "how it could have been." Yet they derive the name Barabbas from the context of Archelaus' acceding, before a shouting crowd in Jerusalem in connection with Passover, to the release of prisoners taken in the recent insurrection incited by Judas and Matthias, both probably called Rabban, for which Josephus has *sophistēs*.

If correct, this means that there never was a real person, Barabbas, who was imprisoned at "the" insurrection during the period shortly before Jesus' crucifixion. There are absolutely no other Jewish, Jewish Christian, or Greek or Roman sources for such an insurrection at this time, just as there are none for the custom of a Roman governor's releasing a prisoner in Jerusalem to the crowd at the festival of Passover.

---

is mentioned, as well as Jerome's quotation of the Gospel of the Hebrews, which has *filius magistri eorum* for Barabbas.

[89] Cf. Brown, *The Death of the Messiah* 1.799, for some Gospel MSS as having two r's for the Greek name Barabbas.

[90] Cf. the change from the ending "n" to "s" in Josephus' rendering of the following biblical names (the nominative is assumed): 1) Berodach- or Merodach- baladan to Baladas in *Ant.* 10.30-31, 34; 2) Bigthan to Bagathōos in 11.207 and 249; 3) Esarhaddon to Asarachoddas in 10.23; 4) Kenan to Cainas in 1.79 and 83; 5) Memucan to Muchaios in 11.193; 6) Rezin to Arases in 9.244 and 253; and 7) Rezon to Razos in 8.204.

[91] Cf. *Ant.* 17.214; *Bell.* 1.655 and 2.10.

The entire episode is rather a Palestinian Jewish Christian creation, designed to express definite religious truths (see Section VII. below).

*   *   *

The ten motifs in the Barabbas narrative in the Gospels of an insurrection, a *bēma*, a crowd, crying out, requests / demands, releasing a prisoner, a festival, Passover, custom and the King of the Jews, all derive from the major insurrection in Jerusalem under Herod the Great as handled by his successor and son, Archelaus, at Passover in 4 BCE. Cumulatively, they present a strong argument for the Markan episode, as well as later developments such as *bēma* found in two of the other Gospels, as based primarily on this historical event. Indeed, the name Barabbas itself may also derive from the same incident.

The following section suggests how the above motifs could have been connected by the Palestinian Jewish Christian who first composed the Barabbas narrative to the time of Jesus' "trial" before Pilate.

IV. The Procurator Vitellius' Release at Passover in Jerusalem

If the reconstruction made above is basically correct, the insurrection in Jerusalem under Herod the Great and Archelaus, including Passover, provided the background for most of the expressions and motifs in the Barabbas narrative of the Gospels. Yet it occurred in 4 BCE, and Jesus' Crucifixion probably around 30 CE.[92] How could the Palestinian Jewish Christian who first orally composed this narrative relate it to the time of Jesus, when there was no insurrection and no release? The answer is most probably to be found in an event which occurred some six years later.

The Roman historian Suetonius wrote his *Lives of the Caesars* in 120 CE.[93] In his account of the emperor Vitellius, he relates that the latter's father Lucius Vitellius became a consul and then was made governor (*praepositus*) of Syria (in 35 CE). There he acted with "supreme diplomacy," and Suetonius considered him a *vir innocens et industrius*.[94]

Two examples of Vitellius' diplomatic manner in dealing with the Jews are the following. The procurator of Judea, Pontius Pilate, severely

---

[92] For the date of the Crucifixion, cf. G. Caird, art. "The Chronology of the NT" in *IDB* 1.603, favoring 30 CE.

[93] Cf. J. Rolfe in the LCL edition of Suetonius, I.ix.

[94] He chided him only for his later infatuation with a certain woman, and flattery of Gaius as a god. Cf. "Vitellius" 2.4 (LCL II.250-251). See also Tacitus, *Annales* 6.32- *in regendis provinciis prisca virtute egit*. Tacitus published his Annals in 116 CE (LCL III.230 and 234).

provoked the inhabitants of Jerusalem, probably in 26 CE, by introducing the images of the Roman emperor on the military standards of the imperial troops.[95] In addition, he later appropriated funds from the sacred treasure called "Corbān" in order to construct an aqueduct for Jerusalem. Since these monies were supposed to be used for Temple sacrifices, thousands of Jews protested, and many were killed in the ensuing uprising (στάσις).[96]

In contrast to such intentionally provocative behavior, Vitellius in 37 CE acceded to Jewish wishes not to march through their land with the images on his troops' military standards. He instead ordered them to take a detour, while he himself went up to Jerusalem and made a sacrifice in the Temple at a festival.[97]

A year earlier, in 36 CE, Pilate had dealt with an uprising (θόρυβος) of the Samaritans at their sacred Mount Gerizim in such an atrocious way that these appealed to Vitellius. They maintained that they had pursued no rebellion (ἀπόστασις), but were rather fleeing from the persecution of Pilate. Vitellius thereupon ordered Pilate to answer to the charges before the emperor Tiberius in Rome.[98]

At this time Vitellius went up to Jerusalem, where the traditional feast (ἑορτή) of Passover was being celebrated. The governor was given a magnificent reception, certainly in great part for having deposed the hated Pilate.[99] Vitellius thereupon completely "remitted" (ἀνίημι) to the inhabitants (of Jerusalem) the taxes / duties on all produce purchased there (*Ant.* 17.90).[100] The same Greek verb, ἀνίημι, is also employed of "remitting" a death sentence.[101]

This tax / duty / market toll was the same one which Herod the Great had levied as part of his oppressive revenue system. "Remission" of it was already demanded at the insurrection in 4 BCE. The Jerusalem

---

[95] Cf. Josephus, *Ant.* 18.55-59, and *Bell.* 2.169-174.

[96] Cf. *Ant.* 18.60-62, with n. "b," and *Bell.* 2.175-177.

[97] *Ant.* 18.120-124. This was probably at Sukkoth or Booths in the fall, for Vitellius then dismissed his army for the winter (124). Against Schürer, *The history* 1.350.

[98] *Ant.* 18.85-89. The term θόρυβος in 85 and 88 occurs also in Matt 27:34.

[99] Pilate was so hated that both he and Herod were included by Judaic tradition in the genealogy of wicked Haman. Cf. for example the First Targum to Esth 5:1 and the Second Targum to 3:1 (Grossfeld, *The First Targum to Esther,* Table E, on p. 144, with 3. as Pilatus and 11. as Herod); Cassel English on 2 Targ. Esth 3:1 (304, with his note); and Ginzberg, *Legends* 6.462.

[100] The same reception is meant in *Ant.* 15.405.

[101] LSJ 143.

crowd at that time had shouted out to Archelaus, sitting on his golden throne on a *bēma* in the Temple, and had demanded that just these "ruthlessly exacted" taxes be removed (*Ant.* 17.205; *Bell.* 2.4). This historical detail, so important for the daily life of the Jerusalemites, helped the Palestinian Jewish Christian author of the Barabbas / Pilate narrative to transfer the motif of "remitting" from 4 BCE via 36 CE, with the governor Vitellius, to the governor Pilate, whom he had just deposed. This is all the more probable because another of the three demands made in 4 BCE, and acceded to, was the "release" (ἀπόλυσις, ἀπολύω) of the prisoners taken by Herod (*Ant.* 17.204; *Bell.* 2.4).

Two other factors beyond the deposition of Pilate and the "remission" described above made Vitellius' visit to Jerusalem at the festival of Passover in 36 CE so memorable for Jews and Jewish Christians. Also out of respect for the religious feelings of the Jews, Vitellius gave an order that the special garments of the high priest, which were only worn on the three major festivals and the Day of Atonement, should now, after forty years, be transferred back from Roman custody in the Antonia fortress to the priests, as had been the case before 4 BCE.[102] The Jews were extremely grateful for this sign of respect for their religious traditions.

Finally, Vitellius at the same time removed Joseph surnamed Caiaphas (*Ant.* 18.95), who had been high priest from 26-36 CE.[103] According to the Gospels, it was he who had presided over the Jewish hearing, the so-called "trial" of Jesus, demanding the death sentence for him (Mark 14:53-65 par.; John 11:49 and 18:13-28) and handing him over to Pilate (Mark 15:1-5 par.; John 18:28-35). This is then directly followed by the Barabbas / Pilate scene.

The fact that Vitellius, the Roman governor who deposed the hated Pilate, made a "remission" at a Passover festival in Jerusalem in 36 CE, and also deposed the high priest Caiaphas, encouraged a Palestinian Jewish Christian to paint the strange picture of a very generous Roman procurator Pilate in Jerusalem only some six years earlier in such warm colors. Pilate is described as trying three times to release innocent Jesus.

The magnificently received Vitellius was highly respected for his sensitivity to Jewish customs, including his handing back to the Jews at Passover the high priestly garments employed "every year" at the three

---

[102] Cf. *Ant.* 18.90-95 and 15.403-408.

[103] *Ant.* 18.35 and n. "a." On the spelling of the name, cf. Schürer, *The history* 2.230, as well as the ossuary found in Talpiot south of Jerusalem, now in the Israel Museum in Jerusalem. It is described in *Jesus & His World*, 139-142.

festivals and the Day of Atonement.[104] The historical fact that he "remitted" taxes in Jerusalem at Passover in 36 CE was connected by the Palestinian Jewish Christian author of the Pilate / Barabbas narrative to the same "remission" demanded and acceded to at Passover in 4 BCE. At that time the "release" of prisoners from the recent insurrection was another of the three demands made by a shouting Jerusalem crowd to Archelaus upon a *bēma* in the Temple. To this the latter also assented. By means of the expression "release / remission," the incidents of 4 BCE and 36 CE were thus related. They were then applied to a Passover scene in Jerusalem set in ca. 30 CE, at which Caiaphas and Pilate, both deposed by Vitellius, play major roles.

This was no different from what the Palestinian Jewish Christian author of Luke 2:1-20 did when he transferred the motif of a census taken in Judea under the Roman legate Quirinius in 6/7 CE back to the time of Jesus' birth, somewhat before Herod's death in 4 BCE. Nor was it different from the Evangelist Matthew's later appropriation of imagery from an incident of the *magus* Tiridates. Coming from the east, he did obeisance to the emperor / king Nero in Rome in 66 CE. Matthew used Tiridates' entourage as part of the background for his portrayal of the magi at Jesus' birth in 2:1-12.[105] The appropriation of motifs and expressions from earlier or later incidents was typical of haggadic storytelling, in which exact chronology was not emphasized.

* * *

The above arguments made in regard to the background materials employed in the Barabbas narrative are cumulative. While they may be questioned individually (some are stronger than others), together they carry great weight. Almost all of the major expressions and motifs in the Barabbas episode can be explained by them. They also help to explain not only the strangely generous effort on the part of Pilate, otherwise known for his extreme cruelty and insensitivity to Jewish customs and religious feelings, to release the prisoner Jesus, sent bound to him. Here the positive character of Vitellius has been transferred back to Pilate. The proposed background also helps to explain the "custom" of a Roman

---

[104] *Ant.* 18.94 – ἑκάστου ἔτους.

[105] On the first, cf. Schürer, *The history* 1.399-427, and the chapter "Die Weihnachtsgeschichte im Lichte jüdischer Traditionen vom Mose-Kind und Hirten-Messias (Lukas 2,1-20)" in my *Weihnachtsgeschichte, Barmherziger Samariter, Verlorener Sohn*, 11-58. On the second, see "The Magi at the Birth of Cyrus, and the Magi at Jesus' Birth in Matt 2:1-12," which originally appeared in *New Perspectives on Ancient Judaism*, 2, 99-114, and later in my *Barabbas and Esther* 95-111.

procurator in Jerusalem who released a prisoner to the crowd at the annual festival of Passover. As remarked in the Introduction, there is not a single attestation in Jewish or non-Jewish sources of such a custom. The Palestinian Jewish Christian creator of the Barabbas incident, like others in his time, conveniently invented a custom, here from Passover information available to him which involved the release of prisoners.

V. The Original Language and Date of the Narrative

The Palestinian Jewish Christian who first orally composed the episode of Pilate's release of the insurrectionist Barabbas and his handing Jesus over to be crucified did so in a Semitic language. This was probably Aramiac, the everyday language of the people, yet Hebrew cannot be completely excluded. If the latter was the case, it would then have been translated almost immediately into Aramaic so that those who did not understand spoken Hebrew could also appreciate it.

One clear sign of Semitic influence in the Barabbas narrative is found at Mark 15:15a, where Pilate wants to "appease" the crowd. Matthew and Luke omit it here, probably considering it difficult to understand. The Greek τὸ ἱκανὸν ποιῆσαι, as noted above, is not a Latinism, but rather reflects the background of the expression in Archelaus' attempt to appease / flatter the crowd at Passover in Jerusalem. The "author" of the Barabbas narrative could not have been dependent on the Aramaic version of this incident as related by Josephus in his *Bellum*, for the work was only published after 70 CE. Rather, he too most probably had knowledge of this memorable incident, involving the death of ca. 3000 people at Passover, from local Palestinian, Aramaic tradition. The collective memory of a people is quite long in regard to atrocious events of such magnitude.

The Aramaic of the above Greek expression may have been the pael of פיס, to quiet, appease, secure the good will of, win the favor of.[106] This is supported by the double meaning of τὸ ἱκανὸν ποιεῖν τινι, to satisfy, or to do someone a favor.[107] Another term, less probable, is רצי, רצא, to appease.[108]

Semitic influence may also be observed in Mark 15:8. The NRSV translates the participle ἀναβάς here as "So the crowd 'came' and began

---

[106] Jastrow 1166-1167, Levy 4.40. "To make / do פיוסא," conciliation (Jastrow 1160), would also be possible, a construction closer to the Greek of Mark 15:15.

[107] BAGD 374, 1.c.

[108] Jastrow 1494. Cf. also חנף, to flatter, or to show favor in court (Jastrow 484-485). The hiphil of the verb שבע (Jastrow 1516), to satisfy, is employed in the United Bible Societies' Hebrew New Testament (p. 138).

to ask Pilate...." Yet the RSV should be preferred, which reads: "And the crowd 'came up' and began to ask Pilate...." I suggest that ἀναβαίνω here translates an original Semitic עלי, עלה, עלא, which became a technical expression, meaning "to go up (to Jerusalem and the Temple) for the festival."[109] It is a vestige of the background of the Barabbas episode in the insurrection under Herod, with which his son Archelaus had to deal. According to Josephus, from his *bēma* in the Temple Archelaus addressed the pilgrims, those who had "come up" for the festival of Passover and were now in the Temple.

The Palestinian Jewish Christian who first composed the Barabbas narrative borrowed the term "to go up" from his source and employed it of the Jerusalem Passover pilgrimage crowd as "going up" from the city to the Temple Mount. Pilate may thus be thought of as somewhere in the large Court of the Gentiles, just as Archelaus sat on his *bēma* there.[110] Or, more probably, the narrator now considered the crowd to have "gone up" for judgment from the Temple towards the fortress of Antonia at its NW corner, where he thought there was a prison (with Barabbas inside), and where he imagined that Pilate resided.[111]

A third indication of an originally Semitic background to the Barabbas narrative is found in Mark 15:13, "And they cried out πάλιν." This is usually translated "again," yet the crowd is not described as having done so before. The Greek is best thought of as rendering the Aramaic תוב, which can also mean "furthermore," "then." Verse 13 should thus be translated: "Then they cried out, 'Crucify him!'"[112] Here

---

[109] Jastrow 1081 d; the Aramaic is on 1082.

[110] Cf. the Judaic tradition that one of the ten "ascents" of the Shekhinah is from the city to the Temple Mount. See *'Avot R. Nat.* A 34 (Schechter 102; Goldin 141-142; Neusner 207).

[111] Cf. the "whole battalion" of Mark 15:16, and Paul as held prisoner in the praetorium of Caesarea before the trial to take place there (Acts 23:35; 24:23). See also the art. "Antonia, Tower of," by K. Clark in *IDB* 1.153-154. It had direct access to the Court of the Gentiles. Josephus in *Bell.* 5.242 says it "looked down" upon the Temple (see also *Ant.* 20.110), and the Roman soldiers stationed there at the pilgrimage festivals guarded against a possible insurrection in the Temple (*Bell.* 5.244). This has nothing to do, of course, with the unsolvable question of where Pilate actually resided in Jerusalem. Just before the outbreak of the Jewish-Roman War in 66 CE, for example, Florus resided in Jerusalem in the palace (of Herod) and held judgment on a tribunal before it (*Bell.* 2.301, 308, 314). Yet that was a good thirty-five years after Pilate's "trial" of Jesus.

[112] Cf. M. Black, Die *Muttersprache Jesu* 112-113. Black is dependent on others such as Wellhausen here. See J. Gnilka, *Das Evangelium nach Markus (Mk 8,27 – 16,20)* (EKKNT 11/2; Zurich, Benziger; Neukirchen-Vluyn: Neukirchener, 1989³) 302, n. 37. See also Jastrow 1650 on תוב; the Hebrew שׁוּב (p. 1528) can have the same

חוב was employed in a different sense than in v 12, "again." This is a part of the narrative artistry of the Palestinian Jewish Christian who first composed the episode.

A fourth sign of the Semitic background of the Barabbas narrative is found in Luke 23:19, βληθεὶς ἐν τῇ φυλακῇ, where the dative ("thrown in") is employed instead of the accusative ("thrown into"), as in v 25: βεβλημένον εἰς φυλακήν.[113] The first Greek expression may represent אתאסר בבית מטרתא, "to be chained / bound in prison," with ב, which was translated literally as ἐν.[114]

The above four Semitic expressions, especially the first, make a Semitic background to the Barabbas narrative very probable.

In regard to the date of the Barabbas narrative, it is probable that the individual units now contained in the Passion Narrative were composed at a very early time.[115] Vitellius' act of "releasing" in Jerusalem at the Passover festival of 36 CE, connected to his deposing Caiaphas and Pilate, inspired a Palestinian Jewish Christian to compose the Barabbas narrative, probably already in the forties. This episode was then inserted into an early Semitic framework of the Passion Narrative, which is still recognizable in Mark 15:1 and 15b. Pilate's conversation with Jesus in vv 2-5 and the Barabbas incident in vv 6-15a were then added to this outer structure to fill out the rather bare data.

The original Semitic Barabbas narrative was very popular, as shown in the major variants now found in the other Gospels. Perhaps already in a larger context, it was then translated by a Hellenistic Jewish Christian into Greek. From there it later became available to the Evangelist Mark, who incorporated it into his Gospel, generally thought to date from shortly before or after 70 CE.[116]

---

meaning. Mark 15:13 is discussed in BAGD 607, yet the third meaning there, "furthermore, thereupon" (p. 606), is closest to that of the Semitic original.

[113] I doubt whether the first is from Luke (cf. BDF, p. 1, n. 2 for Luke's especially confusing εἰς and ἐν).

[114] Cf. Jastrow 98 and 770 for אסר and מטרתא, respectively. "To be thrown into" in Aramaic could be אתרמי ל (Jastrow 1482), but ל would not be translated with ἐν.

[115] Cf. R. Bultmann, *The History of the Synoptic Tradition* 275: "Unlike other material in the tradition, the Passion narrative was very early fashioned into a coherent form...." He speaks beforehand of the separate pieces in it which were "handed down as isolated elements."

[116] Cf. J. Marcus, "The Jewish War and the Sitz im Leben of Mark" 460; D. Lührmann, *Das Markus-Evangelium* 6; and J. Gnilka, *Das Evangelium nach Markus (Mk 1 – 8,26)* (EKKNT 11/1; Zurich, Benziger; Neukirchen-Vluyn: Neukirchener, 1989³) 34.

While no certainty can be attained in the matter, nothing stands in the way of dating the original Semitic form of the Barabbas narrative already in the forties CE.

VI. The Purpose of the Original Narrative, and Mark's Redaction of It

A

The Palestinian Jewish Christian who composed the original, oral narrative with Pilate, Jesus and Barabbas did so primarily for three reasons. They were the following.

1) *Filling a Gap.*

The earliest Passion account noted that the Jewish Sanhedrin ("council") in Jerusalem held an early morning consultation, bound Jesus, led him off, and handed him over to Pilate (Mark 15:1), certainly with the intention that the Roman official condemn him to death. The account continued by relating how Pilate then scourged Jesus and handed him over to be crucified (15:15b).

This is all that was originally known to the first followers of Jesus. There is no reason to doubt the Gospel statement that when Jesus was taken captive in the Garden of Gethsemane, *all* the disciples forsook him and fled for their lives (Mark 14:27, 50 par.). None of Jesus' followers were eyewitnesses to Pilate's interrogation of Jesus, if one occurred at all. Pilate was well-known for constantly ordering executions (including crucifixion) without a trial (Philo, *Leg. Gai.* 302). No one knew the procurator's exact reasons for having Jesus scourged and handed over to be crucified (except for the charge in Mark 15:26). In order to fill this major gap, the short verbal exchange between Pilate and Jesus was created (15:2-5), as well as the following Barabbas incident (vv 6-15a).

Gap-filling was very typical of Palestinian Jewish haggadah. I. Heinemann speaks in this regard of the "creative (re-)writing of history,"[117] and J. Goldin of "imaginative dramatization."[118] This describes very well the later re-molding of the scene of Archelaus on a *bēma* before a shouting crowd in the Jerusalem Temple, including a

---

[117] Quoted in Strack and Stemberger, *Einleitung* 225 as "schöpferische Geschichtsschreibung"; the English in *Introduction* 260 employs "historiography," which is misleading here.

[118] Cf. his *The Song at the Sea* (Philadelphia and New York: The Jewish Publication Society, 1990, original 1971) 27.

demand for the release of prisoners from the recent insurrection. A Palestinian Jewish Christian reworked this raw material in a creative way to fill in the gap described above. The result was the Barabbas episode. It was similar in this respect, for example, to the accounts of Jesus in the Garden of Gethsemane, Peter in the house of the high priest, the beheading of John the Baptist, and the twelve-year-old Jesus in the Jerusalem Temple.[119]

2) *Transferring the Roman Responsibility for Jesus' Death to the Jews.*

A very small number of the self-serving priestly aristocracy in Jerusalem were infuriated because of Jesus' symbolic "cleansing" of the Temple (Mark 11:15-19) and because he severely castigated them for misusing the Temple, God's "vineyard," in his parable of the wicked tenants, told within the Temple precincts (12:1b-9; cf. v 12).[120] Because the Galilean prophet was so popular with his fellow Jews (11:18; 12:12, 37; 14:2; 15:10 – envy), they had to have Jesus taken captive in the Garden of Gethsemane under the cover of night and not openly, during the day (14:49a and 1 – by stealth). The members of the priestly aristocracy wanted to secure their privileged financial status, especially in the "business" of the Temple. They knew that the crowds, particularly at the Passover festival marking the Hebrews' deliverance from slavery in Egypt, could easily be incited to insurrection by a popular prophet (14:2). That would automatically cause Roman military intervention, and possibly also the destruction of the Temple and the loss of their positions and power. Thus they preemptively handed their fellow Jew, Jesus, over to the Roman Pilate. They did this just as Herod Antipas, fearing a revolt because of John the Baptist's eloquence and popularity with the crowds,

---

[119] Cf. my studies "Jesus in Gethsemane (Mark 14:32-42 par.)" in *The Wicked Tenants and Gethsemane* (USFISFCJ 4; Atlanta: Scholars Press, 1996) 156; "Peter's Threefold Denial," *ibid.* 115-120; *Water into Wine and the Beheading of John the Baptist* 74; and "The Child Jesus in the Temple (Luke 2:41-51a)" in *Samuel, Saul and Jesus* 60-61.

[120] On the latter, cf. my essay "The Parable of the Wicked Tenants (Mark 12:1-9)" in *The Wicked Tenants and Gethsemane* 1-64. See also Josephus, *Ant.* 18.64: "Pilate, upon hearing him [Jesus] accused by men of the highest standing among us, ... condemned him to be crucified...." These men can only be the high priests and others in the Sanhedrin. At least in this respect Josephus' testimony on Jesus appears to be trustworthy. While the prediction of Jesus' destroying the Temple and rebuilding it in three days (Mark 14:58; 15:29; see also John 2:19) is a later Christian reference to the Resurrection on Easter Sunday, an earlier form of 13:2, with the divine passive, is probably original (cf. also Acts 6:14). This was another reason the Temple hierarchy felt threatened and wished to be rid of the prophet from Nazareth. Here Jesus stood in the tradition of Jeremiah (Jer 26:6, 8-9, 11-12).

put him to death in Machaerus *before* sedition against the tetrarch could take place.[121]

Yet the primary responsibility for Jesus' execution lay with the Roman Pontius Pilate. He alone could pronounce a death sentence and order his soldiers to crucify someone. It is worth noting that no formal sentence is related in Mark 15:15. This was typical of the very cruel procurator.[122] The sarcastic charge against Jesus, which Pilate had attached to his cross, is most probably historical: "The King of the Jews" (v 26; cf. its repetition in vv 2, 9 and 12).[123] Pilate was only too willing to crucify someone he considered a political rebel, a possible danger to Rome with the only true king, the emperor Tiberius, and to his own position.

The Palestinian Jewish Christian who created the Barabbas episode, however, transferred the main responsibility for Jesus' crucifixion back to his fellow Jews. He did this by asserting that it was not only the chief priests who sought Jesus' death (15:10-11). They induced the (entire) Jewish crowd to cry out to Pilate: "Crucify him!" (vv 13-14). Although the Roman had tried three times to release Jesus instead of Barabbas to the crowd, the procurator finally yielded to their demands (v 15a).

The original narrator made this transfer of responsibility for two major reasons. Jewish Christians now claimed to be the "true" Israel, that God had made a "new" covenant or testament with mankind in Jesus of Nazareth. Those Jews who refused to believe in him as the Messiah were for him no longer truly Israel, they now ostensibly belonged to the "old" covenant. A daughter religion in the state of puberty, Christianity, was rebelling here against its own mother, Judaism. It was seeking to assert its own self-identity, in part by distancing itself from its own roots.

Secondly, already before 70 CE it may have been advantageous for Christians, pacifistic "non-rebels," to lean towards Rome, the occupying military power in Palestine and ruler of the world. The indications leading up to the unsuccessful Jewish rebellion of 66-70 CE already

---

[121] Josephus, *Ant.* 18.116-119. Cf. also Mark 14:1-2, where the chief priests and scribes seek to arrest and kill Jesus *before* the feast of Passover in order to avoid a "tumult" of the people. See also the Sadduccean high priest Ananus, who at a meeting of the Sanhedrin accused James, Jesus' brother, of transgressing the Law, and "delivered" (παραδίδωμι) him and others to be stoned (*Ant.* 20.199-200). Fairminded inhabitants of Jerusalem were so offended by this that they had Ananus deposed (201-203).

[122] Cf. again Philo, *Leg. Gai.* 302: "the executions without trial constantly repeated, the ceaseless and supremely grievous cruelty."

[123] Cf. N. Dahl, *The Crucified Messiah and Other Essays* (Minneapolis: Augsburg, 1974) 23-24, 28.

decades before may have signaled to Christians that it would be advantageous to place as much formal distance between themselves and much of the Zealotic-minded section of the Jewish populace as possible.[124]

3) *Emphasizing Jesus' Innocence.*

In the present form of the Markan Barabbas narrative, it is implied that he was one of the insurrectionists who committed murder in the insurrection (15:7). Luke 23:19 and 25 specifically state this, and John 18:40 labels Barabbas an insurrectionist.

Pilate in contrast asks the crowd in regard to Jesus: "What evil has he done?" (Mark 15:14). Luke 23:22 adds to this: "I have found in him no crime deserving death." In Matthew, Pilate's wife also labels Jesus "that righteous man," and the procurator washes his hands with water and asserts that he is innocent of Jesus' blood (27:19 and 24). Finally, in John 18:38 (cf. 19:4 and 6) Pilate tells "the Jews": "I find no crime in him."

In other words, the Markan form of the narrative and the later developments found in the other three Evangelists show that the scene was designed from the outset to present a dramatic contrast. Barabbas is a dramatic foil to Jesus, whose innocence is even maintained by the heathen Pilate.[125] It is well-known that the color white is best perceived not when a shade of gray, but rather pure black, is placed next to it.

Condemning the innocent and letting the guilty go free is a Judaic motif already found with the verb ἀπολύω in Sus 53 and 2 Macc 4:47. In Jesus' case, it cried out for the justice of God, which Christians saw effected when He raised His Son, taking Jesus to Himself, on Easter Sunday.

* * *

Finally, it should be emphasized that the Palestinian Jewish Christian who first composed the oral Barabbas narrative certainly knew of the role of the suffering servant in Isaiah 53, who died for the godless and the guilty. While this may be behind passages like Mark 14:24, 49, 61 and 15:27, [28] and an episode like Luke 23:39-43, there are no indications

---

[124] I adapt this from my *Barabbas and Esther* 24-25. There I also refer to scattered persecution of Christians by Jews, which may have been another minor factor.

[125] Irony may also be involved here. J. Brooks in *Mark* (The New American Commentary 23; Nashville: Broadman Press, 1991) 252 states in this regard: "Jesus was falsely accused by the Jews and condemned by Pilate for the very thing of which Barabbas was actually guilty." Cf. also Juel, *Mark* 216.

whatsoever that the author of Mark 15:6-15a was thinking of Jesus as the suffering servant of Isaiah 53 here.[126]

B

Various suggestions as to the Markan redaction of the Barabbas narrative have been made. W. Schenk, for example, considers Mark 15:7-8, 11 and 15a to belong to an originally independent story. Mark then supplemented this account with other verses.[127] W. Grundmann believes the original "Vorlage" consisted of vv 1, 3-5, 2, and 12-14, which was then edited by Mark.[128] W. Schmithals considers vv 12-14 to be Markan,[129] while E. Lohmeyer thinks Mark probably inserted "the chief priests" in v 10, which for him does not fit "the chief priests" in v 11.[130]

The repetition of "the chief priests" in 15:11, instead of a simple "*they* stirred up," as part of the verb, may be due to the intention of the original narrator described above. He wished to transfer responsibility for Jesus' death from the Roman Pilate to his fellow (non-believing) Jews, and especially to their leaders. This occurred in part by emphasizing the role of the chief priests through repeating the designation.

Otherwise, I recognize no clear signs of Markan redaction in 15:6-15a.[131] The Evangelist incorporated the narrative between 15:1 and 15b, prefacing it with another episode available to him, vv 2-5. As I indicated in my analysis of the background of 15:6-15a above, there is hardly a single expression or motif in these verses which does not derive from the Archelaus "Vorlage." This strongly speaks against individual verses or parts of them as deriving from Mark.

---

[126] Against for example Gnilka, *Das Evangelium nach Markus (Mk 8,27 – 16,20)* 303; Grundmann, *Das Evangelium nach Markus* 425; and Schmithals, *Das Evangelium nach Markus, Kapitel 9,2 – 16*, 675. On this question, see also Gundry, *Mark* 938.

[127] Cf. his specific arguments in *Der Passionsbericht nach Markus* (Gütersloh: Mohn, 1974) 249.

[128] *Das Evangelium nach Markus* 425, although on 422 he maintains that it is difficult to get back to the history of tradition before Mark and to his redactional activity.

[129] *Das Evangelium nach Markus, Kapitel 9,2 – 16*, 675.

[130] *Das Evangelium des Markus* 338.

[131] An exception could be minor elements such as δέ (Schenk, *Der Passionsbericht des Markus* 249).

* * *

The Palestinian Jewish Christian who first composed the Barabbas episode was a gifted narrator, as shown for example in the inclusio through the term "release" in 15:6 and 15a. He very creatively composed a dramatic scene in which innocence and guilt were strongly contrasted. As a Christian Jew, he fairly attacked a specific group of his fellow Jews, the chief priests, for handing Jesus over to the Roman Pilate to have him executed. This was verbal internecine fighting typical of the time. Unfortunately, he did not consider the possible terrible effects his unfair attack on his fellow Jews would later have when he (unhistorically) also described the Jerusalem crowd as shouting: "Crucify him!" This was then intensified in the church's favorite Gospel, Matthew, where the Evangelist emphasized that "*all* the people answered, 'His blood be on us and on our children!'" (27:25). The most terrible sentence in the entire New Testament, this fictitious assertion became the basis for countless pogroms of Jews by Christians throughout the centuries, especially during the season of Lent, just before Easter.

One purpose of this essay has been to show its *unhistorical* character as well as the major *religious* truth it seeks to express, Jesus' innocence. While this is small consolation to later Jewish victims of Christian persecution based primarily on this narrative, it at least provides contemporary Christians and Jews a new opportunity to analyze and appreciate the episode in regard to what it originally intended to convey.

Sources and Reference Works

I. *The Bible.*

Kittel, *Biblia Hebraica,* ed. R. Kittel et al. (Stuttgart: Privilegierte Württembergische Bibelanstalt, 1951[7]).

Rahlfs, *Septuaginta,* ed. A. Rahlfs (Stuttgart: Württembergische Bibelanstalt, 1962[7]).

Hatch and Redpath, *A Concordance to the Septuagint,* ed. E. Hatch and H. Redpath (Oxford: Clarendon, 1897; reprint Grand Rapids, Michigan: Baker Book House, 1983).

Nestle / Aland, *Novum Testamentum Graece,* ed. E. Nestle, K. Aland, et al. (Stuttgart: Deutsche Bibelgesellschaft, 1990[26]).

The Greek New Testament, ed. K. Aland, M. Black, B. Metzger and A. Wikgren (London: United Bible Societies, 1966).

Hebrew New Testament, by F. Delitzsch (Berlin: Trowitzsch and Son, 1885).

Hebrew New Testament (Jerusalem: The United Bible Societies, 1979).

II. *The Targums.*

Sperber, *The Bible in Aramaic,* ed. A. Sperber (Leiden: Brill, 1959), 4 volumes.

Aberbach and Grossfeld, *Targum Onkelos to Genesis,* trans. M. Aberbach and B. Grossfeld (Denver: Center for Judaic Studies, University of Denver; New York: Ktav, 1982).

McNamara, *Targum Neofiti 1: Genesis,* trans. M. McNamara (The Aramaic Bible, 1A; Edinburgh: Clark, 1992).

Maher, *Targum Pseudo-Jonathan: Genesis,* trans. M. Maher (The Aramaic Bible, 1B; Edinburgh: Clark, 1992).

Drazin, *Targum Onkelos to Exodus*, ed. and trans. I. Drazin (New York: Ktav; Denver: Center for Judaic Studies, University of Denver, 1990).

Grossfeld, *The Targum Onqelos to Exodus*, trans. B. Grossfeld (The Aramaic Bible, 7; Edinburgh: Clark, 1988).

McNamara / Maher, *Targum Neofiti 1: Exodus, Targum Pseudo-Jonathan: Exodus*, trans. M. McNamara and M. Maher (The Aramaic Bible, 2; Edinburgh: Clark, 1994).

Díez Macho, *Neophyti 1*, Vol. I, Genesis, ed. A. Díez Macho (Madrid: Consejo Superior de Investigaciones Científicas, 1968). Vol. II, Exodus, 1970; vol. IV, Numbers, 1974.

Grossfeld, *The Targum Onqelos to Leviticus and The Targum Onqelos to Numbers*, trans. B. Grossfeld (The Aramaic Bible, 8; Edinburgh: Clark, 1988).

Rieder, *Targum Jonathan ben Uziel on the Pentateuch*, ed. with a Hebrew translation by D. Rieder (Jerusalem, 1984), 2 volumes.

Etheridge, *The Targums of Onkelos and Jonathan Ben Uzziel on the Pentateuch with the Fragments of the Jerusalem Targum*, trans. J. Etheridge (New York: Ktav, 1968; original 1862).

Klein, *The Fragment-Targums of the Pentateuch*, ed. and trans. M. Klein (AnBib 76; Rome: Biblical Institute, 1980), 2 volumes.

Harrington and Saldarini, *Targum Jonathan of the Former Prophets*, trans. D. Harrington and A. Saldarini (The Aramaic Bible, 10; Edinburgh: Clark, 1987).

Stenning, *The Targum of Isaiah*, ed. and trans. J. Stenning (Oxford: Clarendon, 1949).

Chilton, *The Isaiah Targum*, trans. B. Chilton (The Aramaic Bible, 11; Edinburgh: Clark, 1987).

Hayward, *The Targum of Jeremiah*, trans. R. Hayward (The Aramaic Bible, 12; Edinburgh: Clark, 1987).

Cathcart and Gordon, *The Targum of the Minor Prophets*, trans. K. Cathcart and R. Gordon (The Aramaic Bible, 14; Edinburgh: Clark, 1989).

Lagarde, *Hagiographa Chaldaice*, ed. P. de Lagarde (Leipzig: Teubner, 1873; reprint Osnabrück: Zeller, 1967).

Merino, *Targum de Salmos*, ed. L. Merino (Madrid: Consejo Superior de Investigaciones Científicas, 1984).

Cassel, P. *An Explanatory Commentary on Esther,* trans. A. Bernstein (Edinburgh: Clark, 1888). Includes an English translation of the two targumim to Esther. Aramaic in *Aus Literatur und Geschichte.* Zweites Targum zum Buche Esther. Im vocalisierten Urtext (Leipzig and Berlin: Friedrich, 1885).

Grossfeld, *The First Targum to Esther,* trans. B. Grossfeld (New York: Sepher-Hermon, 1983).

Grossfeld, *The Targum Sheni to the Book of Esther,* ed. and trans. B. Grossfeld (New York: Sepher-Hermon, 1994).

III. *The Mishnah and Tosefta.*

Albeck, *Shisha Sidre Mishna,* ed. Ch. Albeck (Jerusalem and Tel Aviv: Bialik Institute and Dvir, 1975), 6 volumes.

Danby, *The Mishnah,* trans. H. Danby (London: Oxford University, 1933).

Neusner, *The Mishnah,* trans. J. Neusner (New Haven: Yale University, 1988).

Krauss, *Sanhedrin-Makkot,* ed. and trans. S. Krauss (Die Mischna, IV.4.5; Giessen: Töpelmann, 1933).

Zuckermandel, *Tosephta,* ed. M. Zuckermandel, with a supplement by S. Liebermann (Jerusalem: Wahrmann, 1970).

Lieberman, *The Tosefta.* Seder Mo'ed, ed. S. Lieberman (New York: The Jewish Theological Seminary of America, 1962).

Neusner, *The Tosefta,* trans. J. Neusner et al. (Hoboken, New Jersey: Ktav, 1977-1986), 6 volumes.

IV. *The Talmuds.*

Soncino, *The Babylonian Talmud,* ed. I. Epstein, various translators (London: Soncino, 1952), 18 volumes and index.

Soncino, *The Minor Tractates of the Talmud,* ed. A. Cohen, various translators (London: Soncino, 1965), 2 volumes.

Goldschmidt, *Der Babylonische Talmud,* ed. with a German translation by L. Goldschmidt (Haag: Nijoff, 1933), 9 volumes.

Krotoshin, *Talmud Yerushalmi,* Krotoshin edition (Jerusalem: Shilah, 1969).

Neusner, *The Talmud of the Land of Israel*, trans. J. Neusner et al. (Chicago: University of Chicago, 1982-1995), 34 volumes.

V. *Halakhic Midrashim.*

Lauterbach, *Mekilta de-Rabbi Ishmael*, ed. and trans. J. Lauterbach (Philadelphia: The Jewish Publication Society of America, 1976), 3 volumes.

Epstein / Melamed, *Mekhilta d'Rabbi Šim'on b. Jochai*, ed. J. Epstein and E. Melamed (Jerusalem: Hillel Press, 1955; reprint 1979).

Horowitz, *Siphre ad Numeros adjecto Siphre zutta*, ed. H. Horowitz (Jerusalem: Wahrmann, 1976).

Neusner, *Sifre to Numbers*, trans. J. Neusner (BJS 118-119; Atlanta: Scholars Press, 1986), 2 volumes.

Kuhn, *Der tannaitische Midrasch Sifre zu Numeri*, German by K. Kuhn (Stuttgart: Kohlhammer, 1959).

Finkelstein, *Sifre on Deuteronomy*, ed. L. Finkelstein (New York: The Jewish Theological Seminary of America, 1969).

Hammer, *Sifre.* A Tannaitic Commentary on the Book of Deuteronomy, trans. R. Hammer (YJS 24; New Haven: Yale University, 1986).

Neusner, *Sifre to Deuteronomy.* An Analytical Translation, trans. J. Neusner (BJS 98 and 101; Atlanta: Scholars Press, 1987), 2 volumes.

VI. *Haggadic Midrashim.*

Soncino, *Midrash Rabbah*, ed. H. Freedman and M. Simon (London: Soncino, 1939), 9 volumes and index.

Midrash Rabbah (Vilna: Romm, 1887).

Mirqin, *Midrash Rabbah*, Pentateuch. Ed. and vocalized by M. Mirqin (Tel Aviv: Yavneh, 1981), 11 volumes.

Theodor and Albeck, *Midrash Bereshit Rabba*, ed. J. Theodor and Ch. Albeck (Jerusalem: Wahrmann, 1965), 3 volumes.

Margulies, *Leviticus Rabbah:* Midrash Wayyikra Rabbah, ed. M. Margulies (Jerusalem: Ministry of Education and Culture of Israel, American Academy for Jewish Research, 1953-1960).

Neusner, *Judaism and Scripture*. The Evidence of Leviticus Rabbah, trans. J. Neusner (Chicago Studies in the History of Judaism; Chicago: University of Chicago, 1986).

Midrash Tanḥuma, Eshkol edition (Jerusalem: Eshkol, no date).

Singermann, *Midrasch Tanchuma* (only Genesis), ed. with a German translation by F. Singermann (Berlin: Lamm, 1927).

Buber, *Midrasch Tanḥuma:* Ein agadischer Commentar zum Pentateuch, ed. S. Buber (Vilna: Romm, 1885).

Bietenhard, *Midrasch Tanḥuma B,* German by H. Bietenhard (Judaica et Christiana 5-6; Bern: Peter Lang, 1980-1982), 2 volumes.

Schechter, *Aboth de Rabbi Nathan* (A and B), ed. S. Schechter (Vienna, 1887; reprinted New York: Feldheim, 1945).

Goldin, *The Fathers According to Rabbi Nathan* (A), trans. J. Goldin (YJS 10; New Haven: Yale University, 1955).

Neusner, *The Fathers According to Rabbi Nathan*. An Analytical Translation and Explanation, trans. J. Neusner (BJS 114; Atlanta: Scholars Press, 1986).

Saldarini, *The Fathers According to Rabbi Nathan* (B), trans. A. Saldarini (SJLA 11; Leiden: Brill, 1975).

Mandelbaum, *Pesikta de Rav Kahana,* ed. B. Mandelbaum (New York: The Jewish Theological Seminary of America, 1962), 2 volumes.

Braude and Kapstein, *Pesikta de-Rab Kahana,* trans. W. Braude and I. Kapstein (Philadelphia: The Jewish Publication Society of America, 1975).

Neusner, *Pesiqta de Rab Kahana*. An Analytical Translation, trans. J. Neusner (BJS 122-123; Atlanta: Scholars Press, 1987).

Friedmann, *Pesikta Rabbati,* ed. M. Friedmann (Vienna, 1880; reprint Tel Aviv, 1962-1963).

Braude, *Pesikta Rabbati,* trans. W. Braude (YJS 18; New Haven: Yale University, 1968), 2 volumes.

Friedmann, *Seder Eliahu rabba und Seder Eliahu zuta,* ed. M. Friedmann (Vienna, 1902-1904; reprint Jerusalem, 1969).

Braude and Kapstein, *Tanna debe Eliyyahu,* trans. W. Braude and I. Kapstein (Philadelphia: The Jewish Publication Society of America, 1981).

Buber, *Midrasch Tehillim*, ed. S. Buber (Vilna: Romm, 1891).

Braude, *The Midrash on Psalms*, trans. W. Braude (YJS 13, 1-2; New Haven: Yale University, 1959), 2 volumes.

Donsqi, *Midrash Rabbah. Shir ha-Shirim*, ed. S. Donsqi (Jerusalem: Dvir, 1980).

Eshkol, *Pirqe Rabbi Eliezer*, Eshkol edition (Jerusalem: Eshkol, 1973).

Higger, *Pirqe R. Eliezer*, ed. M. Higger in *Horeb* 8 (1944) 82-119; 9 (1946) 94-116; and 10 (1948) 185-294.

Friedlander, *Pirke de Rabbi Eliezer*, trans. G. Friedlander (New York: Hermon, 1970; original London, 1916).

Milikowsky, *Seder Olam*. A Rabbinic Chronography, ed. and trans. Ch. Milikowsky (1981 Yale University Ph.D. dissertation).

Yalquṭ Shim'oni, vol. I (Jerusalem: Kook, 1973).

Kasher, *Encyclopedia of Biblical Interpretation*, vol. I, Genesis, ed. and trans. M. Kasher (New York: American Biblical Encyclopedia Society, 1953). Vol. VIII, Exodus, 1970.

VII. *Apocrypha, Pseudepigrapha, Philo, Josephus and the Dead Sea Scrolls.*

Apocrypha: see Rahlfs, *Septuaginta*.

OTP. The Old Testament Pseudepigrapha, ed. J. Charlesworth (Garden City, New York: Doubleday, 1983-1985), 2 volumes.

APOT. The Apocrypha and Pseudepigrapha of the Old Testament, II. Pseudepigrapha, ed. R. Charles (Oxford: Clarendon, 1913).

Harrington, *Les Antiquités Bibliques*, ed. D. Harrington, French by J. Cazeaux (SC 229-230; Paris: du Cerf, 1976), 2 volumes.

LCL, *Philo*, Greek and English translation by F. Colson, G. Whitaker, J. Earp and R. Marcus (Cambridge, Massachusetts: Harvard University, 1971), 10 volumes with 2 supplements.

LCL, *Josephus*, Greek and English translation by H. Thackeray, R. Marcus and A. Wikgren (Cambridge, Massachusetts: Harvard University, 1969), 9 volumes.

Charlesworth, *Graphic Concordance to the Dead Sea Scrolls*, ed. J. Charlesworth et al. (Tübingen: Mohr; Louisville: Westminster / John Knox, 1991).

Martínez, *The Dead Sea Scrolls Translated*, trans. F. Martínez (Leiden: Brill, 1994).

Fitzmyer, J., *The Dead Sea Scrolls*. Major Publications and Tools for Study (SBLRBS 20; Atlanta: Scholars Press, 1990).

VIII. *Greek and Latin Writers.*

Herodotus, trans. A. Godley (LCL; Cambridge, Massachusetts: Harvard University Press, 1920 / 1981), 4 volumes.

Isocrates, *Panegyricus*, trans. G. Norlin (LCL; Cambridge, Massachusetts: Harvard University Press, 1961-1962), 3 volumes.

Dio Cassius, *Roman History*, trans. E. Cary (LCL; Cambridge, Massachusetts: Harvard University Press, 1954-1955), 9 volumes.

Dion Chrysostomos, "Orationes," in *Dionis Chrysostomi Orationes*, ed. G. de Budé (Leipzig: Teubner, 1916).

Plutarch, *Lives*, trans. B. Perrin (LCL; Cambridge, Massachusetts: Harvard University Press, 1914 / 1982), 11 volumes.

Suetonius, *Lives of the Caesars*, trans. J. Rolfe (LCL; Cambridge, Massachusetts: Harvard University Press, 1913 / 1989), 2 volumes.

Seneca, "Ad Pavlinvm, De Brevitate Vitae," in vol. 2 of *Moral Essays*, trans. J. Basore (LCL; Cambridge, Massachusetts: Harvard University Press, 1928 / 1994), 3 volumes.

Tacitus, *The Histories*, trans. C. Moore (LCL; Cambridge, Massachusetts: Harvard University Press, 1925 / 1968). *The Annals*, trans. J. Jackson (LCL; Cambridge, Massachusetts: Harvard University Press, 1937 / 1970), 4 volumes.

IX. *Dictionaries and Reference Works.*

BDB, *A Hebrew and English Lexicon of the Old Testament*, by F. Brown, S. Driver and C. Briggs (Oxford: Clarendon, 1962).

Jastrow, *A Dictionary of the Targumim, the Talmud Babli and Yerushalmi, and the Midrashic Literature*, by M. Jastrow (New York: Pardes, 1950), 2 volumes.

Levy, *Neuhebräisches und chaldäisches Wörterbuch über die Talmudim und Midraschim*, by J. Levy (Berlin and Vienna, 1924[2]), 4 volumes.

Krauss, *Griechische und Lateinische Lehnwörter in Talmud, Midrasch und Targum*, by S. Krauss (Berlin: Calvary, 1898-1899).

Hyman, *Torah Hakethubah Vehamessurah.* A Reference Book of the Scriptural Passages Quoted in Talmudic, Midrashic and Early Rabbinic Literature, by Aaron Hyman, second edition by Arthur Hyman (Tel Aviv: Dvir, 1979), 3 volumes.

Schürer, *The history of the Jewish people in the age of Jesus Christ (175 B.C. – A.D. 135),* by E. Schürer, ed. G. Vermes, F. Millar and M. Black (Edinburgh: Clark, 1973-1986), 3 volumes.

Jeremias, *Jerusalem in the Time of Jesus,* by J. Jeremias (London: SCM, 1969).

Strack and Stemberger, *Introduction to the Talmud and Midrash,* by H. Strack and G. Stemberger (Minneapolis: Fortress, 1992). At times I refer to the German, *Einleitung in Talmud und Midrasch* (Munich: Beck, 1982[7]).

Ginzberg, *The Legends of the Jews,* by L. Ginzberg (Philadelphia: The Jewish Publication Society of America, 1968), 6 volumes and index.

JE, *The Jewish Encyclopedia* (New York: Funk and Wagnalls, 1905), 12 volumes.

EJ, *Encyclopaedia Judaica* (Jerusalem: Keter, 1971), 16 volumes.

LSJ, *A Greek-English Lexicon,* by H. Liddell, R. Scott and H. Jones (Oxford: Clarendon, 1966[9]).

BAGD, *A Greek-English Lexicon of the New Testament and Other Early Christian Literature,* by W. Bauer, W. Arndt, F. Gingrich and F. Danker (Chicago: University of Chicago, 1979[2]).

Chambers Murray, latin-english Dictionary, ed. W. Smith and J. Lockwood (Edinburgh, Chambers; London: Murray, 1986).

TDNT, Theological Dictionary of the New Testament, ed. G. Kittel and G. Friedrich (Grand Rapids, Michigan: Eerdmans, 1964-1976), 9 volumes and index.

Str-B, *Kommentar zum Neuen Testament aus Talmud und Midrasch,* by (H. Strack and) P. Billerbeck (Munich: Beck, 1924-1961), 6 volumes.

IDB, The Interpreter's Dictionary of the Bible, ed. G. Buttrick et al. (New York and Nashville: Abingdon Press, 1962), four volumes. Supplementary Volume, ed. K. Crim, 1976.

Nickelsburg, *Jewish Literature Between the Bible and the Mishnah,* by G. Nickelsburg (Philadelphia: Fortress, 1981).

Jesus & His World. An Archaeological and Cultural Dictionary, ed. J. Rousseau and R. Arav (Minneapolis: Fortress Press, 1995).

Index of Modern Authors

Aberbach, M. 13

Albeck, Ch. 5

Amram, D. 10, 33

Arav, R., and Rousseau, J. 24, 26,

.... 52, 56, 64-65, 160

Aus, R. 2, 67, 104, 129,

.... 135, 138, 140,

.................................143, 161, 166, 168

Bacher, W. 12, 37

Bahrdt, K. 53

Barclay, W. 27, 45

Barrett, C. 27, 41

Bauer, J. 152

Beare, F. 109

Becker, J. 2, 44, 47

Becker, U. 1-2, 20, 27, 38,

.... 41, 43-45, 47

Berg, W. 51, 55, 126

Berger, A. 25

Betz, O. 55, 57, 100

Billerbeck, P. (Str-B) 2, 10-11, 22,

.................................24, 27, 34-36, 60,

........................97, 111, 123, 128, 155

Black, M. 19, 163

Blinzler, J. 11, 35

Bokser, B. 54

Brandon, S. 13

Braude, W. 96

Brooks, J. 168

Brown, R. 21, 27, 38, 55,

.... 135-136, 149, 156-157

Bultmann, R. 47, 164

Caird, G. 158

Carson, D. 21

Charlesworth, J. 114

Clark, K. 41, 163

Clemen, K. 126

Cohn, H. 10

Collins, J. 113-114

Colson, F. 3, 122

Cotter, W. 52

Dahl, N. 167

Derrett, J. 20-22, 27, 135

Dibelius, M. 83, 131

Dobsevage, I. 132

Donsqi, S. 77

Edersheim, A. 51

Ehrman, B. 40

Eisler, R. 1, 45

Eissfeldt, O. 8

Feldman, L. 24, 121

Fitzmyer, J. 52

Fröhlke, F. 152

Gärtner, B. 55

Gaster, T. 79

Ginzberg, L. 7, 17, 38,
................................72, 96, 117, 159

Gnilka, J. ... 47, 123, 126, 163-164, 169

Goldin, J. 62, 165

Gould, E. 70

Grundmann, W. 41, 109, 123, 169

Guilding, A. 55, 133

Gundry, R. 51, 109, 135, 169

Gutbrod, W. 12

Harrington, D. 109

Hartmann, L. 25

Hayward, R. 96

Heil, J. 51, 96

Heinemann, I. 166

Heitmüller, W. 1

Hengel, M. 13, 16, 20, 22

Herr, M. 129

Hooker, M. 51, 55, 65, 129

Howard, C. 13

Jacobs, J. 39, 132

Jeremias, J. 19-20, 25, 153

Juel, D. 136, 168

Jung, J. 23-24

Kertelge, K. 126

Kilpatrick, G. 109

Klostermann, E. 83, 109

Köster, H. 44, 46-47

Kohler, K. 5, 13, 16, 21

Krupp, M. 5

Kuhn, K. 6, 9-10, 32

Lagrange, M.-J. 21, 65

Lane, W. 66, 83, 130

Lapide, P. 53, 57, 128

Lévi, I. 113

Levy, J. 5

Leroy, H. 47

Levine, E. x

Lightfoot, J. 33

Lindars, B. 21, 27, 38, 47

Lohmeyer, E. 131, 169

Lührmann, D. 40, 123, 164

Luz, U. 109

Macgregor, G. 42, 44-45

Madden, P. 52

Malbon, E. 55

Mann, C. 66, 129

Marcus, J. 123, 164

Martin, B. 38

McDonald, J. 2-3, 40, 47

McNeile, A. 1

Meyer, H. 20-21, 45

Meyer, R. 18

Mitchell, A. x

Morris, L. 21, 27

Neirynck, F. 135

Neusner, J. .... x, 32

Nickelsburg, G. 15, 95, 121-122

Nicolas, B. 25

Oswald, N. x

Puech, E. 113-114

Raditsa, L. 25

Reitzenstein, R. 126

Riesner, R. 64-65

Rouse, W. 122

Safrai, S. 53

Sahm, U. 65

Sanders, J. 38

Schachter, J. 36

Schalit, A. 142, 145

Schenk, W. 169

Schlatter, A. 109, 149

Schmithals, W. 123, 126, 130, 169

Schnackenburg, R. 1, 27, 47

Schneider, J. 41

Schniewind, J. 70

Schöndorf, H. 27

Schürer, E. 24, 117, 119, 140,
.... 142-143, 155-157, 159-161

Schwarz, O. 27

Schweizer, E. 109

Seligsohn, M. 13

Slotki, J. 4, 6

Stegner, W. 55, 61, 90, 96, 126-128

Stemberger, G. 54

Stern, E. 13

Strathmann, H. 1

Taylor, N. 123

Taylor, V. 53, 66, 128

Tigay, J. 10

Townshend, R. 121

van der Loos, H. 53

van Iersel, B 83

von Campenhausen, H. 1

von der Osten-Sacken, P. ....x, 9, 54

Winter, P. 135
Wright, G.................................. 53-54
Wright, R. 22

Yarbro Collins, A. 51-52, 104, 117

About the Author

Roger David Aus, b. 1940, studied English and German at St. Olaf College, and theology at Harvard Divinity School, Luther Theological Seminary, and Yale University, from which he received the Ph.D. degree in New Testament Studies in 1971. He is an ordained clergyman of the Evangelical Lutheran Church in America, currently serving the German-speaking Luthergemeinde in Berlin-Reinickendorf, Germany. The Protestant Church of Berlin-Brandenburg (Berlin West) kindly granted him a short study leave in Jerusalem, Israel, in 1981. His study of New Testament topics always reflects his great interest in, and deep appreciation of, the Jewish roots of the Christian faith.

South Florida Studies in the History of Judaism

240001	Lectures on Judaism in the Academy and in the Humanities	Neusner
240002	Lectures on Judaism in the History of Religion	Neusner
240003	Self-Fulfilling Prophecy: Exile and Return in the History of Judaism	Neusner
240004	The Canonical History of Ideas: The Place of the So-called Tannaite Midrashim, Mekhilta Attributed to R. Ishmael, Sifra, Sifré to Numbers, and Sifré to Deuteronomy	Neusner
240005	Ancient Judaism: Debates and Disputes, Second Series	Neusner
240006	The Hasmoneans and Their Supporters: From Mattathias to the Death of John Hyrcanus I	Sievers
240007	Approaches to Ancient Judaism: New Series, Volume One	Neusner
240008	Judaism in the Matrix of Christianity	Neusner
240009	Tradition as Selectivity: Scripture, Mishnah, Tosefta, and Midrash in the Talmud of Babylonia	Neusner
240010	The Tosefta: Translated from the Hebrew: Sixth Division Tohorot	Neusner
240011	In the Margins of the Midrash: Sifre Ha'azinu Texts, Commentaries and Reflections	Basser
240012	Language as Taxonomy: The Rules for Using Hebrew and Aramaic in the Babylonia Talmud	Neusner
240013	The Rules of Composition of the Talmud of Babylonia: The Cogency of the Bavli's Composite	Neusner
240014	Understanding the Rabbinic Mind: Essays on the Hermeneutic of Max Kadushin	Ochs
240015	Essays in Jewish Historiography	Rapoport-Albert
240016	The Golden Calf and the Origins of the Jewish Controversy	Bori/Ward
240017	Approaches to Ancient Judaism: New Series, Volume Two	Neusner
240018	The Bavli That Might Have Been: The Tosefta's Theory of Mishnah Commentary Compared With the Bavli's	Neusner
240019	The Formation of Judaism: In Retrospect and Prospect	Neusner
240020	Judaism in Society: The Evidence of the Yerushalmi,Toward the Natural History of a Religion	Neusner
240021	The Enchantments of Judaism: Rites of Transformation from Birth Through Death	Neusner
240022	Åbo Addresses	Neusner
240023	The City of God in Judaism and Other Comparative and Methodological Studies	Neusner
240024	The Bavli's One Voice: Types and Forms of Analytical Discourse and their Fixed Order of Appearance	Neusner
240025	The Dura-Europos Synagogue: A Re-evaluation (1932-1992)	Gutmann
240026	Precedent and Judicial Discretion: The Case of Joseph ibn Lev	Morell
240027	Max Weinreich Geschichte der jiddischen Sprachforschung	Frakes
240028	Israel: Its Life and Culture, Volume I	Pedersen
240029	Israel: Its Life and Culture, Volume II	Pedersen
240030	The Bavli's One Statement: The Metapropositional Program of Babylonian Talmud Tractate Zebahim Chapters One and Five	Neusner

240031	The Oral Torah: The Sacred Books of Judaism: An Introduction: Second Printing	Neusner
240032	The Twentieth Century Construction of "Judaism:" Essays on the Religion of Torah in the History of Religion	Neusner
240033	How the Talmud Shaped Rabbinic Discourse	Neusner
240034	The Discourse of the Bavli: Language, Literature, and Symbolism: Five Recent Findings	Neusner
240035	The Law Behind the Laws: The Bavli's Essential Discourse	Neusner
240036	Sources and Traditions: Types of Compositions in the Talmud of Babylonia	Neusner
240037	How to Study the Bavli: The Languages, Literatures, and Lessons of the Talmud of Babylonia	Neusner
240038	The Bavli's Primary Discourse: Mishnah Commentary: Its Rhetorical Paradigms and their Theological Implications	Neusner
240039	Midrash Aleph Beth	Sawyer
240040	Jewish Thought in the 20th Century: An Introduction in the Talmud of Babylonia Tractate Moed Qatan	Schweid
240041	Diaspora Jews and Judaism: Essays in Honor of, and in Dialogue with, A. Thomas Kraabel	Overman/MacLennan
240042	The Bavli: An Introduction	Neusner
240043	The Bavli's Massive Miscellanies: The Problem of Agglutinative Discourse in the Talmud of Babylonia	Neusner
240044	The Foundations of the Theology of Judaism: An Anthology Part II: Torah	Neusner
240045	Form-Analytical Comparison in Rabbinic Judaism: Structure and Form in *The Fathers* and *The Fathers According to Rabbi Nathan*	Neusner
240046	Essays on Hebrew	Weinberg
240047	The Tosefta: An Introduction	Neusner
240048	The Foundations of the Theology of Judaism: An Anthology Part III: Israel	Neusner
240049	The Study of Ancient Judaism, Volume I: Mishnah, Midrash, Siddur	Neusner
240050	The Study of Ancient Judaism, Volume II: The Palestinian and Babylonian Talmuds	Neusner
240051	Take Judaism, for Example: Studies toward the Comparison of Religions	Neusner
240052	From Eden to Golgotha: Essays in Biblical Theology	Moberly
240053	The Principal Parts of the Bavli's Discourse: A Preliminary Taxonomy: Mishnah Commentary, Sources, Traditions and Agglutinative Miscellanies	Neusner
240054	Barabbas and Esther and Other Studies in the Judaic Illumination of Earliest Christianity	Aus
240055	Targum Studies, Volume I: Textual and Contextual Studies in the Pentateuchal Targums	Flesher
240056	Approaches to Ancient Judaism: New Series, Volume Three, Historical and Literary Studies	Neusner
240057	The Motherhood of God and Other Studies	Gruber
240058	The Analytic Movement: Hayyim Soloveitchik and his Circle	Solomon

240059	Recovering the Role of Women: Power and Authority in Rabbinic Jewish Society	Haas
240060	The Relation between Herodotus' *History* and Primary History	Mandell/Freedman
240061	The First Seven Days: A Philosophical Commentary on the Creation of Genesis	Samuelson
240062	The Bavli's Intellectual Character: The Generative Problematic: In Bavli Baba Qamma Chapter One And Bavli Shabbat Chapter One	Neusner
240063	The Incarnation of God: The Character of Divinity in Formative Judaism: Second Printing	Neusner
240064	Moses Kimhi: Commentary on the Book of Job	Basser/Walfish
240066	Death and Birth of Judaism: Second Printing	Neusner
240067	Decoding the Talmud's Exegetical Program	Neusner
240068	Sources of the Transformation of Judaism	Neusner
240069	The Torah in the Talmud: A Taxonomy of the Uses of Scripture in the Talmud, Volume I	Neusner
240070	The Torah in the Talmud: A Taxonomy of the Uses of Scripture in the Talmud, Volume II	Neusner
240071	The Bavli's Unique Voice: A Systematic Comparison of the Talmud of Babylonia and the Talmud of the Land of Israel, Volume One	Neusner
240072	The Bavli's Unique Voice: A Systematic Comparison of the Talmud of Babylonia and the Talmud of the Land of Israel, Volume Two	Neusner
240073	The Bavli's Unique Voice: A Systematic Comparison of the Talmud of Babylonia and the Talmud of the Land of Israel, Volume Three	Neusner
240074	Bits of Honey: Essays for Samson H. Levey	Chyet/Ellenson
240075	The Mystical Study of Ruth: *Midrash HaNe'elam* of the Zohar to the Book of Ruth	Englander
240076	The Bavli's Unique Voice: A Systematic Comparison of the Talmud of Babylonia and the Talmud of the Land of Israel, Volume Four	Neusner
240077	The Bavli's Unique Voice: A Systematic Comparison of the Talmud of Babylonia and the Talmud of the Land of Israel, Volume Five	Neusner
240078	The Bavli's Unique Voice: A Systematic Comparison of the Talmud of Babylonia and the Talmud of the Land of Israel, Volume Six	Neusner
240079	The Bavli's Unique Voice: A Systematic Comparison of the Talmud of Babylonia and the Talmud of the Land of Israel, Volume Seven	Neusner
240080	Are There Really Tannaitic Parallels to the Gospels?	Neusner
240081	Approaches to Ancient Judaism: New Series, Volume Four, Religious and Theological Studies	Neusner
240082	Approaches to Ancient Judaism: New Series, Volume Five, Historical, Literary, and Religious Studies	Basser/Fishbane
240083	Ancient Judaism: Debates and Disputes, Third Series	Neusner

240084	Judaic Law from Jesus to the Mishnah	Neusner
240085	Writing with Scripture: Second Printing	Neusner/Green
240086	Foundations of Judaism: Second Printing	Neusner
240087	Judaism and Zoroastrianism at the Dusk of Late Antiquity	Neusner
240088	Judaism States Its Theology	Neusner
240089	The Judaism behind the Texts I.A	Neusner
240090	The Judaism behind the Texts I.B	Neusner
240091	Stranger at Home	Neusner
240092	Pseudo-Rabad: Commentary to Sifre Deuteronomy	Basser
240093	FromText to Historical Context in Rabbinic Judaism	Neusner
240094	Formative Judaism	Neusner
240095	Purity in Rabbinic Judaism	Neusner
240096	Was Jesus of Nazareth the Messiah?	McMichael
240097	The Judaism behind the Texts I.C	Neusner
240098	The Judaism behind the Texts II	Neusner
240099	The Judaism behind the Texts III	Neusner
240100	The Judaism behind the Texts IV	Neusner
240101	The Judaism behind the Texts V	Neusner
240102	The Judaism the Rabbis Take for Granted	Neusner
240103	From Text to Historical Context in Rabbinic Judaism V. II	Neusner
240104	From Text to Historical Context in Rabbinic Judaism V. III	Neusner
240105	Samuel, Saul, and Jesus: Three Early Palestinian Jewish Christian Gospel Haggadoth	Aus
240106	What is Midrash? And a Midrash Reader	Neusner
240107	Rabbinic Judaism: Disputes and Debates	Neusner
240108	Why There Never Was a "Talmud of Caesarea"	Neusner
240109	Judaism after the Death of "The Death of God"	Neusner
240110	Approaches to Ancient Judaism	Neusner
240112	The Judaic Law of Baptism	Neusner
240113	The Documentary Foundation of Rabbinic Culture	Neusner
240114	Understanding Seeking Faith, Volume Four	Neusner
240115	Paul and Judaism: An Anthropological Approach	Laato
240116	Approaches to Ancient Judaism, New Series, Volume Eight	Neusner
240119	Theme and Context in Biblical Lists	Scolnic
240120	Where the Talmud Comes From	Neusner
240121	The Initial Phases of the Talmud, Volume Three: Social Ethics	Neusner
240122	Are the Talmuds Interchangeable? Christine Hayes's Blunder	Neusner
240123	The Initial Phases of the Talmud, Volume One: Exegesis of Scripture	Neusner
240124	The Initial Phases of the Talmud, Volume Two: Exemplary Virtue	Neusner
240125	The Initial Phases of the Talmud, Volume Four: Theology	Neusner
240126	From Agnon to Oz	Bargad
240127	Talmudic Dialectics, Volume I: Tractate Berakhot and the Divisions of Appointed Times and Women	Neusner
240128	Talmudic Dialectics, Volume II: The Divisions of Damages and Holy Things and Tractate Niddah	Neusner
240129	The Talmud: Introduction and Reader	Neusner

240130	*Gesher Vakesher:* Bridges and Bonds	Green
	The Life of Leon Kronish	
240131	Beyond Catastrophe	Neusner
240132	Ancient Judaism, Fourth Series	Neusner
240133	Formative Judaism, New Series: Current Issues and Arguments	
	Volume One	Neusner
240134	Sects and Scrolls	Davies
240135	Religion and Law	Neusner
240136	Approaches to Ancient Judaism, New Series, Volume Nine	Neusner
240137	Uppsala Addresses	Neusner
240138	Jews and Christians in the Life and Thought of Hugh of	
	St. Victor	Moore
240140	Jews, Pagans, and Christians in the Golan Heights	Gregg/Urman
240141	Rosenzweig on Profane/Secular History	Vogel
240142	Approaches to Ancient Judaism, New Series, Volume Ten	Neusner
240143	Archaeology and the Galilee	Edwards/McCullough
240144	Rationality and Structure	Neusner
240145	Formative Judaism, New Series: Current Issues and Arguments	
	Volume Two	Neusner
240146	Ancient Judaism, Religious and Theological Perspectives	
	First Series	Neusner
240147	The Good Creator	Gelander
240148	The Mind of Classical Judaism, Volume IV, The Philosophy	
	and Political Economy of Formative Judaism: The Mishnah's	
	System of the Social Order	Neusner
240149	The Mind of Classical Judaism, Volume I, Modes of Thought::	
	Making Connections and Drawing Conclusions	Neusner
240150	The Mind of Classical Judaism, Volume II, From Philosophy	
	to Religion	Neusner
241051	The Mind of Classical Judaism, Volume III, What is "Israel"?	
	Social Thought in the Formative Age	Neusner
240152	The Tosefta, Translated from the Hebrew: Fifth Division,	
	Qodoshim, The Order of Holy Things	Neusner
240153	The Theology of Rabbinic Judaism: A Prolegomenon	Neusner
240154	Approaches to Ancient Judaism, New Series, Volume Eleven	Neusner
240155	Pesiqta Rabbati: A Synoptic Edition of Pesiqta Rabbati Based	
	upon all Extant Manuscripts and the Editio Princeps, V. I	Ulmer
240157	Caught in the Act: Walking on the Sea and the Release of	
	Barabbas Revisited	Aus

South Florida Academic Commentary Series

243001	The Talmud of Babylonia, An Academic Commentary,	
	Volume XI, Bavli Tractate Moed Qatan	Neusner
243002	The Talmud of Babylonia, An Academic Commentary,	
	Volume XXXIV, Bavli Tractate Keritot	Neusner
243003	The Talmud of Babylonia, An Academic Commentary,	
	Volume XVII, Bavli Tractate Sotah	Neusner

243004	The Talmud of Babylonia, An Academic Commentary, Volume XXIV, Bavli Tractate Makkot	Neusner
243005	The Talmud of Babylonia, An Academic Commentary, Volume XXXII, Bavli Tractate Arakhin	Neusner
243006	The Talmud of Babylonia, An Academic Commentary, Volume VI, Bavli Tractate Sukkah	Neusner
243007	The Talmud of Babylonia, An Academic Commentary, Volume XII, Bavli Tractate Hagigah	Neusner
243008	The Talmud of Babylonia, An Academic Commentary, Volume XXVI, Bavli Tractate Horayot	Neusner
243009	The Talmud of Babylonia, An Academic Commentary, Volume XXVII, Bavli Tractate Shebuot	Neusner
243010	The Talmud of Babylonia, An Academic Commentary, Volume XXXIII, Bavli Tractate Temurah	Neusner
243011	The Talmud of Babylonia, An Academic Commentary, Volume XXXV, Bavli Tractates Meilah and Tamid	Neusner
243012	The Talmud of Babylonia, An Academic Commentary, Volume VIII, Bavli Tractate Rosh Hashanah	Neusner
243013	The Talmud of Babylonia, An Academic Commentary, Volume V, Bavli Tractate Yoma	Neusner
243014	The Talmud of Babylonia, An Academic Commentary, Volume XXXVI, Bavli Tractate Niddah	Neusner
243015	The Talmud of Babylonia, An Academic Commentary, Volume XX, Bavli Tractate Baba Qamma	Neusner
243016	The Talmud of Babylonia, An Academic Commentary, Volume XXXI, Bavli Tractate Bekhorot	Neusner
243017	The Talmud of Babylonia, An Academic Commentary, Volume XXX, Bavli Tractate Hullin	Neusner
243018	The Talmud of Babylonia, An Academic Commentary, Volume VII, Bavli Tractate Besah	Neusner
243019	The Talmud of Babylonia, An Academic Commentary, Volume X, Bavli Tractate Megillah	Neusner
243020	The Talmud of Babylonia, An Academic Commentary, Volume XXVIII, Bavli Tractate Zebahim A. Chapters I through VII	Neusner
243021	The Talmud of Babylonia, An Academic Commentary, Volume XXI, Bavli Tractate Baba Mesia, A. Chapters I through VI	Neusner
243022	The Talmud of Babylonia, An Academic Commentary, Volume XXII, Bavli Tractate Baba Batra, A. Chapters I through VI	Neusner
243023	The Talmud of Babylonia, An Academic Commentary, Volume XXIX, Bavli Tractate Menahot, A. Chapters I through VI	Neusner
243024	The Talmud of Babylonia, An Academic Commentary, Volume I, Bavli Tractate Berakhot	Neusner
243025	The Talmud of Babylonia, An Academic Commentary, Volume XXV, Bavli Tractate Abodah Zarah	Neusner
243026	The Talmud of Babylonia, An Academic Commentary, Volume XXIII, Bavli Tractate Sanhedrin, A. Chapters I through VII	Neusner

243027	The Talmud of Babylonia, A Complete Outline, Part IV, The Division of Holy Things; A: From Tractate Zabahim through Tractate Hullin	Neusner
243028	The Talmud of Babylonia, An Academic Commentary, Volume XIV, Bavli Tractate Ketubot, A. Chapters I through VI	Neusner
243029	The Talmud of Babylonia, An Academic Commentary, Volume IV, Bavli Tractate Pesahim, A. Chapters I through VII	Neusner
243030	The Talmud of Babylonia, An Academic Commentary, Volume III, Bavli Tractate Erubin, A. ChaptersI through V	Neusner
243031	The Talmud of Babylonia, A Complete Outline, Part III, The Division of Damages; A: From Tractate Baba Qamma through Tractate Baba Batra	Neusner
243032	The Talmud of Babylonia, An Academic Commentary, Volume II, Bavli Tractate Shabbat, Volume A, Chapters One through Twelve	Neusner
243033	The Talmud of Babylonia, An Academic Commentary, Volume II, Bavli Tractate Shabbat, Volume B, Chapters Thirteen through Twenty-four	Neusner
243034	The Talmud of Babylonia, An Academic Commentary, Volume XV, Bavli Tractate Nedarim	Neusner
243035	The Talmud of Babylonia, An Academic Commentary, Volume XVIII, Bavli Tractate Gittin	Neusner
243036	The Talmud of Babylonia, An Academic Commentary, Volume XIX, Bavli Tractate Qiddushin	Neusner
243037	The Talmud of Babylonia, A Complete Outline, Part IV, The Division of Holy Things; B: From Tractate Berakot through Tractate Niddah	Neusner
243038	The Talmud of Babylonia, A Complete Outline, Part III, The Division of Damages; B: From Tractate Sanhedrin through Tractate Shebuot	Neusner
243039	The Talmud of Babylonia, A Complete Outline, Part I, Tractate Berakhot and the Division of Appointed Times A: From Tractate Berakhot through Tractate Pesahim	Neusner
243040	The Talmud of Babylonia, A Complete Outline, Part I, Tractate Berakhot and the Division of Appointed Times B: From Tractate Yoma through Tractate Hagigah	Neusner
243041	The Talmud of Babylonia, A Complete Outline, Part II, The Division of Women; A: From Tractate Yebamot through Tractate Ketubot	Neusner
243042	The Talmud of Babylonia, A Complete Outline, Part II, The Division of Women; B: From Tractate Nedarim through Tractate Qiddushin	Neusner
243043	The Talmud of Babylonia, An Academic Commentary, Volume XIII, Bavli Tractate Yebamot, A. Chapters One through Eight	Neusner
243044	The Talmud of Babylonia, An Academic Commentary, XIII, Bavli Tractate Yebamot, B. Chapters Nine through Seventeen	Neusner

243045	The Talmud of the Land of Israel, A Complete Outline of the Second, Third and Fourth Divisions, Part II, The Division of Women, A. Yebamot to Nedarim	Neusner
243046	The Talmud of the Land of Israel, A Complete Outline of the Second, Third and Fourth Divisions, Part II, The Division of Women, B. Nazir to Sotah	Neusner
243047	The Talmud of the Land of Israel, A Complete Outline of the Second, Third and Fourth Divisions, Part I, The Division of Appointed Times, C. Pesahim and Sukkah	Neusner
243048	The Talmud of the Land of Israel, A Complete Outline of the Second, Third and Fourth Divisions, Part I, The Division of Appointed Times, A. Berakhot, Shabbat	Neusner
243049	The Talmud of the Land of Israel, A Complete Outline of the Second, Third and Fourth Divisions, Part I, The Division of Appointed Times, B. Erubin, Yoma and Besah	Neusner
243050	The Talmud of the Land of Israel, A Complete Outline of the Second, Third and Fourth Divisions, Part I, The Division of Appointed Times, D. Taanit, Megillah, Rosh Hashannah, Hagigah and Moed Qatan	Neusner
243051	The Talmud of the Land of Israel, A Complete Outline of the Second, Third and Fourth Divisions, Part III, The Division of Damages, A. Baba Qamma, Baba Mesia, Baba Batra, Horayot and Niddah	Neusner
243052	The Talmud of the Land of Israel, A Complete Outline of the Second, Third and Fourth Divisions, Part III, The Division of Damages, B. Sanhedrin, Makkot, Shebuot and Abldah Zarah	Neusner
243053	The Two Talmuds Compared, II. The Division of Women in the Talmud of the Land of Israel and the Talmud of Babylonia, Volume A, Tractates Yebamot and Ketubot	Neusner
243054	The Two Talmuds Compared, II. The Division of Women in the Talmud of the Land of Israel and the Talmud of Babylonia, Volume B, Tractates Nedarim, Nazir and Sotah	Neusner
243055	The Two Talmuds Compared, II. The Division of Women in the Talmud of the Land of Israel and the Talmud of Babylonia, Volume C, Tractates Qiddushin and Gittin	Neusner
243056	The Two Talmuds Compared, III. The Division of Damages in the Talmud of the Land of Israel and the Talmud of Babylonia, Volume A, Tractates Baba Qamma and Baba Mesia	Neusner
243057	The Two Talmuds Compared, III. The Division of Damages in the Talmud of the Land of Israel and the Talmud of Babylonia, Volume B, Tractates Baba Batra and Niddah	Neusner
243058	The Two Talmuds Compared, III. The Division of Damages in the Talmud of the Land of Israel and the Talmud of Babylonia, Volume C, Tractates Sanhedrin and Makkot	Neusner
243059	The Two Talmuds Compared, I. Tractate Berakhot and the Division of Appointed Times in the Talmud of the Land of Israel and the Talmud of Babylonia, Volume B, Tractate Shabbat	Neusner
243060	The Two Talmuds Compared, I. Tractate Berakhot and the Division of Appointed Times in the Talmud of the Land of Israel and the Talmud of Babylonia, Volume A, Tractate Berakhot	Neusner

243061	The Two Talmuds Compared, III. The Division of Damages in the Talmud of the Land of Israel and the Talmud of Babylonia, Volume D, Tractates Shebuot, Abodah Zarah and Horayot	Neusner
243062	The Two Talmuds Compared, I. Tractate Berakhot and the Division of Appointed Times in the Talmud of the Land of Israel and the Talmud of Babylonia, Volume C, Tractate Erubin	Neusner
243063	The Two Talmuds Compared, I. Tractate Berakhot and the Division of Appointed Times in the Talmud of the Land of Israel and the Talmud of Babylonia, Volume D, Tractates Yoma and Sukkah	Neusner
243064	The Two Talmuds Compared, I. Tractate Berakhot and the Division of Appointed Times in the Talmud of the Land of Israel and the Talmud of Babylonia, Volume E, Tractate Pesahim	Neusner
243065	The Two Talmuds Compared, I. Tractate Berakhot and the Division of Appointed Times in the Talmud of the Land of Israel and the Talmud of Babylonia, Volume F, Tractates Besah, Taanit and Megillah	Neusner
243066	The Two Talmuds Compared, I. Tractate Berakhot and the Division of Appointed Times in the Talmud of the Land of Israel and the Talmud of Babylonia, Volume G, Tractates Rosh Hashanah and Moed Qatan	Neusner
243067	The Talmud of Babylonia, An Academic Commentary, Volume XXII, Bavli Tractate Baba Batra, B. Chapters VII through XI	Neusner
243068	The Talmud of Babylonia, An Academic Commentary, Volume XXIII, Bavli Tractate Sanhedrin, B. Chapters VIII through XII	Neusner
243069	The Talmud of Babylonia, An Academic Commentary, Volume XIV, Bavli Tractate Ketubot, B. ChaptersVII through XIV	Neusner
243070	The Talmud of Babylonia, An Academic Commentary, Volume IV, Bavli Tractate Pesahim, B. Chapters VIII through XI	Neusner
243071	The Talmud of Babylonia, An Academic Commentary, Volume XXIX, Bavli Tractate Menahot, B. Chapters VII through XIV	Neusner
243072	The Talmud of Babylonia, An Academic Commentary, Volume XXVIII, Bavli Tractate Zebahim B. Chapters VIII through XV	Neusner
243073	The Talmud of Babylonia, An Academic Commentary, Volume XXI, Bavli Tractate Baba Mesia, B. Chapters VIII through XI	Neusner
243074	The Talmud of Babylonia, An Academic Commentary, Volume III, Bavli Tractate Erubin, A. ChaptersVI through XI	Neusner
243075	The Components of the Rabbinic Documents: From the Whole to the Parts, I. Sifra, Part One	Neusner
243076	The Components of the Rabbinic Documents: From the Whole to the Parts, I. Sifra, Part Two	Neusner
243077	The Components of the Rabbinic Documents: From the Whole to the Parts, I. Sifra, Part Three	Neusner

243078	The Components of the Rabbinic Documents: From the Whole to the Parts, I. Sifra, Part Four	Neusner
243079	The Components of the Rabbinic Documents: From the Whole to the Parts, II. Esther Rabbah I	Neusner
243080	The Components of the Rabbinic Documents: From the Whole to the Parts, III. Ruth Rabbah	Neusner
243081	The Components of the Rabbinic Documents: From the Whole to the Parts, IV. Lamemtations Rabbah	Neusner
243082	The Components of the Rabbinic Documents: From the Whole to the Parts, V. Song of Songs Rabbah, Part One	Neusner
243083	The Components of the Rabbinic Documents: From the Whole to the Parts, V. Song of Songs Rabbah, Part Two	Neusner
243084	The Components of the Rabbinic Documents: From the Whole to the Parts, VI. The Fathers According to Rabbi Nathan	Neusner
243085	The Components of the Rabbinic Documents: From the Whole to the Parts, VII. Sifré to Deuteronomy, Part One	Neusner
243086	The Components of the Rabbinic Documents: From the Whole to the Parts, VII. Sifré to Deuteronomy, Part Two	Neusner
243087	The Components of the Rabbinic Documents: From the Whole to the Parts, VII. Sifré to Deuteronomy, Part Three	Neusner
243088	The Components of the Rabbinic Documents: From the Whole to the Parts, VIII. Mekhilta Attributed to Rabbi Ishmael, Part One	Neusner
243089	The Components of the Rabbinic Documents: From the Whole to the Parts, VIII. Mekhilta Attributed to Rabbi Ishmael, Part Two	Neusner
243090	The Components of the Rabbinic Documents: From the Whole to the Parts, VIII. Mekhilta Attributed to Rabbi Ishmael, Part Three	Neusner
243092	The Components of the Rabbinic Documents: From the Whole to the Parts, IX. Genesis Rabbah, Part One, Introduction and Chapters One through Twenty-two	Neusner
243093	The Components of the Rabbinic Documents: From the Whole to the Parts, IX. Genesis Rabbah, Part Two, Chapters Twenty-three through Fifty	Neusner
243094	The Components of the Rabbinic Documents: From the Whole to the Parts, IX. Genesis Rabbah, Part Three, Chapters Fifty-one through Seventy-five	Neusner
243095	The Components of the Rabbinic Documents: From the Whole to the Parts, X. Leviticus Rabbah, Part One , Introduction and Parashiyyot One through Seventeen	Neusner
243096	The Components of the Rabbinic Documents: From the Whole to the Parts, X. Leviticus Rabbah, Part Two, Parashiyyot Eighteen through Thirty-seven	Neusner
243097	The Components of the Rabbinic Documents: From the Whole to the Parts, X. Leviticus Rabbah, Part Three, Topical and Methodical Outline	Neusner
243098	The Components of the Rabbinic Documents: From the Whole to the Parts, XI. Pesiqta deRab Kahana, Part One, Introduction and Pisqaot One through Eleven	Neusner
243099	The Components of the Rabbinic Documents: From the Whole to the Parts, XI. Pesiqta deRab Kahana, Part Two, Pisqaot Twelve through Twenty-eight	Neusner

243100   The Components of the Rabbinic Documents: From the Whole to
the Parts, XI. Pesiqta deRab Kahana, Part Three, A Topical
and Methodical Outline   Neusner

243101   The Components of the Rabbinic Documents: From the Whole to
the Parts, IX. Genesis Rabbah, Part Four, Chapters Seventy-six
through One Hundred   Neusner

243102   The Components of the Rabbinic Documents: From the Whole to
the Parts, IX. Genesis Rabbah, Part Five, A Methodical and
Topical Outline; Bereshit through Vaere, Chapters One through
Fifty-seven   Neusner

243103   The Components of the Rabbinic Documents: From the Whole to
the Parts, IX. Genesis Rabbah, Part Six, A Methodical and
Topical Outline; Hayye Sarah through Miqqes, Chapters
Fifty-eight through One Hundred   Neusner

South Florida International Studies in Formative Christianity and Judaism

242501   The Earliest Christian Mission to 'All Nations'   La Grand
242502   Judaic Approaches to the Gospels   Chilton
242503   The "Essence of Christianity"   Forni Rosa
242504   The Wicked Tenants and Gethsemane   Aus
242505   Messiah-Christos   Laato
242506   Romans 9–11: A Reader-Response Analysis   Lodge

South Florida-Rochester-Saint Louis Studies on Religion and the Social Order

245001   Faith and Context, Volume 1   Ong
245002   Faith and Context, Volume 2   Ong
245003   Judaism and Civil Religion   Breslauer
245004   The Sociology of Andrew M. Greeley   Greeley
245005   Faith and Context, Volume 3   Ong
245006   The Christ of Michelangelo   Dixon
245007   From Hermeneutics to Ethical Consensus Among Cultures   Bori
245008   Mordecai Kaplan's Thought in a Postmodern Age   Breslauer
245009   No Longer Aliens, No Longer Strangers   Eckardt
245010   Between Tradition and Culture   Ellenson
245011   Religion and the Social Order   Neusner
245012   Christianity and the Stranger   Nichols
245013   The Polish Challenge   Czosnyka
245014   Islam and the Question of Minorities   Sonn
245015   Religion and the Political Order   Neusner
245016   The Ecology of Religion   Neusner